DATE DUE

DEC 1 2 2009	
JAN 1 9 2010	

BRODART, CO.   Cat. No. 23-221-003

MAKING ENEMIES

MAKING ENEMIES

Humiliation and International Conflict

Evelin Lindner

Foreword by Morton Deutsch

Contemporary Psychology

Chris E. Stout, Series Editor

PRAEGER SECURITY INTERNATIONAL

Westport, Connecticut • London

Library of Congress Cataloging-in-Publication Data

Lindner, Evelin, 1954-

Making enemies: humiliation and international conflict / Evelin Lindner; foreword by Morton Deutsch.

p. cm.—(Contemporary psychology, ISSN 1546-668X)

Includes bibliographical references and index.

ISBN 0-275-99109-1 (alk. paper)

1. Humiliation. 2. Social conflict—Psychological aspects. 3. International relations—Psychological aspects. I. Title. II. Series: Contemporary psychology (Praeger Publishers)

BF575.H85L56 2006

327.101'9—dc22   2006015399

British Library Cataloguing in Publication Data is available.

Library of Congress Catalog Card Number: 2006015399

ISBN: 0–275–99109–1

ISSN: 1546–668X

First published in 2006

Praeger Security International, 88 Post Road West, Westport, CT 06881

An imprint of Greenwood Publishing Group, Inc.

www.praeger.com

Printed in the United States of America

The paper used in this book complies with the Permanent Paper Standard issued by the National Information Standards Organization (Z39.48–1984).

10 9 8 7 6 5 4 3 2 1

CONTENTS

FOREWORD

I first met Dr. Evelin Lindner in December 2001 when she was the speaker at a Colloquium of the Peace Education Program at Teachers College, Columbia University. I was attracted to the Colloquium by the title of her talk, "Humiliation and the Roots of Violence." When she spoke, I was impressed by the importance and originality of her ideas. She showed how humiliation—a profound emotion that, unfortunately, has been little studied by psychologists—often plays a critical role in leading to destructive international and interpersonal conflicts. Her talk was illustrated by fascinating examples drawn from her rich and varied international experiences in such countries as Rwanda, Somalia, Egypt, Germany, and the United States.

As a result of her talk, she was invited to teach a course on the psychology of humiliation in the Program on Conflict Resolution at Columbia University's Teachers College. Her course was extremely well-received by the students and faculty. During the summer of 2002, I read many of Dr. Lindner's papers and had an opportunity to talk with her about her work. I urged her to write a book that would present her ideas to a wider social science audience as well as to policy makers and the lay public.

I consider this book to be a very valuable and original contribution to understanding how the experience of humiliation can lead to destructive interaction at the interpersonal and international levels. It has profound and devastating effects. It shakes the foundation of one's identity by devaluing one's worth and by undermining one's inherent human right to care and justice.

Dr. Lindner develops with great insight the important idea that our awareness of humiliation as a powerful and pervasive experience in human affairs has emerged only recently. She attributes this emergence to two phenomena: *egalization* and *globalization.* Egalization (a term coined by Lindner) refers to the development of the political ideal of equal dignity during the eighteenth century, as reflected in the American and French revolutions. Globalization refers to the increasing interdependence and interconnectedness of peoples throughout the world. A woman in Afghanistan who has always accepted her husband's right to beat her feels humiliated when she learns through television that, in other parts of the *global village,* women are viewed as equal to men and husbands are imprisoned for beating their wives.

Dr. Lindner is a very thoughtful person who has read widely and deeply in the social sciences. She has also had a rich, varied experience in many countries as a psychotherapist, counselor, researcher, and global citizen, immersing herself in and embracing diverse cultures.

The book should interest a wide audience. Psychologists and other social scientists will find new ideas to enrich their understanding of how humiliation contributes to destructive conflict and violence at the international as well as interpersonal levels. Policy makers will not only be exposed to these new ideas but also to their policy implications. And, beyond the foregoing, all readers—whether they have a professional interest or not—will find much of value to their personal lives.

Morton Deutsch

E.L. Thorndike Professor Emeritus of Psychology and Education, and Director Emeritus of the International Center for Cooperation & Conflict Resolution (ICCCR), Teachers College, Columbia University

PREFACE

One of the most savored activities I have in my work life is serving as Series Editor for Contemporary Psychology for Praeger. It affords me the enviable position of being able to be the first to read inspired works by inspiring people. Dr. Evelin Lindner and this book are wonderful evidence of my good fortune.

I first had the opportunity to read her work when she was a contributing author in another book project—*The Psychology of Resolving Global Conflicts*—a venture in which I had been blessed to be able to collaborate with and learn from Mari Fitzduff, PhD. In that work, Dr. Lindner gave what I now consider to be a prelude to what has grown to become this book.

I am captivated with this topic, the perspective, and the amount of work (both theoretical and "practical" if you will) that Dr. Lindner has covered herein. I do not think it is overstating the point to dare say her work is groundbreaking in its breadth and synthesis of cultures and events. Her research and her work are sober yet sympathetic, fascinating, and persuasive. One comes to fully understand that humiliation serves as a *most* common denominator in conflict and violence. I was humbled to have been a signatory in the reaffirmation of the United Nations' Declaration on Human Rights upon its 50th anniversary. In that document, the corrosive role that humiliation plays in violations of human rights and dignity was recognized as well.

Dr. Lindner blends in the complexity of cultural relativity with the concomitant complexity of the balance involved in respecting ethic traditions and cultural mores. Just as I have written about the cyclic consequences of quid pro quo retaliations that ratchet up to skirmishes and civil wars and the difficult to interrupt cycle of revenge that can act as a perpetuating influence in conflicts, however, initial causes and subsequent retributions may change over time. Dr. Lindner articulates the causal relationship of "humiliation entrepreneurs" and their resultant humiliation cycles that create terroristic events, wars, and genocides. Personally, this book will be of great help in the work that I do through my Center for Global Initiatives—be it humanitarian relief, medical/psychological services, or even international public health initiatives.

I have written in the past of psychology's "seduction-of-reduction" fetish, for it is somehow comforting (albeit misleading) to think that if we reduce the sophistication of a situation, we can then come to understand it. And if we can understand it, we like to think that we can control the phenomenon. I think that Dr. Lindner's work instructs us in the important lesson that we need to seek first to understand, however, not via reductionism, but through the likely more difficult approach of fully appreciating the contemporary and historic context, systemic influences, cultural customs, and motivations as they all come to bear on humiliation's role in mind-set, emotion, and behavior. Refreshingly, this book is not so much focused on then "controlling" as it is "responding" to volatile situations. Ideally it is more intelligent to prevent, but perhaps the best we can strive for is to at least be intelligent enough to be aware. We can thank Dr. Lindner for this. Perhaps then the rest is up to us?

Chris E. Stout
Kildeer, IL

ACKNOWLEDGMENTS

This book builds on my global life of the past 30 years and, more recently, a four-year study at the University of Oslo on *The Feeling of Being Humiliated: A Central Theme in Armed Conflicts.* The project was funded by the Royal Norwegian Ministry of Foreign Affairs and the Norwegian Research Council, and its task was to study the role of humiliation in the recent mass slaughters in Rwanda, Somalia, and other twentieth century genocides, and I am deeply grateful for their commitment to this critical issue.

I received generous international support from over 500 academics and practitioners in anthropology, history, philosophy, political science, psychology, and sociology, and I thank them all. Among my many generous colleagues in America, I am especially grateful to Professor Morton Deutsch of Columbia University, who authored the Foreword to this book and without whom it would not have been completed; Dr. David A. Hamburg, President Emeritus of the Carnegie Corporation; Alan B. Slifka, founder of the Alan B. Slifka Program in Intercommunal Coexistence at Brandeis University; and Professor Lee D. Ross, cofounder of the Stanford Center on Conflict and Negotiation. To my many generous colleagues in Europe, I would like to express my profound gratitude, especially to Professor Dennis Smith of Loughborough University, U.K., and to Associate Professor Reidar Ommundsen, Professor Jan Smedslund, and the other dedicated members of the Department of Psychology at the University of Oslo.

The political insights offered in this book are the result of decades of having lived and worked all over the world—in Africa, America, China, Egypt, Germany, Israel, Malaysia, New Zealand, Norway, and Thailand—and I extend especially warm thanks to all my international interlocutors, neighbors, and hosts, many of whom must struggle daily to carry on the work of peace, or just to carry on, under the most difficult circumstances. As for its psychological insights, I owe them in large part to the many clients I have treated in my practice as a clinical psychologist, and I am deeply indebted to them.

I would like to thank Kathleen Morrow for her invaluable help in making the manuscript readable.

Finally, I thank my parents, whose personal courage gave my work its direction and motivation.

INTRODUCTION

As a weapon of war and a tactic of torture, the power of humiliation to destroy everyone and everything in its path makes it "the nuclear bomb of the emotions." The goal of this book is to explore the explosive role this seldom-studied emotion plays at every level of human conflict, from our global politics to our private lives.

Very little has been written specifically on humiliation and how to avoid or defuse it to stop violence. However, the emotion is gaining visibility, especially now, with world attention on Middle East affairs. Thomas Friedman, *New York Times* columnist, for example, in many of his texts, pinpoints "humiliation" and "dignity" as being *the* issue in the Middle East, and the driving force behind Jihad.

Ten years ago, I began to wonder why social psychologists did not focus more attention on the distinct and destructive impact of humiliation on human relations. The lack of research left many questions about this important phenomenon unanswered: What do we feel when we feel humiliated? How does the feeling affect what we think of ourselves and others? Is the feeling different when we are humiliated as an individual, a group, or a nation? What is our response to humiliation? Does our response depend on our character or our culture? Why is our response often violent? What pushes us past violence to terror, war, and genocide? How do we stop the cycle of humiliation and retaliation once it starts?[1]

The more I studied the humiliation experience, the more I realized that finding the answers to these questions was critical to the peace of our planet and everyone on it. And so, for the last ten years, I have been formulating a *theory of humiliation* and helping to create a new multidisciplinary field in academia that incorporates principles and scholarship from the disciplines of anthropology, history, philosophy, political science, social psychology, and sociology.[2] To help develop this agenda, I founded and help build the Human Dignity and Humiliation Studies network (http://www.humiliationstudies.org), a global consortium of distinguished academics and practitioners who have joined with me to pursue this vital work.

The first step in developing the theory was to decide on a working definition. The word *humiliation* refers to three different elements of the experience—the perpetrator's act, the victim's feeling, and the social process. The listener (or in this case, the reader) must infer which element or combination of elements is being described, and what is understood may often be different from what is intended. To add to the confusion, different cultures, different groups within a culture, and different individuals within a group often disagree as to whether or not an experience rises to the level of a humiliation. Since all such decisions and distinctions depend on subjective judgments, each side of a dispute will typically insist on applying the word to its own experience and denying it to the other.

A contemporary definition of humiliation can be based on the human rights ideal of equal dignity for all. The first paragraph of Article 1 of the Universal Declaration of Human Rights, which was adopted by the United Nations General Assembly on December 10, 1948, reads: "All human beings are born free and equal in dignity and rights. They are endowed with reason and conscience and should act towards one another in a spirit of brotherhood." In this context, "humiliation" is the enforced lowering of any person or group by a process of subjugation that damages their dignity; "to be humiliated" is to be placed in a situation that is against one's interest (although, sadly, not always against one's will) in a demeaning and damaging way; and "to humiliate" is to transgress the rightful expectations of every human being and of all humanity that basic human rights will be respected.

This is a modern definition that is very different from the word's earlier meaning. *Humiliation* is rooted in the Latin *humus* (earth), *humilis* (low), and *humiliare* (to make low), from whence came the English *humble* (having a low estimate of one's importance), *humility* (having a modest opinion of oneself), and *humiliate* (to make low or humble). Since their inception, these words reflected the rigid ranking of human worth that was the accepted social order of that time. To put one's inferiors "down" and to be put "down" by one's superiors was in many instances a matter of honor and duty.

But with the Age of Enlightenment came a different view of human worth and a different meaning of humiliation—"to lower or depress the dignity or self-respect, to mortify." As old ideas of natural order were overtaken by new ideas of natural rights, humiliation was transformed from an "honorable social medicine" into a "dishonorable social disease." Stripping away one's dignity became as profound a violation as stripping away one's flesh, and humiliation was redefined as a mortal wounding of one's very being.

Unfortunately, this transition has not been easy. The human rights ideal teaches the downtrodden and underprivileged of the world that their plight is a violation of their rights, and that what was accepted before as "normal" should be rejected now as humiliating. In Rwanda, Hutus lived under a hierarchical system ruled by the Tutsi elite for hundreds of years, and this social order was regarded as "normal"; it was only recently, in the light of changing moral views and the Hutu rise to power, that humiliation became a burning wound that led to a genocidal frenzy against the Tutsi *inyenzi* ("cockroaches").

Furthermore, the human rights definition of humiliation is far from being accepted everywhere, and the conflict between honor codes and the moral framework of human rights in itself elicits feelings of humiliation. In "honor killings," for example, a family whose daughter was raped may try to regain its honor by killing the girl; advocates of human rights are appalled by what they regard as a humiliating devaluation of women, while defenders of family honor are offended by what they regard as the advocates' humiliating devaluation of their culture.

When a humiliated mind is left to reflect on its own destruction, it may become convinced that it must inflict even greater pain on the perpetrator. So begins a vicious cycle of violation and vindication that both sides believe they are obligated to pursue. Terror, war, and genocide can result if this belief is fed by "humiliation entrepreneurs" who exhort their followers to exact revenge with grand narratives of humiliation and retaliation. Neither side can break free because being the first to back down would be a further humiliation, so they remain trapped in a self-perpetuating cycle of mayhem and murder.

Because these humiliation cycles are so difficult to stop, it is vital that we resist the temptation to start them. This is the lesson the world learned from the greatest aberration in modern history, the Third Reich, which was a reaction in large part to Germany's humiliating defeat in World War I and the terms of the the Treaty of Versailles. Hitler's promise to avenge and avert such disgrace, and his grand narrative of Aryan humiliation at the hands of Germany's neighbors and "World Jewry," swept him from political obscurity to global domination. But the victors in World War II did not make the same mistake, and, through the courage of the Marshall Plan (whatever its motives), Germany's second defeat did not lead to revenge but to its rebirth as a respected member of the European community.

Germany was fortunate to have resolved this cycle in a few decades because memories of invasion, expulsion, persecution, and subjugation can remain at the center of group identities for centuries. Research shows that memories of humiliation do not age but stay surprisingly fresh.[3] At the group level, memories of humiliation are sometimes rekindled as "chosen trauma"[4] to justify mayhem. The 1389 defeat at the Battle of Kosovo fueled Serb nationalism and wars in

Croatia, Bosnia, and Kosovo. By the same token, memories of the rescue from past humiliation or historic victories over humiliation define national and religious celebrations of pride and joy.

When political scientists analyze what underlies cycles of violence and terror, they usually speak of individual depravity and social deprivation, both of which play critical roles. But if we look at the evolution of these human disasters, whether in Europe, Africa, Asia, or anywhere around the world, we consistently find that the force that keeps fueling the extremists, silencing the moderates, and driving the conflict to spiral out of control is humiliation. During my fieldwork in Somaliland, with its culture of extreme pride and history of extreme violence, I learned an old Somali proverb, *Hadellca xun ayaa ka xanuun kulul xabada,* which means "Humiliation is worse than death; in times of war, words of humiliation hurt more than bullets."

Destructive as they are, we cannot put an end to all acts and feelings of humiliation. "Perpetrators" may not know or intend that any harm will be done, or may do harm indirectly by trying to do good, as is often the case with international aid workers; "victims" may not know or agree that any harm has been done, or may feel harmed indirectly by the suffering of others, as is often the case with international terrorists; and "perpetrators" may believe that they are actually "victims" when their privileges are revoked and their status is "lowered" to one of equal dignity. What we can do, however, is strive to eliminate our institutionalized processes, minimize our intentional acts, and refocus our misdirected feelings of humiliation.

From a human rights perspective, only certain claims of humiliation and demands for redress are deemed "legitimate," but from both scholarly and pragmatic perspectives, it is unwise to label any such feelings as "right" or "wrong" because feelings are feelings, pain is pain, and we ignore them at our own risk. At the same time, we must remember that to recognize feelings, analyze consequences, and consider solutions is not to legitimize, accept, or condone them. But for our own sake and safety, we must give serious study and attention to all feelings of humiliation, because even if the injury is imaginary, the revenge is just as real.

I believe that the importance of humiliation is now beginning to gain more recognition as a result of globalization and the "flattening" of the world. As people come closer together, both physically and digitally, their expectations of equal dignity and opportunity rise, and any attempt to lower the expectations of any one group becomes an offense against all groups, and a threat to the hope of a new and better social order. In this new global context, the actions and reactions of individuals and nations are magnified, and it becomes all the more critical not to introduce the humiliation dynamic into our conflicts over human rights, natural resources, cultural identity, territorial integrity, economic competition, and political cooperation.

Those who live in traditional societies still defined by hierarchies of power and honor may take offense at having their social systems described as the "old order." But the terms "new" and "old" do not signify "better" and "worse"—they only describe social solutions that emerge to suit the context of a given time, place, and set of circumstances. Strategies can be "right" in one context and "wrong" in another, so a new solution is simply one that is better adapted to a new context. Honor codes had a respected place when the world was defined by borders and boundaries, but the advent of cable television, the Internet, and cellular phones have signaled the emergence of a *global village,*[5] and the human rights ideal is best adapted to this new world.

When the norms of human rights prevail, the wounds that were caused by an old humiliation may be healed by a new humility if it is shared, inclusive, and embedded in relationships that respect each other's strengths and accept each other's weaknesses. That may sound unduly optimistic, but Nelson Mandela was able to unite South Africa, one of the most bitterly divided nations on Earth, by the example of his own humility and humanity towards his vanquished enemies (in this book I treat Nelson Mandela in an *ideal type* fashion and focus on his constructive strategies, which, I feel, are not minimized by various criticisms that people may be directing at him as a person).

As a psychologist who has practiced all over the world and studied its cultures, I have learned that humiliation is a story as ancient as human history and as fresh as tomorrow's headlines. It is the thread that ties all intractable conflicts together. If the search for peace is to succeed, then we must understand that humiliated hearts and minds are the deadliest weapons of mass destruction, and we must agree that it is time for the world to begin to disarm.

Organization of this Book

This book is organized in three main parts. The first part is entitled "Humiliation at Work in the Mind." The first chapter unfolds the *mental landscape* that forms the background for any dynamic of humiliation. The second chapter describes how humiliation is regarded as a highly legitimate tool in traditional honor societies, but becomes a profoundly illicit violation of dignity when the concept of human rights permeates the moral and ethical framework. "Globalization and Egalization," the last chapter of Part I, describes how globalization has the potential to elicit humility and suggests that we need *egalization* (I coined this term and explain it later), or the undoing of humiliation, in order to build a decent global society.

Part II is entitled "Humiliation at Work in the World." Its first chapter discusses how *misunderstandings* can elicit feelings of humiliation. The ensuing chapter addresses humiliation's roles in international *conflict,* followed by a chapter on *humiliation, terrorism,* and *torture.*

Part III is entitled "Why Humiliation Does Not Work." The chapter about *addiction* to humiliation addresses how victims of humiliation may become addicted to the experience and pull their neighbors into malign cycles of humiliation. The following chapter discusses the *antidote* to humiliation, or ways to avoid or defuse humiliation. Part III ends with an outlook into the *future*.

In writing this book, I tried to avoid jargon to make the work accessible to as many people as possible. To make the writing more immediate and vivid, vignettes and examples from psychotherapy and research are used throughout the book. The names are not real, and the identities of the people are obscured to protect their privacy except where I obtained their consent. I have translated many of the examples into English and usually do not indicate what the original language was. I often paraphrase and summarize.

Several important themes could not be expanded because of space limitation. For example, how does social and cultural change unfold? Or, how does the individual interact with the group and vice versa? Individuals have feelings—can groups have feelings? I propose that a process of organization and mobilization is necessary in order to "transport" dynamics of humiliation from the individual to the group level.

I should, furthermore, make my personal stance in relation to human rights clear at the outset. I promote human rights ideals that conceive of human worthiness and dignity as equal for every human being. However, I stand in for human rights not because I enjoy presenting myself as an arrogant Westerner who humiliates the non-West by denigrating their honor codes of ranked human worthiness. On the contrary, to my view, people who endorse honor codes may not be looked down upon; my conceptualization is that honor codes had their respected place in a world that did not yet experience the coming together of humankind into *one single* family. However, we live in a new reality, the vision and emerging reality of a *global village,* and this new reality can, according to my view, best be tackled with human rights norms. I believe that human rights represent a normative framework that is better adapted to an emerging global village.

This book addresses the American readership particularly (see especially Chapter 5), since the United States, as sole superpower, has the capacity to tip the world toward demise, even with the best of intentions. (I beg non-American readers for their understanding for this focus.)

I conclude this introduction with a thought from history. In 1905, Norway and Sweden stood at the brink of war. Norway wished to liberate itself from the "union" with Sweden (for Norway "union" was a euphemism for "Swedish occupation"). The great Norwegian researcher, explorer, diplomat, and Nobel Peace Prize winner Fridtjof Nansen (1861–1930), a crucial player in the peaceful dissolution of this "union," said:

We are just as little desirous of inflicting humiliation as we are of suffering it. Such desires, aside from being bad politics, are the mark of inferior breeding. It is, therefore, reasonable and politic for us—to try to help Sweden by concessions and liberality, so that the dissolution of the Union may be carried through without the Swedish people's feeling humiliated.[6]

PART I

HUMILIATION AT WORK IN THE MIND

CHAPTER 1

The Mental Landscape

Humiliation is about *putting down* and *holding down.* The word humiliation comes from humus, which means *earth* in Latin. On September 11, 2001, the Twin Towers were taken down to the ground, to the dust of the earth. What the towers stood for was *debased* and *denigrated.* On April 9, 2003, another set of dynamics of humiliation unfolded before the eyes of the world. The statue of Saddam Hussein in Paradise Square in Baghdad was brought down to the ground.

The images broadcast around the world began with some young Iraqis trying to tear the statue down and enlisting American help. An American armored vehicle arrived on the scene and pulled the statue down to the cheers of the people. The statue fell only halfway at first, leaving the statue with Saddam Hussein's head hanging down. This was the beginning of a strong symbolic marking of the ultimate humiliation of Saddam Hussein and his regime. Disgusted, the Iraqis threw whatever they could gather at the statue. When the core of the statue fell to the ground, the Iraqis chanted and jubilated, jumped up and down, and danced on the statue's body. They smacked this image of their former dictator with their shoes, a highly offensive gesture of humiliation in Iraq (meaning something like "I throw the dust under my feet into your face!"). Half an hour later, they dragged his head down. A tyrant was debased and denigrated, the first dynamic of humiliation to unfold in this scene. An Iraqi guest in the BBCWorld studio expressed his delight in the symbolic debasement of Saddam Hussein.

However, a second dynamic of humiliation had occurred moments earlier. Just as a group of young Marines was about to help tear down the status of Saddam

Hussein, one of them climbed up and draped an American flag over Saddam's face—and in Iraq, America, and all over the world, people gasped in horror. Then, another Marine climbed up to remove it and replace it with an Iraqi flag —and in Iraq, America, and all over the world, people sighed in relief. This was truly a *global moment* for the *global village* where we all could see how easily a moment of thoughtlessness could turn potential allies into accidental enemies.

The world community witnessed the power of humiliation as it unfolded, with two perspectives intertwined in the same event. *Debasement, denigration,* and *degradation* are words that contain the prefix *de-* which signifies *down from* in Latin, *from great heights down to the ground.* In the case of the Twin Towers, thousands of innocent victims paid with their lives for a powerful "message of humiliation" sent to the mighty masters of today's world in the act of "taking down" a symbol of the rich West. Taking down and humiliating Saddam Hussein's statue sent a powerful message to him and his followers that his supremacy was broken.

The first case, the Twin Towers tragedy, we consider a disaster; the second, the deposing of a tyrant, a victory. It seems that humiliation can work for both "good" and "evil." Yet, this is not the case. We will understand this better in the further course of this book. What is lacking so far in this description is a differentiation of humiliation and humility. As laid out earlier, humiliation is not the only word with roots in Latin "humus," earth. There is also *humility* and *humbleness.* Both can be wonderful assets. It is not humiliation that is the opposite of arrogance, but connection in shared humility. Humility and humbleness stand for the humble acknowledgement of limits and the absence of arrogated superiority and hubris.

The following story may help make the distinction between humility and humiliation clearer.

Julius Paltiel, a Norwegian Jew I met in October 2002, was imprisoned in the "SS Strafgefangenenlager Falstad" during World War II. Falstad is situated in breathtakingly beautiful country in the middle of Norway, not far away from Trondheim. Falstad, a large, forlorn building constructed around a rectangular courtyard, was once a special school for handicapped boys. However, in 1941, it was taken over by the German occupiers and turned into a detention camp for political prisoners.

Paltiel told me about an incident that occurred at Falstad when one of the prisoners—a cultivated German Jew with a beautiful voice—was asked to sing. SS officers and prisoners, including Julius Paltiel himself, stood in the courtyard, listening. The prisoner sang several traditional German songs so touchingly that the German SS officers—who usually shouted orders and insults—listened in complete silence.

After a quarter of an hour of this beautiful sound, there was a pause. Complete silence that ended when a dog began to howl. This "woke up" the SS officers who immediately attempted to cover up their vulnerability by inflicting humiliation on the prisoners. They began by announcing that no Jew was capable of singing so beautifully—the proof was supposedly provided by the dog's howling: even an animal could recognize how bad the Jewish singing was.

The officers ordered the Jewish prisoners to go to a tree in the middle of the courtyard, shake off its remaining autumn leaves and, lying on their bellies, take the leaves one-by-one into their mouths and crawl to the corners of the court-yard. The non-Jewish prisoners were ordered to watch and shout. However, many turned their backs.

The beautiful, touching songs seemed to have undermined the hierarchy of *Übermensch* and *Untermensch* the SS officers worked so hard to maintain. The songs humbled the SS officers and, for a moment, introduced humility. However, they could not accept the truth that they were mere humans among other humans, capable of being touched by the singing of another mere mortal. When the singing stopped, they remembered the ideological frame they subscribed to, one that made them the masters, allegedly ordained by nature to rule over these lesser beings. Interestingly, they did not beat the prisoners "mindlessly" or treat them with mere physical brutality. Instead they chose to transmit a highly sym-bolic and intelligent "message" to both prisoners and themselves, one that reinstated physically, mentally, and emotionally the hierarchy of *Übermensch*/ *Untermensch*, sending the prisoners literally *down*, down to the dust of the ground to carry out "services" that were so *low* that there could be no doubt of who was the master.

Earlier we said that it seems that humiliation can work for both good and evil. Now we see that it might be feasible to assign the words "humbling" and "humil-ity" to the good manifestation of lowering or being lowered and reserve the term humiliation for its evil expression.

Top and Bottom: How the Vertical Dimension Can Be Used

The word *humiliation* paints a vivid, three-dimensional picture. The prisoners of Falstad and the employees in the Twin Towers tragically met perpetrators who perceived them to be arrogating superiority and were cruelly and devastatingly brought down. To avoid such atrocities in the future, we must understand the inner workings of the phenomenon of humiliation, even if it is painful and diffi-cult to step into perpetrators' shoes.

Whatever language, we always find a downward spatial orientation connected with words that signify humiliation. Consider the words *de-gradation, ned-verdi-gelse* in Norwegian, *Er-niedrig-ung* in German, or *a-baisse-ment* in French. The syllables *de, ned, niedrig,* and *bas* all mean *down from, low,* or *below. To put down, degrade, denigrate, debase, demean, derogate, lower, lessen,* or *belittle*—all these words are built on the same spatial, orientational metaphor, namely that some-thing or somebody is pushed down and forcefully held there. These spatial metaphors are found in all languages; they are global. This suggests that the mental landscape that entails the vertical scale is global, too.

Figure 1 depicts the mental landscape of arrogation, humiliation, and humility. The Aryan *Übermensch* arrogates superiority, defining himself as positioned far above *lesser* beings called *Untermenschen* or *subhumans*. (*Über* means *above* in German, *unter* means *below*, and *Mensch* means *human being*.) The *Übermensch* is a *higher* human being and the *Untermensch* a *lesser* human being. In the middle of this mental landscape we can imagine a line of equality, humility, and humbleness—the shared humanity so despised by the Übermensch. The Übermensch lives in a world where human beings differ in value and worth; some are of higher value, others of lesser value. The Übermensch puts in place a vertical scale of human worth ranging from above to below. I call this the *hierarchy of human worthiness*, the *vertical scale of human worth and value*, or the *vertical scale of human worth*.

Our physical environment includes heaven and the blue skies above, with the floor of our home down at our feet and the basement even *lower*. Below even that is the darkness down inside the Earth. Why do we organize the world thus in our minds? Perhaps it is the force of gravity that keeps our feet on the ground and

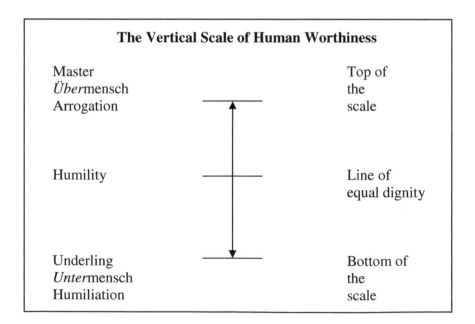

Figure 1.1
The Vertical Scale of Human Worthiness[1]

Source: Initially developed in Lindner, 2001c.

suggests a vertical ordering of the physical world. If we were designed to hover about irregularly without gravity keeping us put, we would probably not emphasize the concepts of *up* and down.

Objective observers from other parts of the universe may find our preoccupation with up and down a bit silly, asking (quite logically) why we insist that the surface of planet Earth is down and the Sun up. Yet, earth dwellers all share the experience of gravity, so the vertical scale provides a useful common reference frame. It is so much a part of our consciousness that we use it for an unconscious metaphor for good and bad and high and low and apply this scale to the value and worth of things and beings. Lakoff and Johnson (1999) address this activity when they speak about *moral ranking*.

We apply such rankings to our evaluations of both the abiotic and the biotic worlds. Gold, worth much, is high up on the scale of worth and value, silver is a little lower, and dirt is worth little and is somewhere far down. When we turn to the biotic world, we see divine powers usually being placed at the absolute top, somewhere in heaven, far above humans. The human scale begins just below gods and angels. At its "pinnacle" the human scale champions divinely ordained masters and continues downward until it reaches the lowest underlings, who are often seen as of little more value than animals.

Even animals are ranked—many put the lion (the "king of animals") at the top, with "vermin" at the bottom of the scale. I have not encountered any culture or language that does not use such rankings. History is full of examples in which the scale of human value was applied literally. Having one's head higher than the emperor's was forbidden in the former Chinese empire and many others. Even today, we encounter the vertical scale in our lives, minds, and hearts. Recently, a businessman told me about his visit to Africa. He was trying to hire employees and was annoyed by the way some of the applicants sat during his interviews. One very tall young African man almost slipped out of his chair, exhibiting a sloppiness that seemed to make him unfit for any serious job. It was not until the businessman learned that in this African culture it is regarded as unfitting to have one's head higher than a person of older age and rank that he was able to properly interpret the so-called "sloppiness" of his prospective employees as an attempt to show respect, to avoid humiliating their future boss.

Lesser and Higher Beings: The Vertical Scale as Applied to Human Worth

We all, through the language we learn as children, apply the vertical dimension to our thinking about the relative value of things and beings. This might seem harmless enough, yet it can bring immense suffering and pain. Slavery and apartheid, for example, stringently institutionalized this vertical ranking. Human rights advocates, on the other hand, aim to dismantle such practices, to collapse the gradient between *top* and *bottom* into *one single line of equal dignity.*

There is nothing automatic about how the vertical scale operates to rank human beings. It is not a natural law, like gravity. The vertical scale's use on human worthiness is purely ideological, dependent upon the world view or philosophy that individuals and cultures construct for its expression. Some philosophies accept the scale's use to justify a hierarchical ordering of society. Other philosophies encourage society's members to meet at a middle line of equal dignity. In the course of human history, innumerable variations on such philosophies have been tried out, and disagreements about how the vertical scale should be applied have often been disruptive and harmful.

For many centuries Jews, to give one of many possible examples, had to deal with the accusation that they "arrogate superiority" and needed to be "taught a lesson" about "where they belong." Eastern Europe's pogroms and the Holocaust were fueled by the desire of some extremists to teach the Jews to "come down" and think of themselves as inferior beings. The truth was that these Jews, far from arrogating superiority, were merely trying to survive. Any impartial observer could see that the accusations against them were wrong, cruel, and evil scapegoating. Whatever privileges Jews had acquired were hard-earned or brought about by their exclusion from other ways of living (denial of the right to own land, for example).

We can, therefore, see two opposing applications of the vertical scale. From the Jewish point of view there was no arrogation of undue superiority, but rather a hard and uphill struggle for life under harsh circumstances. Their persecutors saw a totally different landscape, one that justified atrocities throughout Western history. The interesting point is that the Jews, their tormenters, and uninvolved bystanders all used the same vertical scale, though differently.

Genocide is perhaps the cruelest example of the application of the vertical scale to human beings. Genocide is about killing. However, ugly as that definition is, it is inaccurate. If genocide were merely about killing, bringing victims to death would be "sufficient."[2] Yet, killing is only the last act, and there are victims who almost yearn for it. The perpetrators of genocide care much more about humiliating their victims than they do about killing them. In the genocide in Rwanda, grandmothers were forced to parade naked in the streets before being killed, and daughters were raped in front of their families. As the following quotations illustrate, victims were willing to pay for bullets and begged to be shot rather than slowly humiliated to death.

> There had not been enough guns to go around, and in any case bullets were deemed too expensive for the likes of Tutsis: the ubiquitous flat-bladed machetes (pangas), or any farm or kitchen implement, would do the job just as well. Thus the Rwandan tragedy became one of the few genocides in our century to be accomplished almost entirely without firearms. Indeed, it took many strong and eager arms to carry out the strenuous work of raping, burning, and hacking to death a half-million people (and mutilating many thousands more by slicing off their hands, their breasts, their

genitals, or their ears) with pangas, kitchen knives, farm hoes, pitchforks, and hastily improvised spiked clubs.[3]

Some killers tortured victims, both male and female, physically or psychologically, before finally killing them or leaving them to die. An elderly Tutsi woman in Kibirira commune had her legs cut off and was left to bleed to death. A Hutu man in Cyangugu, known to oppose the MRND-CDR, was killed by having parts of his body cut off, beginning with his extremities. A Tutsi baby was thrown alive into a latrine in Nyamirambo, Kigali, to die of suffocation or hunger. Survivors bear scars of wounds that testify better than words to the brutality with which they were attacked. Assailants tortured Tutsi by demanding that they kill their own children and tormented Hutu married to Tutsi partners by insisting that they kill their spouses. Victims generally regarded being shot as the least painful way to die and, if given the choice and possessing the means, they willingly paid to die that way.

Assailants often stripped victims naked before killing them, both to acquire their clothes without stains or tears and to humiliate them. In many places, killers refused to permit the burial of victims and insisted that their bodies be left to rot where they had fallen. Persons who attempted to give a decent burial to Tutsi were sometimes accused by others of being "accomplices" of the enemy.[4] The Hutu widow of a Tutsi man killed at Mugonero in Kibuye expressed her distress at the violation of Rwandan custom, which is to treat the dead with dignity. Speaking of Pastor Elizaphan Ntakirutimana of the Adventist church, she stated:[5] "What gives me grief is that after the pastor had all these people killed, he didn't even see to burying them, including his fellow pastors. They lay outside for two weeks, eaten by dogs and crows."[6]

Genocide is about humiliating the personal dignity of the victims, denigrating their group to a subhuman level. The Rwandan genocide of 1994 provides a gruesome catalogue of intricate practices designed to *bring down* the victims' dignity. The most literal way of achieving this debasement was, as Human Rights Watch reports, and as I heard described many times, cutting off the legs of tall Tutsis to *shorten* not only their bodies, but "bring down" their alleged *arrogance.*

The verb *to arrogate,* the opposite of the verb *derogate,* is part of the linguistic web of humiliation. Both verbs are built on the Latin verb *rogare,* which means *to ask. Rogare* can be combined with the prefix *de,* which means *down from,* or the prefix *ad,* which means *toward.* To *arrogate superiority* means to appropriate superiority (Latin *to ask toward*), and to *derogate* means to belittle, denigrate, and minimize a person (Latin *to ask down from*). Tutsis were perceived to have *arrogated superiority,* and by cutting their legs *short* they were derogated, cruelly forced to *come down.*

It is extremely important to understand the arbitrariness, the ideological bases, of the application of the vertical scale on human worthiness. There is no "fixed" or "natural" connection between human worthiness and lesser and higher categorizations. Although everybody has this scale mentally available, it is a principle or a tool that can be used in different ways. One can choose to use this tool to extend a gradient between lesser and higher beings or one can reject this use, choosing to collect all humankind at *one middle line of equal dignity.* This tool is like a hammer that can be used to hit nails into the wall, or to pry them out. It is a tool that is always there even when some of its potential uses are outlawed. Those who consider the vertical ranking of human worth legitimate regard humiliation as morally justified humbling. Their thinking is: "I degrade you, I push you down the scale of human worth and value, and you deserve it and better accept it." Those who regard such ranking as illegitimate say, "You are being degraded, pushed down the scale of human worth and value, however, you do not deserve it and must not accept it."

A note of hope: The vertical scale is much more than a source of suffering. It can also generate wonderful wisdom, based on humility. To use the hammer metaphor, humiliation equates with hitting nails into the wall, and humility with prying them out again. The Adolf Hitlers stand for cruel humiliation and the Nelson Mandelas for wise humility. In the following chapters, we delve deeper into the workings of the vertical scale and the extent to which it permeates and determines our lives.

Summary

This chapter highlights the fact that the vertical scale is a tool that has been used to rank human worth and value throughout human history, sometimes in horrific ways. I also make the point that this use is not compulsory. It can be rejected. A vertical scale may be applied to human worth and value in many ways—it can generate rigid caste systems or it can generate a sense of the equal dignity and humble solidarity of all humans.

CHAPTER 2

ONCE THE CURE, NOW THE DISEASE

Nazi Germany is not the only society that operated on the assumption that it is legitimate to rank humans as beings of more or less worth and value, although Nazi culture exhibited unusual cruelty in the way it implemented this belief. The Holocaust was of unspeakable horror. The vertical scale was applied so as to push certain categories of people out of humanity entirely, into the abyss of "subhuman vermin." Other genocidal killers, as well, have dehumanized their victims, labeling them as vermin and pests. In Rwanda, in 1994, the Tutsis were humiliated as "cockroaches," or "inyenzi."

However, I do not want to discuss the unspeakable cruelty of ranking people as subhuman at this point. I would like to shed light on something perhaps even more difficult to accept, namely the *normalcy* with which the vertical scaling of human worth was regarded as legitimate throughout human history. For thousands of years, humanity believed in hierarchically ordering human value, calling it the *order of nature* or *divine order.* The cradle of democracy, the Greek city state of about 2,000 years ago, was adamant that women and slaves could not have a voice. Closer to our own time, the American *Declaration of Independence,* which stipulated that "all men [sic] are created equal and have 'unalienable rights' to life, liberty and the pursuit of happiness," was signed by people who owned slaves.

Know Your Place! How Humiliation Can Lack the Connotation of Violation

Human history may be interpreted as a discourse circling around questions concerning the vertical scale: whether and how the vertical scale is known to people, whether they are aware they have a choice in how to apply it, and to what extent they believe certain applications may be legitimate (in the spirit of a Weberian *ideal-type* approach[1]).

For millions of years, hominids evolving towards *Homo sapiens* roamed the globe as hunters and gatherers. They lived in small bands of approximately 200 individuals who enjoyed rather egalitarian societal institutions and remarkably high qualities of life. There is no proof of organized fighting among hunters and gatherers.[2] "The Hobbesian view of humans in a constant state of 'Warre' is simply not supported by the archaeological record."[3] The absence of evidence for homicide does not prove that it did not occur, but it would be safe to posit that organized killing did not occur until much later (suggesting that "man" is perhaps not aggressive by "nature," but rather by circumstance).

It is certainly wrongheaded to idealize hunters and gatherers or to romanticize them as harmonious golden age dwellers. Yet, in the face of dissonance, conflict, disharmony, disease, or danger, their core ethos, their core moral sentiment, seems to have been egalitarian. In other words, human worth and value were not ranked hierarchically in any deeply institutionalized form. Every individual faced the world more or less from a stance of pristine pride. Throughout approximately 90 percent of human history, hunters and gatherers populated the planet at their leisure.

However, there came a time when they were confronted with the fact that the globe has a limited surface and that abundance was not guaranteed. In some ways we could call this "hitting of the wall" humankind's *first round of globalization*— the species had managed to populate the entire globe, or at least the known and easily habitable parts of it. Anthropologists call this set of circumstances *circumscription.*[4]

Circumscription meant that there was no longer enough—not enough space and not enough resources. Our planet is small and gives the illusion of being unlimited only as long as one has not yet reached its limits. Though the problem had been building up slowly over many prehistoric eons, it reached a critical moment at one very "brief" historic moment, namely when the global climate changed dramatically 11,600 years ago. The Pleistocene's last ice age ended and the Holocene period of relatively warm, wet, stable, CO_2 rich environment began.

However, *Homo sapiens* had developed specific tool kits over a long time and were preadapted, thus "prepared." When sudden climatic change transformed the planet, scholars agree, the practice of agriculture over a large fraction of suitable surface began. "The spread of agriculture throughout the world resulted from a single, strong, manipulation."[5]

The emergence of a supportive environment enabled the experiment of intensification, the domestication of plants and animal. Through *intensification,* human populations were able to increase their resources when the old method of simply wandering off into untouched abundance was no longer feasible. (Some populations chose a second alternative—that of raiding their neighbors.) Through the environmentally stimulated adaptation of agriculture and intensifications, humans began to *subdue* the Earth. We read in the Bible, Genesis 1:28 (New International Version of the Bible), "God blessed them and said to them, 'Be fruitful and increase in number; fill the Earth and subdue it. Rule over the fish of the sea and the birds of the air and over every living creature that moves on the ground.'" In other words, for 10,000 years (until very recently) humankind was profoundly satisfied with its agrarian survival strategy, convinced that it was following divine order.

Zygmunt Bauman writes that from the time humans began to practice agriculture, nature—the entire unprocessed, pristine world—became our enemy.

> ...the world of nature...had to be beheaded and deprived of autonomous will and power of resistance.... The world was an object of willed action: a raw material in the work guided and given form by human designs.... Left to itself, the world had no meaning. It was solely the human design that injected it with a sense of purpose. So the earth became a repository of ores and other "natural resources," wood turned into timber and water—depending on circumstances—into an energy source, waterway, or the solvent of waste.[6]

Humiliation as "Honorable Medicine"

Following Baumann's logic, we can see that humans began to turn other humans into underlings and slaves in the same way they turned *wood* into *timber. Intensification* set off a chain of events that slowly evolved into an increasingly stark vertical scale of human value, or power distance,[7] with *higher* beings, the *masters,* at the *top* and *lesser* beings, the slaves and *underlings,* at the *bottom.* For the period of the last 10,000 years this order defined most communities and societies.

This hierarchical order was regarded as profoundly legitimate, either divinely ordained or prescribed by nature. It was held dear as the backbone of civilization, and its maintenance was deemed to be indispensable for human life. Within a hierarchical order, "holding down" underlings is deemed a necessary injury inflicted on lower beings, lest they forget their position and disturb the holy order. Surgery hurts but must be endured because it is "good for you," so oppression "had" to be perpetrated and the accompanying pain accepted.

Maintaining the hierarchical gradient was hard work, but those involved were convinced that the efforts were well invested. If you did not hold your subordinates in their *subposition,* you risked being called *lazy.* The "lazy kings" (*les rois fainéants*) of the sixth and seventh centuries in France, for example, were ridiculed because they allowed their immediate subordinates, the *maires du palais,* the managers of the palace, to usurp power. One of these maires du palais, indeed, eventually took over the throne in the year 751.

Marvin Harris provides a description of the laborious task of keeping a vertical ranking of human worthiness in place. He writes about the necessity of having "specialists" who perform ideological services in support of the status quo:

> The elaborate religions of the Inca, Aztecs, ancient Egyptians, and other nonindustrial civilizations sanctified the privileges and powers of the ruling elite. They upheld the doctrine of the divine descent of the Inca and the pharaoh and taught that the balance and continuity of the universe required the subordination of commoners to persons of noble and divine birth. Among the Aztecs, the priests were convinced and sought to convince others that the gods must be nourished with human blood. They personally pulled out the beating hearts of the state's prisoners of war on top of Tenochtitlán's pyramids. In many states, religion has been used to condition masses of people to accept deprivation, to look forward to material rewards in the afterlife, and to be grateful for small favors from superiors lest ingratitude call down a fiery retribution in this life or in a hell to come.[8]

Seduction, as well as coercion, was used, according to Harris.

> A considerable amount of conformity can be achieved by inviting the ruled to identify with the governing elite and to enjoy vicariously the pomp of state occasions. Public spectacles such as religious processions, coronations, and victory parades work against the alienating effects of poverty and exploitation. In Rome, the masses were controlled by encouraging them to watch gladiators, chariot races, circuses, and other mass spectator events.[9]

Morton Deutsch writes about the basic ways by which high power groups can keep low power groups low:

> …control over the instruments of systematic terror and of their use; control over the state which establishes and enforces the laws, rules and procedures which regulate the social institutions of the society; control over the institutions (such as the family, school church, and media) which socialize and indoctrinate people (such as the family, school, church, and the media) to accept the power inequalities; and interactive power in which there are repeated individual behaviors by those who are more powerful which confirm the subordinate status of those in low power. In addition, there are the self-fulfilling prophecies in which the behavior of the oppressed, resulting from their oppression are used by the oppressor to justify the oppression; and the distorted relation between the oppressor and the oppressed.[10]

Thus the normalcy of the vertical scale's application as a legitimate social classification system of human worthiness began roughly 10,000 years ago with the invention of agriculture[11] and in subsequent *civilizations* as they emerged in Mesopotamia, along the Nile, and in many other places. In his book *Early Civilizations,* Bruce Trigger reminds us that "because of the pervasiveness of inequality, no one who lived in the early civilizations questioned the normalcy of this condition. If egalitarianism was known, it was as a feature of some of the despised, barbarian societies that existed beyond the borders of the 'civilized' world."[12] During long stretches of human history that inequality—the vertical ranking of human worth—was much more than a reluctantly tolerated evil; it was hailed as the very core of civilization. Equality was "barbaric."

Once Low, Always Low! Peripheral Characteristics Can Be Ranked and Essentialized

I prefer to use the term *vertical ranking of human worth and value,* rather than *inequality, hierarchy,* or *stratification.* The significant point for my discussion is not the absence or presence of hierarchy, inequality, or stratification, but the ranking of human worth. Hierarchy, inequality, and stratification can very well coexist with the absence of ranking. Robert W. Fuller[13] describes this in his book *Somebodies and Nobodies.* According to Fuller, humiliation is not the *use* of rank, but the *abuse* of rank. The pilot in a plane or the captain of a ship are masters over their passengers when in the sky or at high sea. Clear hierarchy and stark inequality characterize these situations. The pilot and the captain, however, need *not* look down on their passengers as lesser beings.

In other words, using concepts such as hierarchy, inequality, or stratification could be somewhat misleading, inviting objections such as, "There have always been differences between people! Human beings have never been the same and never will be! Are you a dreamer who believes that we could or should all be the same? This is not only impossible, but boring!" Such objections are irrelevant to the discussion of this book and represent a grave miscomprehension of its focus, which is whether human worth and value can be ranked. Diversity and difference can, without a problem, go with sameness of value and worth; there is no automatic mechanism that necessarily links diversity and difference to rankings. The vertical scale of human worth is conceptually independent of hierarchy, inequality, or stratification.

A system that condones the vertical scale of human value *essentializes* hierarchy, inequality, and stratification. In such a social framework, a street sweeper not only does a lowly *job,* the lowliness of the task is essentialized as the inner core of his entire being: He or she *is* a lowly *person.* Something that could very well be peripheral to this person's essence, namely the task of sweeping the street, is turned into her core definition: this person is deemed to be of lower human value and worth. This essentialization is what we find in many, if not most, traditional societies. A street sweeper and a bank director could easily be seen as fellow human beings of equal dignity, differentiated only by their occupations. However, in traditional societies, this basically neutral difference is ranked as lesser and higher. *My Fair Lady,* the musical, illustrates beautifully how Professor Higgins regards the poor flower girl Elisa as a *lower human being,* even after she has learned *higher manners.* Her essence, in his view, is fixed in lowliness through her initial poor status in society. For Professor Higgins nothing can turn Elisa into a human being of worthiness equal to him and his class.

Affaire d'honneur! Honor Is Nothing but Ranked Pride and Dignity

The concept of *honor* was, and still is, linked to the vertical scale. The German SS officers under Hitler learned that humiliating "Untermenschen," holding them to the ground, sometimes literally, was an honorable and noble duty. *Meine Ehre heißt Treue* or "my honor is loyalty" was the German motto, loyalty to the "Führer's" vision of a world of Aryan Übermenschen. Young German soldiers in Falstad, together with millions of Germans, were imbued with the ideology that pushing and holding down those who "belonged" below was their honorable obligation. An officer who disobeyed this mandate would not only risk losing his life, he would be risking the loss of his honor. Obedience to the Führer's will was his supreme honorable duty, not merely for the sake of his immediate superordinates or political leaders, but for the sake of the entire German people, even (in his mind) of the global order as a whole. The Aryan race was the savior of the world and young German soldiers learned that it was their highest duty to safeguard Aryan superiority and secure a bright future for the entire globe.

During long stretches of history, humiliation was reason enough for honorable gentlemen to risk their lives in duels or duel-like wars. Honor was not only inescapable, but also ranked. Aristocrats had *more* honor than other people, but everybody cared for the honor allotted to him in the appropriate way. Thomas Scheff, researcher on the sociology of emotions, tells a story in Yiddish and English that illustrates how the honor of masters was not the same as the honor of underlings (2002 in Oslo). "Two Jews get into a fight," Tom recounts. "Neither manages to win the quarrel. Finally, they agree to have a duel." This, explains Tom, is the first joke, because duels were something for aristocrats, not for insignificant Jewish underlings. "Next morning, before dawn, one of the opponents arrives at the little clearing in the forest where the duel was to take place. There he waits. He waits. And he waits. His opponent does not come. He simply does not show up! Finally, a messenger arrives with a note from the opponent saying he is late and that the other should start without him!"

In traditional honor-based societies, each social stratum, be it called caste, class, group, or subgroup, cultivates indigenous idiosyncratic sets of honor definitions related to the vertical scale. The honor of a slave is different from the honor of a master, but both defend their honor against attempts to humiliate them, to bring them lower. The servant or slave who works in the emperor's private suite attaches his honor to this important rank and resists being degraded to the quarries (note the words *servant* and *to serve* stem from the Latin word *servus,* meaning *slave*). The master, equally, resists being debased into the second rank; he succumbs only if otherwise he would be debased even further.

Honor is a more collective feeling and institution than pristine pride or dignity. It is a learned response to institutionalized pressures. Honor is worn like armor, and people may defend their group's honor against humiliators (for example, in duels) merely as a duty, without feeling much personal emotion. I once counseled an Egyptian lawyer who had studied in Europe and had almost forgotten his roots in the Egyptian countryside where blood feuds were common. One day, to his great surprise and shock, he was visited by villagers who told him that he was next in line to be killed. He knew neither why nor by whom. He had not done anything to elicit other people's hatred. His place in the genealogy of his extended family was sufficient to give him a place in the honor game.

Honor, furthermore, is linked to gender. In an honor society, men are defined as the principal actors, no matter how functionally important female activities might be. He is the *actor,* she is his *object.* He is the defender of honor. He is defined as responsible, self-reflexive, and rational. He is expected to protect *his* women, at least as long as he values them as a *resource,* as prizes and symbols of his honor, or as mothers of his children. A woman who lives in an honor society learns that she either is not a human being at all or is a lowly human being. In the first case, she is perceived as a passive recipient of male actions, as "material" to be used or thrown away by him; she is on the same level as household items or domesticated animals. Also in the second case she is seen as a passive recipient, this time on a level with children or slaves. It is, therefore, in blood feud societies that she can move freely around; only men are "worthy" of being killed "honorably," not women.

Some honor cultures in the Arab World and Africa regard the woman's hymen as a symbol of the family's honor. This is one justification for the practice of female genital mutilation—through this practice, the family's honor (in which she shares) is "protected." In many traditional honor societies, a female is a token, or representative, of the family or group to which she belongs. Daughters or sisters are valued as "gifts" for marriage into other families *her* males want as allies. Only "undamaged," "honorable" girls make honorable gifts.

In conclusion, honor is conceptualized here as a form of ranked pride or dignity, with every stratum in a hierarchical society having its own honor code. Honor, unlike pride and dignity, is often played out as a group phenomenon—usually heavily gendered—more than an individual feeling. People may even find themselves caught in games of honor beyond their control—*affaires d'honneur* important to their group without themselves identifying much with these affaires as individuals.

Do Not Complain! Pain of Humiliation Can Be Accepted as "Prosocial Suffering"

In social and societal structures of honor, any pain or suffering endured by those near or at the bottom of the pyramid of power is deemed to be *necessary* or even *prosocial suffering.* For thousands of years, the suffering of underlings was regarded as "good" for them and for the health of society as a whole. Vaccinations or surgical operations, albeit painful, are accepted as good for patients. Similarly, underlings' pain was seen as good for society by those subscribing to the vertical scale of human value, including many of the underlings themselves.

The concept of a *just war* is another example of the idea that short-term pain can bring long-term benefits. All the pain elicited in the 2003 war in Iraq was deemed by many as regrettable but prosocial, a necessary prelude to a better future.

More so, there have been situations throughout history in which pain was valued on *its own account,* not just as a regrettable yet necessary side effect. Medieval flagellants were happy to whip themselves, to lower their bodies to the ground, and to crawl on their knees for miles. They inflicted these, and worse, humiliations on themselves as acts of penance, to advance themselves morally and to honor God, demonstrating the sincerity of their reverence. Through such self-lowering they reckoned they climbed up on the human ranking scale, up, nearer divinity. They wished to gain worth and value through closeness to God. Their self-inflicted humiliation elevated them on the vertical scale.

Such practices can still be found today, for example, in current Shia celebrations. Bowing to divinity enhances one's moral standing and reputation as long as the object of worship is a widely accepted divinity and not some obscure sectarian guru (bowing to a kitchen knife, or other trivial objects, would be ridiculous and send the practitioners to a madhouse rather than boost their reputation). The Christian God is believed to have reached out to humans by giving his son through the most humiliating death available at the time, namely crucifixion. God lowered himself so as to connect to humanity.

Stockholm Syndrome! Lowliness Can Be Widely Accepted

Throughout history, underlings accepted their lowly lot, often even defending it. Women, for example, kept their heads down for large parts of human history. In Europe, women risked being branded, punished, and even burnt as witches if they dared to arrogate more importance than was "due" them. A woman had to "know her place." She was not supposed to define her lowly condition as humiliation in the sense of violation. On the contrary, she was expected to accept it with "due humbleness" and "female modesty." It was her "honor" to be of service. Her duty, she taught her daughters, was to "respect" this order, not humiliate it by disobedience. Rebellion against female lowliness was regarded as disrespectful to the overall order.

Many women internalized these rules, believing that they represented the right order of the universe. It would be a mistake to believe that only men accused women of failing in modesty, women kept each other down as well. In the last years of Queen Elizabeth I, up to 53 percent of all charges against witches were made by other women.[14] In large parts of the world, women today still believe that they are born inferior.

The history of former slaves or colonized or minority peoples is full of examples of acceptance of inferiority. A member of a low caste in India might see her fate as God's will that should not be opposed. Many colonized *subjects* (*jacere* is Latin for *to throw,* and the prefix *sub* means *under*) deemed their colonizers to be more "civilized." Many yearned to become "more French than the French," or "more British than the British." Frantz Fanon[15] wrote a book entitled *Black Skin, White Masks,* where he describes how he was once very proud of being almost "French," of climbing *up* the vertical scale of human value. What he initially overlooked was that his new-won pride validated his former lowliness. You cannot be proud of being up without judging your former status as *down.*

There are many terms describing this *identification with the oppressor. Learned helplessness* is "a term coined by Martin Seligman to define that helplessness that is a learned state produced by exposure to noxious, unpleasant situations in which there is no possibility of escape or avoidance."[16] Likewise, the *Stockholm syndrome* is "an emotional bond between hostages and their captors, frequently observed when the hostages are held for long periods of time under emotionally straining circumstances. The name derives from the instance when it was first publicly noted, when a group of hostages was held by robbers in a Stockholm bank for five days."[17] *Identification with the oppressor* is not always an individual process; it can also be a societal process. As discussed before, many underlings turned their lowliness into a "culture." Johan Galtung's notion of *penetration,* or "implanting the top dog inside the underdog,"[18] illustrates the fact that acceptance of subjugation may become a culture of its own. Ranajit Guha's understanding of the term *subaltern* also points to this process.[19]

However, it would be arrogant to frame underlings as passive victims. Lowliness and helplessness can also be displayed out of conviction. As discussed before, many underlings accepted their lot as God's will or nature's order. They were not coerced or seduced into believing in their own lowliness; they shared their superiors' views on the legitimacy of ranking human essence in a way that turned them into lesser beings.

Break the Will of the Child! Parents Can Reproduce Underlings

Parents were central to the reproduction of obedient underlings. Alice Miller[20] spelled out how, in the period that led up to the two World Wars, leading pedagogues regarded *breaking the will of the child* as an essential part of responsible child rearing. Lakoff and Johnson describe this philosophy as the *strict father model* (as opposed to the *nurturant parent model*):

> The father has authority to determine the policy that governs the family. He has moral authority and his commands are to be obeyed. He teaches his children right from wrong by setting strict rules for their behavior and by setting a moral example in his own life. He enforces these moral rules by reward and punishment. The father also gains his children's cooperation by showing love and by appreciating them when they obey the rules. But children must not be coddled, lest they become spoiled. A spoiled child lacks the appropriate moral values and the moral strength and discipline to live independently and meet life's challenges. The mother has day-to-day responsibility for the care of the household, raising the children; and upholding the father's authority. Love and nurturance are a vital part of family life, but they should never outweigh parental authority, which is an expression of love and nurturance—tough love. As children mature, the virtues of respect for moral authority, self reliance, and self-discipline allow them to incorporate their father's moral values, empowering them to be self-governing and self-legislating.[21]

The result is a weakening and not a strengthening of the child. Evidence from three areas of psychological research—attachment theory, socialization theory, and family violence studies—shows that the strict father model "...tends to produce children who are dependent on the authority of others, cannot chart their own moral course very well, have less of a conscience, are less respectful of others, and have no greater ability to resist temptations."[22] Thus, the strict father model seems to produce what Theodor Adorno[23] called the *authoritarian personality* whose principal characteristic is obedience and a willingness to blindly follow orders, irrespective of their moral contents.

Be "Civilized"! How Humiliation May Elicit Shame and Humility

Earlier I mentioned humility and humbleness and their place vis-à-vis humiliation in the mental landscape of the vertical scale of human worth. Norbert Elias[24] describes this in his seminal book *The Civilizing Process*. Emile Durkheim, Karl Marx, Max Weber, and historians such as Marc Bloch developed similar lines of reasoning. Elias explains that the process of subjugation may have had a civilizing effect on rough and haughty knights, lords, and commoners. He studied the French court and how feudal lords were seduced into bowing to the absolute ruler. Unruly, proud local warlords were "civilized" by being taught the lessons of shame. According to Elias, pacified and civilized people learn to feel embarrassed; they learn "social anxiety." The *civilized habitus* that Elias describes could also be called the "successfully humiliated habitus."[25] The French court, the Indian caste system, the Chinese system of kowtowing, and the Japanese bow all express and reinforce strong hierarchies, all constructed around practices of ritual humbling.

Shame can be defined as a humbling experience a person agrees to; humiliation describes those experiences a person does not agree to. Shame seems to be lowering accepted by the receiver and interpreted as due humbling. A "civilized" person might blush when he breaks wind inadvertently. He might feel ashamed even if nobody notices because he has learned to subscribe to the notion that farting is a transgression of decent civilized behavior.

Human beings are intersubjective beings: we see ourselves as others see us, and we can feel either pride or shame when we look at ourselves with others' eyes. Shame, guilt, and humility all have prosocial aspects. Shame is what keeps us within the limits of the social contract.[26] We all hope that shame will deter our neighbors from lying to and stealing from us. We trust that our neighbors will feel guilty, feel moral shame, and not have an affair with our spouses. We all hope that our neighbors will bow in humility to the rules that make it possible for us to live in community with one another. We hope that shame and guilt will limit social disruption. Humility has been enshrined in most religions as a necessary virtue to spiritual development. Shame, guilt, and humility are associated with the action of bowing. Arrogant people believe they can reach the sky and do what is not possible to normal mortals. Humble people, on the other hand, recognize that there are limits. Shaming may thus work for the good of the larger society. Corporations and governments are often "shamed" into abiding by the promises of humility they made. They are asked if they are not ashamed of cutting down the trees that are the backbone of a healthy global climate, of destroying biodiversity, the very gene pool that may one day provide humankind with all the medicine it needs.

In other words, one person may feel ashamed and humbled without feeling humiliated; another person may feel humiliated but not ashamed. Shame can take either of two pathways—the path of self-humiliation and self-destructive depression or the prosocial path of self-humbling and allowing oneself to grow into a more mature human being.

Humiliation as Prescribed Lowliness: The Old Order of Honor

A slave who lives in a world where beating slaves is part of the divine order does not suffer the same emotional pain as an individual who lives in a more liberal culture might suffer after incurring a beating. Likewise, a woman who lives in a culture where it is codified by law that husbands ought to beat disobedient wives does not endure the same painful emotions a battered wife in a culture that values female autonomy might endure.

Norway ranks Number One on the Gender-Related Development Index. Nevertheless, as recently as the end of the nineteenth century, Norwegian law gave husbands the right to beat insubordinate wives. Even today, there are women who believe that being beaten by their husbands is normal. The chapter addressing gender-based violence in the *State of World Population 2005* report informs us that 94 percent of women in Egypt indicated that they thought it was acceptable to be beaten, and the next figure came from Zambia with 91 percent of women.[27] "One of the reasons women remain silent is that in many societies violence against women is accepted as a 'normal' aspect of gender relations. In some countries, a large proportion of women believe wife beating may be justified for reasons such as refusing to have sex or not preparing food on time."[28]

Which effects do such *legitimizing myths*[29] have? *Cognitive appraisal theory of emotions* addresses this question. In a culture that legitimizes wife beating, a disobedient wife is regarded as sinning against her husband and against the whole social order. It is thus possible that such a wife accepts the pain of the beating because she regards it as justified and prosocial. It is likely, in fact, that a huge amount of humiliation has been endured quietly by human beings throughout history for precisely this reason.

In long-standing hierarchical societies, the underling and master relationship is static—both believe their relationship to be the natural order of things. Underlings may be happy or unhappy, but they do not view their inferior status as a significant variable in their happiness equation. They accept their position in the same way they accept that some people are taller than others, that time passes, or that we grow old and die. People may not be happy about these facts of life, but there is little any of us can do about them.

Many of my female clients (and some male ones) were caught in a struggle against "prescribed lowliness." Eighteen-year-old Nadia was regularly beaten by her mother, who shouted: "Why did we send you to school to give you haughty ideas? So you could forget the rightful place of a woman? We should never have sent you to school! A woman bears her husband's children and obeys him! That is her role! Stop whining!"

Stop! How Humiliation Turns into Painful Violation: The New Order of Dignity

William Ian Miller informs us that "the earliest recorded use of *to humiliate*, meaning to mortify or to lower or to depress the dignity or self-respect of someone, does not occur until 1757."[30] In other words, in the English-speaking world, humiliation was not seen as hurtful until about 250 years ago. English-speaking people were not isolated in their attitudes. For millennia, people around the world believed that it was normal and morally correct to have masters and underlings, and that masters were entitled to be treated as higher beings and underlings deserved to be shown "where they belonged." Even when underlings rebelled, it was to replace the master rather than to dismantle the hierarchy.

The emergence of the modern meaning of the word *humiliation* (1757) co-occurs with a number of other transitions. The author of *The Invention of the Self,*

John O. Lyons,[31] for example, analyzed travelers' descriptions of their experiences and found that around 1750 the authors began to insert themselves as subjects with a personal perspective on what they observed.[32] This change closely preceded the American Declaration of Independence (July 4, 1776) and the French Revolution (August 4, 1789), rallying points for the development of the human rights movement. Undoubtedly, the ideas that culminated in today's concepts of human rights predate 1757. Religions such as Christianity and Islam teach ideals of equality. However, these ideals did not move to the forefront of Western consciousness until about 250 years ago.

Human rights ideals are not the sole property of the West, but, I propose, the West was the first region to be impacted by what I call the second round of *globalization,* which brought about a new set of global realities. Those realities eroded the old *age of honor (with fear as defining negative emotion)* and gave way to the new *age of dignity (with humiliation as defining negative emotion).* The new moral sentiment condemns handling fellow human beings in ways that degrade their innate value. Self-empowered, dignified individuals are the ideal of the new human rights paradigm. Individuals operating within this paradigm are encouraged to stand up in civil disobedience if blackmailed and extorted by fear. This new dignified individual easily feels humiliated if equal dignity is violated, producing a new kind of defiance.

After 10,000 years of hierarchical domination, a very sudden and very major transition is currently occurring, its beginning marked by the 1757 change of the meaning of the word humiliation. The new *Zeitgeist* urges the dismantling of the vertical gradient of human worth. What masters and underlings once colluded in calling *benevolent patronage* is now criticized as *brutal domination.* Virtually nowhere in the modern world is *subjugating* people or *putting/pushing/holding down* people regarded as reason for pride and satisfaction today.

William Ury, an anthropologist and director of the Harvard University Project on Preventing War, drew up *a simplified depiction of history;* see Table 2.1. In this effort, he pulls together elements from *anthropology, game theory,* and *conflict studies* to describe three major types of society: *simple hunter-gatherers, complex agriculturists,* and the current *knowledge society.* In Ury's system, simple hunter-gatherers live in a world of coexistence and open networks, within which conflicts are negotiated, rather than addressed by coercion. The abundance of wild food represents an expandable pie of resources that does not force opponents into win-lose paradigms. Complex agriculturalists, on the other hand, live in a world of coercion. They lead their lives within closed hierarchical pyramids of power on land that represents a fixed pie and pushes antagonists into win-lose situations governed by strict rules.

Knowledge society resembles the hunter-gatherer model because the pie of resources—knowledge—appears to be infinitely expandable, lending itself to win-win conflict solutions. This type of society rejects the tightly knit hierarchical

Table 2.1
A Simplified Depiction of History[33]

Conditions	Type of Society		
	Simple hunter-gatherers	Complex agriculturists	Knowledge society
Basic resource	Expandable pie (wild foods)	Fixed pie (land & power)	Expandable pie (knowledge)
Basic logic of conflict	Both-gain or both-lose	Win-lose	Both-gain or both-lose
Basic form of organization	Open network	Closed pyramid	Open network
Basic form of decision making	Negotiation	Orders	Negotiation
	↓	↓	↓
	Coexistence	Coercion	Coexistence

Source: Ury 1999, p. 108.

structure in favor of the open network espoused by our earliest ancestors. Negotiation and contract replace command lines, and coexistence is the primary
strategy.

"Subjugating Human Beings Is Illegitimate!" How the Sentence of Humiliation Evolved

We can integrate Ury's chart and the practice of humiliation, starting by
reflecting on the sentence, "Subjugating people is illegitimate" or, in an expanded
version, "Subjugating, abasing, instrumentalizing, or putting down human
beings is illegitimate and labeled humiliation, whereby humiliation means the
illicit violation of equal dignity." This sentence feels morally "right" for human
rights advocates in the twenty-first century.

This sentence contains three parts: (a) "subjugation," (b) "human beings," and
(c) "illegitimacy." What we see here is a fascinating core discourse, one that
underpins many debates, not only the one carried out here, on historical development, but also on such topics as communism, democracy, and capitalism.

By varying the last element (c), we can build another sentence, namely "subjugating people is legitimate." We have unearthed, like archaeologists, a sentence
that was accepted as morally "right" throughout the past 10,000 years in most
societies. Where this sentence is accepted, the use of the word humiliation does
not entail any connotation of violation. This sentence is still widely spoken and
heard, but it is rapidly losing legitimacy.

We can also manipulate the second element (b) of the sentence, "human beings," replacing it, for example, with the word "nature," producing two sentences: (1) "subjugating nature is legitimate" and (2) "subjugating nature is illegitimate." The first sentence, "subjugating nature is legitimate," dictated eons of human thought and action. The newer version of this sentence, "subjugating nature is illegitimate," lies at the core of modern talk about sustainability. "Subjugating nature is illegitimate" is the human rights ideal applied to the biosphere. One may call it the *biosphere rights ideal.*

Finally, we can manipulate the first element of the sentence and ask whether the practice of "putting down" and "subjugating" has always been known to humankind. Perhaps it was, albeit at varying degrees of proficiency. Language was, perhaps, the first application of the idea that something can be put down; after all, we *subject* nature to our linguistic labels. The Latin root of the word *subject* reveals it: *ject* stems from *jacere, to throw,* and *sub* means *under.* Chimpanzees know how to use tools, fashioning twigs to gather larvae out of tree holes. They can, in other words, instrumentalize nature for their own advantage, albeit in an extremely restricted manner. Admittedly, early *Homo sapiens* were not very proficient tool users either, compared to modern humans. Early attempts to subjugate nature were, therefore, remarkably modest. With time, however, humankind excelled at the "trade" of subjugation.

We can conclude that at the core of the notion of humiliation we find the *theoretical possibility* that something can be put, pushed, or held down. Once human beings conceived of this theoretical possibility, they *transformed* it into manifold practices. Initially, only abiotic nature was put and held down. Later the idea was *expanded* to include the domestication of animals and also *human beings* were held down.

Using traffic as a metaphor to illustrate the historic evolution of the concept and practice of humiliation and human rights, we see that as long as there was ample space, everybody moved along without taking much notice of the other drivers. Under conditions of abundance, hunters and gatherers enjoyed pristine pride. In early agricultural empires with denser populations, however, the powerful usurped the right to pass first. Honor dictated that big vehicles drove through first at a crossroad, while the smaller ones wait in due reverence. A master regarded it as legitimate to push out the smaller ones, who accepted this treatment as divinely ordained. Occasionally somebody attempted to acquire a larger vehicle. If he succeeded, he is the new master with all the rights of a master, since revolutions toppled the masters, but not the system. However, apart from the threat of revolution, a threat that required constant attention from the masters, this system rendered a certain extent of public stability, calm, and order. At some point, around the time the word "humiliation" began to connote violation, a discussion arose about (to stay with the metaphor) managing traffic more effectively by using traffic lights. Equal dignity for all means that every driver, irrespective of the size of the vehicle, has the same rights before the new traffic lights. The size of the vehicle, its color, and its price do not affect the driver's status or rights.

Table 2.2 integrates my analysis of humiliation into Ury's *simplified depiction of history.* Let me also transpose this analysis of human history onto the graphics presented in Figure 2.1. The horizontal line in the center represents pristine pride. This line is not meant to convey that all human beings are equal, if by equal we mean identical. It does, however, convey a world view that condemns the hierarchical ranking of the differences among human beings in terms of worth and value. This horizontal line depicts the core principle of the egalitarian hunter and gatherer communities that reigned for the first 90 percent of human history. The horizontal line at the top represents the master in the old honor cultures; the line at the bottom represents the underlings in those cultures. With these elements in place, we can visualize the human rights movement as an attempt to collapse the top and bottom lines back into the central line, which, in modern terms, represents equal dignity and humility. The entire diagram underscores the invitation currently being issued by human rights advocates to both masters and underlings to join in shared humility and equal humanity.

The world view of honor, or the old order of honor, is a collective concept. The world view that is based on the notion of dignity is a concept that emphasizes individualism. The ideas of human rights themselves are not new; belief in

Table 2.2
"A Simplified Depiction of History" with Humiliation Added

	Simple hunter-gatherers I	Complex agriculturists II	Knowledge society III
Type of society and period in human history	Pride	Honor	Dignity
The application of the idea that something can be put down, instrumentalized, or subjugated	Humankind undertakes its first tentative attempts of applying the idea of subjugation and, by making tools, instrumentalizes nature.	Humankind expands the practice of subjugation on to human beings; some human beings, slaves and underlings, are transformed into "tools" at the hands of others, the masters.	Humankind turns against the practice of ranking human beings into lesser and higher beings, and declares the practices of the past ten thousand years to be illegitimate.
The evolution of the sentence of humiliation	The subjugation (of nature)	and of human beings (no longer only nature)	is defined as illegitimate (no longer as legitimate).

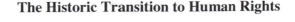

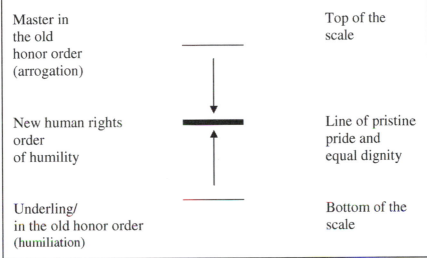

The Historic Transition to Human Rights

Master in
the old
honor order
(arrogation)

Top of the
scale

New human rights
order
of humility

Line of pristine
pride and
equal dignity

Underling/
in the old honor order
(humiliation)

Bottom of the
scale

Figure 2.1
The Historic Transition to Human Rights

the equal dignity of all humans was present in Christianity, Islam, and many other early philosophies. What is new is the widespread acceptance of these ideals. We live today in the midst of a historic transition that our forefathers would have found almost unfathomable. Ideas and moral sentiments that were marginal for millennia have gained unprecedented importance. Ideas that previously lingered at the periphery of the human condition have moved onto the center stage and define the essence of humanity, impacting an increasing number of hearts and minds worldwide.

Dignity Is Untouchable! Human Rights Render Humiliation Illicit

The first paragraph of Article 1 of the Universal Declaration of Human Rights, which was adopted by the United Nations General Assembly on December 10, 1948, reads: "All human beings are born free and equal in dignity and rights. They are endowed with reason and conscience and should act towards one another in a spirit of brotherhood."

This Article does not imply that there are no differences among people. People may have different skin colors, different genders, different religious creeds, and different ethnic backgrounds. However, all human beings, solely by being human, possess the same level of worth and value. *Nobody* is a lesser being, and nobody is a higher being. Nobody is allowed to humiliate and degrade others.

Today, human rights can no longer be viewed as simply another intellectual concept. Human rights ideals elicit gut feelings of the "undueliness" of humiliation when people are treated as *lesser* beings. Human rights ideals introduce a new form of feelings of humiliation that was not present at any prior point in human history. Human rights link dignity and humiliation in new ways. Thus, human rights introduce feelings, feelings of humiliation, when dignity is being degraded.

Why Humiliation Is More Hurtful in the Context of Human Rights

In human rights–based societies humiliation becomes more hurtful and a more important topic for research. This is because the *four* basic kinds of humiliation known to honor cultures become conflated into *one* kind of humiliation when viewed through a human rights lens.

Humiliation in honor societies—we may call it *honor humiliation*—can be categorized in four variants (see Table 2.3).[35] A master uses *conquest humiliation* to subjugate formerly equal neighbors into a position of inferiority. When the hierarchy is in place, the master uses *reinforcement humiliation* to keep it in place. The latter may range from seating orders and bowing rules to brutal measures such as customary beatings or killings. A third form of humiliation, *relegation humiliation,* is used to push an already low-ranking underling even further down. *Exclusion humiliation* means excluding victims altogether, exiling, or even killing them.

Human rights turn all four types of humiliation into the latter one because all human rights violations exclude victims from humanity. This situation produces intense pain and suffering because losing one's dignity means being excluded from the family of humankind altogether. I call this type of humiliation *human rights humiliation* or *dignity humiliation;* it is a deeply destructive and devastating experience that attacks people at their cores. It is from this viewpoint that practices of humiliation once considered "normal," such as beating and "breaking the will," acquire medical labels such as *victimhood* or *trauma.*[36]

Table 2.3 depicts humiliation as practiced in hierarchical honor societies as opposed to the understanding of humiliation in a human rights context.

Be Aware of Changes! All Aspects of Life Are Affected by the Call for Equal Dignity

The human rights movement is both a passive recipient of the shape imposed upon it by its historic and contemporary context and an active force that shapes

Table 2.3
Four Variants of Humiliation[34]

	Honor humiliation	Human rights dignity humiliation
Conquest humiliation: When a strong power reduces the relative autonomy of rivals, previously regarded as equals, and forces them into a position of long-term subordination. Creation of hierarchy or addition of a new upper tier within a hierarchical order.	X	—
Relegation humiliation: When an individual or group is forcefully pushed downwards within an existing status hierarchy.	X	—
Reinforcement humiliation: Routine abuse of inferiors in order to maintain the perception that they are, indeed, inferior.	X	—
Exclusion humiliation: When an individual or group is forcefully ejected from society, for example through banishment, exile, or physical extermination.	X	X

Source: Adapted from Smith 2001, p. 543.

its historic and contemporary environment. Many conceptual shifts mark this transition. In the following paragraphs, I touch upon a few of these concepts: *victimhood, trauma and conflict, objectivity,* and *consciousness,* terms that derive new meanings.

New definitions clash with old definitions! How conflict, victimhood, and trauma draw on the notion of undue humiliation

Victimhood and trauma apply only when victims become consciously aware that they have suffered victimhood and trauma. Individuals often have to make long mental and emotional journeys from honor humiliation to human rights steered dignity humiliation to define themselves as victims.

The common case of the social worker who wants to save a woman from being beaten by her husband comes to mind. The social worker defines the woman as a victim. However, the woman claims that her husband beats her to prove he loves her. Virtually every social worker has experienced the deep frustration of this experience. In other words, people who are under the control of a dominant group, even if this domination is hurtful, may not see themselves as *traumatized victims.* They may even define themselves as "protected children." Even some of Saddam Hussein's followers bought into his self-definition as a benevolent patron. Morton Deutsch writes:

The socially privileged, typically, assume that they have the right to control the interactions in their relationship with members of subordinated groups. Challenging this assumption can be risky for a subordinate and, as a consequence, they usually go unchallenged. The repeated, everyday experience of being treated as an inferior produces a public image of being an inferior, which may be internalized as an image of self-inferiority. In the socially privileged, in contrast, such interactions will produce a public image of superiority and a corresponding self-image. Such nonegalitarian everyday interactions between the socially dominant and the oppressed help to keep the system of oppression in place by the public images and self-images they produce and perpetuate.[37]

As repeatedly stated, human rights has enshrined the idea that every human being has an inner core of dignity that ought not be humiliated. In that way dignity humiliation is posited at the very core of victimhood and trauma inflicted by human beings on their fellows. The situation is very different in the case of earthquakes and other natural disasters. In those situations there is no perpetrator, so the aspect of humiliation is missing (unless one believes in God wishing to humiliate his sinful followers.) Victimhood and trauma are less intense in natural disasters than when the same pain is flowing from fellow human beings, particularly when this happens in the framework of human rights. The reason for this is that the phenomenon of humiliation is deeply relational.

The first question asked about the 2003 blackout in North America was "Was it terrorism?" The relief was almost palpable when it became clear that there was no terrorism involved. The hardship was identical, but it was easier to bear when people knew that the inconvenience was not the result of another terrorist "message of humiliation" (see for work on the *controllability dimension* Keith Allred and James Averill[38]).

When a person suffers at the hands of other human beings, she has in principle four choices. (1) She may define this suffering as a kind of natural disaster (being beaten by a disturbed or drunk person, for example), or (2) she may accept it as a "prosocial honorable lesson" or "prosocial humbling" (as discussed earlier, being beaten, in honor contexts, is often seen as equivalent to having surgery or a vaccination that "hurts but must be endured"), or (3) she may not accept it as a prosocial honorable lesson (being beaten as a slight of honor that calls for humiliation for humiliation), or (4) she might see it as an illegitimate humiliation of dignity (being beaten as a violation of dignity that ought to be opposed in a dignified Mandela-like fashion). Only in the third and fourth cases does a person see herself as a traumatized victim.

How does this dynamic play out in the context of conflict? As long as I accept being beaten as a prosocial honorable lesson, there is concord between me and my dominators. The word *concord* stems from Latin *cum* which means *with* and *cord* which means *heart*. Concord means that our hearts are with each other.

The word *conflict*, however, comes from verb *flectere*, to *bend*, to *curve*. In conflict, *discord* displaces concord and may lead to confrontation. The word *confrontation* entails the Latin word *frons* which means *forehead*. In confrontation, foreheads are placed *against* each other, in opposition. Thus, the term *conflict*, similar to the terms *victimhood* and *trauma*, is dependent on the particular framing of reality adopted by the players and the overall social mind-set within which the incident occurs. Morton Deutsch explains:

> Discontent and the sense of injustice may be latent rather than manifest in a subordinated group. Neither the consciousness of oneself as victimized or disadvantaged nor the consciousness of being a member of a class of disadvantaged may exist psychologically. If this be the case, consciousness-raising tactics are necessary precursors to the developing of group cohesion and social organization. The diversity of consciousness-raising tactics have been illustrated by the variety of techniques employed in recent years by women's liberation groups and black power groups. They range from quasi-therapeutic group discussion meetings through mass meetings and demonstrations to dramatic confrontations of those in high-power groups. It is likely that a positive consciousness of one's disadvantaged identity is most aroused when one sees someone, who is considered to be similar to oneself, explicitly attacked or disadvantaged and sees him resist successfully or overcome the attack; his resistance reveals simultaneously the wound and its cure.[39]

Every psychotherapist has seen divorce cases that evolve in this way: For years, a woman tries to make her husband understand that he must respect her dignity, while he thinks she merely is a little "sensitive" or "hysterical." For long periods she suffers from psychosomatic symptoms and depression, seemingly supporting his views. When she finally files for divorce, he is surprised and hurt, while she tells him that she has talked to him for years, in vain. The woman probably does not call her private uprising "conflict." If her husband were to understand her and apologize for being slow to embrace the ideal of equal dignity, there would be no conflict. If asked, she might say the man created the conflict by his loyalty to the old order that says that a quiet woman is a good and happy woman. As long as she was quiet, he saw no need for change and was reluctant to "bend" to fit new world views. Both sides experience irreconcilable types of humiliation—honor humiliation on the part of the husband, and dignity humiliation on the part of his wife.

The person who has learned to consider herself a victim of undue humiliation (in contrast to due shaming or humbling) at the hands of other people also has four options. (1) She may turn her rage inwards, become depressed and apathetic, and even turn to drug abuse (like the depressed wife suffering from psychosomatic symptoms). In that case the conflict is almost invisible.[40] If, however, this person chooses to turn her rage outwards, we have several outcomes. (2) She may explode in hot desperate and self- and other-destructive rage. Passionate murder and/or suicide might be the result. (3) She can go down a Hitler-like path and organize humiliation entrepreneurship. Hitler attempted to redress humiliation by inflicting humiliation on the supposed humiliators, achieving only another spiral in the cycle of humiliation. In Rwanda feelings of humiliation were systematically incited. Terrorists attract followers with humiliation narratives. There is no need to buy expensive weapons when feelings of humiliation are hot, neighbors kill neighbors with knives (Rwanda), and civil planes are turned into missiles (9/11). Therefore I labeled feelings of humiliation the "nuclear bomb of the emotions." (4) Mandela, in contrast, made constructive use of energy in his rage for social change. He facilitated the birth of a new social order based on respect for individual dignity. Central to his effort was the inclusion of the humiliator, the white upper class, as coprotectors of human rights. In other words, Mandela solved the conflict by peacefully but firmly making Frederik Willem de Clerck and his followers (in the case of the couple this would be the unwilling husband) understand that the old order was dying. The only way the formerly privileged could bend this conflict into concord and *convergence* was by relinquishing their outdated framings of reality. Mandela attempted to attain *shared humility* without humiliation.

In Iraq, there will be convergence only if the Arab World frames the second Iraq war as *liberation.* Conflict will ensue as long as the Arab World frames the military action as *humiliating invasion.* In this event, conflict may remain invisible and be lived out as depression and apathy on the part of Iraqis and Arab citizens and those who identify with them (1). However, simmering rage may also lead to hot retaliation (2) or Hitler-like reactions, such as terrorism against the West (3), or (4) Mandela-like or Gandhi-like outcomes if such leaders are available. This is what people mean when they speak of winning not just the war, but also the peace.

Even truth is being humbled! Epistemology is affected by the idea of equal dignity

The human rights movement aims at dismantling the vertical gradient that creates masters and underlings. *Epistemology* (the study of systems of thinking) is one of many fields affected. Modernist thought has roots in the enlightenment (the rise of human thought from the "dark" or "medieval" ages), characterized by new methods of logic (Descartes, Locke, Kant), empiricism (Bacon), and the emerging scientific method (Newton). The Enlightenment was a revolution, an uprising of individual rationality against "all forms of totalitarianism—royal and religious."[41] The old master, *faith in God-chosen sovereign rulers and their opinions,* was replaced by a new master, *faith in experts as guardians of reason.*

Yet, enlightenment soon faced another challenge. Particularly subversive was the claim that all human beings are equal in their capacity to engage in rational activity. Within this claim hid the seeds for a second revolution, undermining the victories of the earlier one. The insistence in blanket equality meant the *experts* had to yield to the *common man* (and soon the common *man* had to make room on equal terms for his *female* equivalent). As Serge Moscovici puts it:

> ...at the beginning, people took an interest in the biases of social knowledge and compared "experts" with "novices," leaning on the distinction between "truth" and "mere opinion." Now, the notion of collective and social representations presupposes that all people are "rational," that they are rational because they are social, and so on.[42]

No Rankings! Equal Dignity Can Be Ascribed to Stages

The conceptualization of history in this book has been criticized by scholars who wish to avoid *looking down* on people.[43] They reject the notion of *historic stages* because they feel that this smacks of arrogant ranking. They believe in extending respect by highlighting egalitarian diversity, both synchronic and diachronic, rather than insinuate ranking. I agree with the goal. However, I believe there is an easier way of avoiding arrogance than by suppressing the fact of long-term global change.

Hunter and gatherer lifestyles evolved under circumstances of *abundance,* whereas agriculture was an attempt to expand the pie of resources through intensification when abundance had turned to limitation. Modern societies, in turn, are deeply influenced by the coming into being of *one single global village,* which posits yet another novel set of circumstances. In each case, humanity coped and copes creatively, each time within another set of limitations, using the preexisting tool kit and expanding on it. The identification of stages is not to be confused with the arrogant view that the last stage is the best. It may simply be the best under current circumstances. Each stage benefited from being familiar with the physical and mental tool kit that came before.

Earlier I stated that it is an ideological decision whether or not to apply a vertical scale to human worthiness so as to draw up a hierarchical gradient. The same pertains to human history. Human communities and societies—both present and throughout history—do not need to be ranked hierarchically. I certainly do not intend to rank them. However, the wish to abstain from ranking does not force us to relinquish describing differences, even systematic differences that build on each other. It is not necessary to abandon analysis of stepwise discourses just to avoid rankings. Differences, even differences that can be narrated as steps or stages, may be posited as equal in worth and value.

I find it hope-inducing that archeological evidence of systematic war is lacking prior to 10,000 years ago. If systematic war was a side effect of human adaptation to the peculiar conditions of the past 10,000 years, my hope is increased that humankind might be able to build a better world under the new, more benign conditions of a global knowledge society. I find it respect-maximizing when I can humbly recognize the inner logic in practices such as honor killings while extending an invitation to the defenders of such practices into a new, more benign moral universe of human rights ideals.

The conceptualization of history in this book uses a Weberian ideal-type approach. What is described as a sequential development is also synchronic, even within each community and within each individual. Within societies that take it for granted that they are based on human rights, considerable remnants of the honor order linger on. Likewise, in societies such as Pakistan, Egypt, and Mexico, supposedly adhering to the collective honor code, we meet the most clear-sighted human rights defenders. The process is even confounded within the minds and hearts of individuals. The staunchest feminist may give her car key to her husband because she believes he can protect the family better than she can. When the doorbell rings unexpectedly in the middle of the night, she might send her husband to the door. A Western woman, supposedly so "liberated," may be astonished at her Somali sister who, newly arrived in the West, displays more courageous "feminism" than she would ever dare. Different mind-sets exist side by side in the *global village,* in the same society, and even in the same mind.

Summary

I tried to demonstrate in this chapter how rankings of human worth and value evolved throughout human history. Such rankings and the debate about their legitimacy or illegitimacy form important parts of human world views, both diachronically throughout history and synchronically in contemporary times.

- During long stretches of history it was almost universally accepted as the *normal order of things* that human beings were ranked along a vertical scale, with those of *more* worth at the top and those of *less* value at the bottom.

- In an honor society, each level has its own honor. *To humiliate* means maintaining this hierarchical order by "reminding" those further down of their "due" place.

- Humiliation was a universally accepted and honorable tool—and still is in many places—to keep *stability, law, and order,* which was the order of vertically ranking human value and essence.

- Many an underling assisted by what could be called "voluntary self-humiliation," wrapped in various definitions of honor.

- The present is characterized by a transition to a new order of equal dignity for all that contradicts previously existing norms of ranked worthiness. Therefore, this phenomenon calls for exceptional and innovative attention.

Related Reading

Few researchers have studied humiliation explicitly. In many cases the term "humiliation" is not differentiated from other concepts; humiliation and shame, for example, are often used exchangeably, among others by Silvan S. Tomkins

(1962–1992)[44] whose work is carried further by Donald L. Nathanson.[45] Nathanson describes humiliation as a combination of three innate affects out of altogether nine affects, namely as a combination of shame, disgust, and "dissmell" (Tomkins' term) (Nathanson in a personal conversation, October 1, 1999).

In Lindner's work, humiliation is addressed on its own, differentiated from other concepts. Humiliation is, for example, not regarded simply as a variant of shame. Dennis Smith, professor of sociology at Loughborough University, UK, was introduced to the notion of humiliation through Lindner's research and has incorporated the notion into his work in a fascinating way.[46]

The view that humiliation may be a particularly forceful phenomenon is supported by the research of, for example, Suzanne M. Retzinger and Thomas J. Scheff,[47] who studied shame and humiliation in marital quarrels. They show that the suffering caused by humiliation is highly significant and that the bitterest divisions have their roots in shame and humiliation. Also W. Vogel and Aaron Lazare[48] document *unforgivable humiliation* as a very serious obstacle in couples' treatment. Robert L. Hale[49] addressed *The Role of Humiliation and Embarrassment in Serial Murder*. Humiliation has also been studied in such fields as love, sex and social attractiveness, depression, society and identity formation, sports, history, literature, and film.

Donald C. Klein[50] carried out very insightful work on humiliation in, for example, *The Journal of Primary Prevention* that devoted special issues to the topic of humiliation in 1991, 1992, and 1999. Linda Hartling and Tracy Luchetta[51] pioneered a quantitative questionnaire on humiliation (Humiliation Inventory), which probes the extent to which respondents had felt harmed by such incidents throughout life, and how much they feared such incidents.

Scheff and Retzinger extended their work on violence and Holocaust and studied the part played by *humiliated fury* in escalating conflict between individuals and nations;[52] the term "humiliated fury" was coined by Helen Block Lewis.[53] Consider Scheff[54] and Philippe Masson,[55] Stéphane Vachon,[56] Viktor V. Znakov,[57] and see, furthermore, Israel W. Charny[58] and his analysis of excessive power strivings. Psychiatrist James Gilligan,[59] as well, focuses on humiliation as a cause for violence, in his book *Violence: Our Deadly Epidemic and How to Treat It*.

Vamik D. Volkan and Joseph Montville carried out important work on psychopolitical analysis of intergroup conflict and its traumatic effects.[60] Furthermore, Ervin Staub's work is highly significant.[61] See also the journal *Social Research* in 1997,[62] whose special issue was stimulated by the *Decent Society* by Avishai Margalit.[63]

Richard E. Nisbett and Dov Cohen[64] examined an honor-based notion of humiliation. The honor to which Cohen and Nisbett refer is the kind that operates in the more traditional branches of the Mafia or, more generally, in blood feuds. William Ian Miller[65] wrote a book entitled *Humiliation and Other Essays on Honor, Social Discomfort, and Violence,* where he links humiliation to honor as understood in *The Iliad* or Icelandic sagas, namely humiliation as violation of honor.

There is significant literature in philosophy on *the politics of recognition,* claiming that people who are not recognized suffer humiliation, which leads to violence.[66] Max Scheler[67] set out these issues in his classic book *Ressentiment.* In his first period of work, for example, in his book *The Nature of Sympathy,*[68] he focuses on human feelings, love, and the nature of the person. He states that the human person is a loving being, *ens amans,* who may feel *ressentiment.*

This overview does not exhaust the contributions to be found in the literature on the topic of humiliation—or rather on related issues, since, to my awareness, only Miller, Hartling, and the two above-mentioned journals explicitly put the word and concept of humiliation at the center of their attention. Later other authors are also introduced and cited.

However, when we turn to issues that are related to humiliation, then a wide field of research opens up: Research on mobbing and bullying touches upon the phenomenon of humiliation. Research on mobbing and bullying leads to the field of prejudice and stigmatization, which in turn draws on research on trauma and posttraumatic stress disorder, aggression, power and conflict, stress, and, last but not least, emotions.

Conflict and peace are topics that have been widely studied; thousands of publications are to be found that cover a wide range of conflicts, from interpersonal to intergroup and international conflict. The search word *terrorism* renders thousands of hits in databases.

In cases where humiliation shall be studied in cross-cultural settings, cross-cultural psychology has to be included in this brief overview, and the anthropological, sociological, and philosophical embeddedness of processes of humiliation in different cultural contexts has to be addressed, too. If humiliation between groups or even nations is to be studied, then history and political science play a central role as well.

CHAPTER 3

GLOBALIZATION AND EGALIZATION

If we imagine the world as a container with a height and a width, *globalization* has to do with the horizontal dimension, the shrinking width. *Egalization,* a term I coined, concerns the vertical dimension. So-called "globalization critics" oppose a lack of egalization entailed in the current design of globalization. Globalization critics want our world not only to shrink in "width," but also to become "flatter." Globalization entails a push toward egalization, albeit with a painful time lag and in a hurtfully uncoordinated way. In his last book, Thomas Friedman describes how the current round of globalization (he calls it *Globalization 3.0*) contributes to making the world *flatter.*[1] Let us first turn to globalization.

Virtually every news program in the world starts with a turning globe, constantly reminding viewers that we are all inhabitants of planet Earth. None of our ancestors had this view. The astronaut's gaze back at our great blue home is unique and unprecedented in human history. This perspective seduces, invites, and pushes us to become aware of the fact that we live on *one tiny planet* in a vast universe and, increasingly, are moving into *one single global village.* The human world is pulled together both in reality and in our minds (this *coming together* is what I define as globalization). This process pokes holes in the fences and frontiers that used to keep opposing groups safely separated. This merging is not always blissful. Feelings among players who are forced to live more closely gain intensity when misunderstandings arise or expectations are disappointed. Feelings of humiliation can be more swiftly elicited than ever before.

Globalization is not the first historic incidence of *unification.* The creation of larger units is not new. Big empires have formed from smaller units. The Roman Empire, for example, was huge. But, one element in our current global situation is profoundly new—human beings are, for the first time in history, in the process of *consciously* understanding that planet Earth is small, limited, vulnerable, and not expandable.

Past empires were held together by strong centers that ruled over underlings through fear and seduction. They saw themselves in opposition to the rest of the world that was not yet conquered or not worth conquering. For most of human history, the outer boundaries of the human world were fluid. Like early hunters and gatherers who may have thought that they had unlimited "free" space, early conquerors thought that somewhere there were unlimited numbers of underlings to subjugate. Empires did not run out of opportunities to expand or to conquer; there were no limits to their imaginations.

In contrast, today's *global village* is held together by our growing awareness *of the minuteness of the globe, its limits, and of our interdependence.* "We may have all come on different ships, but we're in the same boat now," said Martin Luther King, Jr.

Earth was never anything but a tiny planet in a vast universe. It is not the planet that has changed. Humankind has just arrived (or is in the process of arriving) at a deeper understanding of its reality. We came to this understanding through the help of a long tradition of toolmaking that ultimately led to spaceships, airplanes, and telephone cables—technologies that revolutionized our perspectives on the world. We are able to take pictures from space, airplanes shrink distances between the continents, and communication technology makes networks such as the Internet possible.

The facts and imageries produced by these technologies profoundly affect relations between *us* and *them.* The rifts that used to separate us from them are affected by this unifying drive of globalization. *In-groups* and *out-groups* coalesce into *one single in-group.* There are no longer several *villages,* but one single global village.

Imagery, of course, precedes reality. A global village of happy neighbors is far from being a reality. Several recent debates in anthropology and related disciplines picture the world as fragmented, paradoxical, and ambiguous. The currently bustling academic industry around the idea of globalization,[2] for an early, influential contribution) focuses on the largely technology-driven processes that contribute to increasing contact across boundaries and the diminished importance of space. This focus on unbounded processes has contributed to a reconceptualization of the social world in which flux, movement, and change are the rule, not the exception.[3]

No history lesson helps us, because the notion of *one global village* turns the whole of humanity into one single in-group (with inner diversity) on one tiny planet, something that never occurred before. Humanity's task at this crucial juncture is to study the potentially *benign* and *malign* results of this new reality and find ways to strengthen the benign tendencies and mitigate and marginalize the malign ones.

Are You One of Us? Globalization Can Elicit New Feelings of Humiliation

Central to the future of globalization is the fact that human beings tend to differentiate in-groups from out-groups, us from them, and moral *inclusion* from moral *exclusion*. Bluntly, there are two kinds of morals, an *inside* moral and an *outside* moral. What *my* people deserve is not the same as what *your* people deserve. The reach of morals is also called the *scope of justice*. Peter T. Coleman defines it as follows: "Individuals or groups within our moral boundaries are seen as deserving of the same fair, moral treatment as we deserve. Individuals or groups outside these boundaries are seen as undeserving of this same treatment."[4]

A wealth of social-psychological research relates to the phenomenon of in-group and out-group categorizations. *Social identity theory*, a hotly discussed field, examines phenomena of us versus them. The famous Robbers' Cave Experiment by Muzafer Sherif involved boys in a summer camp.[5] The boys were split into two groups and asked to engage in competitive activities with conflicting goals (for example, zero sum games such as football). Intergroup hostility evolved astonishingly fast, almost automatically. Experiments confirm that the same dynamics hold for adults. Even worse, this splitting tendency is so strong that conflicting goals are not needed to establish the in-group/out-group dichotomy.

In such circumstances, can there ever be *cooperation* across lines? Research indicates that the only remedies for humanity's *splitting tendency* are common superordinate goals that are attainable and determined by common consent among equals. Three conditions must be fulfilled to allow the citizens of the global village to cooperate across fault lines. We must (1) identify with *common superordinate goals* that are (2) *realistically reachable,* and (3) *social inequality must be avoided* in the process.[6]

First requirement for cooperation: Common superordinate goals

In *Creating Super-Ordinate Goals,* Michael Harris Bond, a cross-cultural psychologist based in Hong Kong, writes:

> Social polarizations may be transcended through groups' and their members' uniting successfully around a common purpose or goal (Sherif and Cantril 1947). This might involve local tasks such as constructing community facilities. Community service projects, especially if involving younger students from various ethnic groups serving members of various other ethnic groups, may be especially effective in building trust and good-will across group lines.... National tasks, such as protecting the shared environment or indeed, fighting off an invader, will accomplish the

same unification. Social capital will then develop out of the experience of working together and subsequently out of shared pride in the ongoing benefit from the actual accomplishments themselves.[7]

The increasing understanding of the vulnerability of our planet represents an incentive for *global citizens* to identify with the common superordinate goal of safeguarding our fragile common home. The rising awareness of the planet's tiny size and fragile biosphere coalesces with processes of globalization to provide an experience that binds people together and pushes for cooperation. Globalization, understood in this way, could be said to represent a benign trend that furthers global cooperation. Furthermore, globalization may operate in an even more *benign way* by making people *humble* before these newly identified goals. The majority of lay people, at least until very recently, were not very enlightened about the nature of the Universe. According to our everyday experience, the Earth is flat with small variations for hills or mountains. It is difficult to understand that the Earth is spherical. Previously, proofs were difficult to obtain. In contrast, very recently, virtually everybody on the globe is exposed to the pictures from space of a revolving Earth ball.

Ironically, the human tool kit, meant to heighten human standing, ultimately humbles it. Telescopes disseminate the message that haughtiness on the part of *Homo sapiens* is misplaced. It is unsettling for any intelligent being to ponder whether *Homo sapiens* is chosen by God or merely lost in space. Anyone who thinks along such lines, even with the tiniest shred of doubt, is about to lose faith in fixed order. Masters are not sure anymore whether *up* is really their divinely ordained place; underlings question whether they are divinely ordained to remain down. The thought that planet Earth may be better off without humans may be the most humbling. Perhaps we will die out like the dinosaurs, and nature will sigh with relief. All aspects of globalization that highlight humanity's insignificance and vulnerability humble us, making us more cautious and less prone to inflict *proud subjugation* and *mindless violation*.

A friend, a veterinarian who works in Scandinavia, told me the following (in October 2002):

> Recently, I heard a talk at a conference about artificial insemination. The American speaker explained that his research showed that bulls produce higher quality semen when it is procured with an artificial vagina rather than through the use of electro-ejaculation, whereby the bull receives a small electroshock to trigger ejaculation. The drawback with the artificial vagina is that the bull has to be trained to use it.
>
> After the talk, the American speaker and his colleagues explained that they would continue with electro-ejaculation. I was flabbergasted. First, the speaker explains that using an artificial vagina renders better results and then he declares that he recommends the inferior method. I asked him if he knew that electro-ejaculation was banned in Norway and Sweden for ethical reasons. The speaker and his people replied: "We are free to do what we want!"

At this point, the friend who told me this story almost shouted, "This is the freedom of the fool who cuts off the branch on which he sits. How can foolishness be freedom? These people are so blinded by their arrogance in regard to nature that they do not recognize that a little humility would serve their interests much better! These people humiliate their animals and in my eyes also themselves."

New humility sabotages fixed order and makes arrogance an outdated stance. The Scandinavian veterinarian has heard the message, and his American colleagues have not. They haughtily believe that "freedom" means power over the limitations of nature. The new humility reinforces the many little processes that coalesce in globalization; it transforms acts intended as acts of confident subjugation into overconfident violation.

We may conclude that the emergence of new common superordinate goals powered by the facts and imageries of the vulnerability of planet Earth comprises a benign tendency in globalization. However, there is a problem that can turn *malignant*. The humility that is required to tackle the newly detected superordinate goals—though propelled by processes of globalization—does not emerge simultaneously in all hearts and minds. Wherever humility is wanting, feelings of humiliation heat up on all sides. Isolationist Americans, accused of haughtiness, may feel insulted and humiliated when others point fingers at them. The United States formally rejected Canadian Prime Minister Paul Martin's suggestion that it needed to heed "the conscience of the world" (December 9, 2005, Montreal). And those who do the finger-pointing feel insulted, humiliated, and enraged by the American definition of freedom. Since feelings of humiliation undermine cooperation, the uncoordinated acquisition of this new humility, though urgently needed, can be said to introduce malign or at least *detrimental* tendencies in the short term that have to be mitigated if cooperation is to be attained.

Second requirement: Common superordinate goals must be attainable

Samuel L. Gaertner and John F. Dovidio[8] stipulate that an environment that rests on a win-win situation may be expected to lend itself to cooperation, while zero sum circumstances may increase the likelihood of divisions among people. As I mentioned earlier, Ury[9] describes the global information society as a culture in which the pie of resources is expandable. Unlike land, knowledge—ideas, new thoughts, and novel inventions—has no limits. Agriculturalists depend on land, forcing them to adopt win-lose games. Modern information bearers, on the other hand, find themselves in win-win situations; there is always another innovation out there waiting to be invented (I am not speaking of crude economic growth here, on the contrary). The innovative ideas that power modern technologies that in turn power globalization also render a benign win-win push towards cooperation.

We can, therefore, assume that the second requirement for cooperation—
attainability—exists as a benign tendency in today's world. It would seem beneficial to strengthen these benign tendencies and encourage creativity.

Third requirement: Superordinate goals must be combined with conditions of equality

Social psychology emphasizes equality (which I prefer to call equal dignity) as a
precondition for cooperation because inequality generates ill feelings. Richard G.
Wilkinson[10] discovered that social inequality deteriorates the quality of social
bonds, producing psychosocial stress for all, particularly those of lower status.

The Dictionary of Geography defines deprivation as "lacking in provision of
desired objects or aims":

> Within the less developed countries deprivation may be acute; the necessities of life
> such as water, housing, or food may be lacking. Within the developed world basic
> provisions may be supplied but, in comparison with the better-off, the poor and
> the old may well feel a sense of deprivation. This introduces the concept of *relative
> deprivation* which entails comparison and is usually defined in subjective terms....
> The idea of a *cycle of deprivation* refers to the transmission of deprivation from one
> generation to the next through family behaviors, values, and practices. This idea
> has been extensively debated and discussed.[11]

As long as people live far apart with little information about one another, they
remain unaware of inequalities. Those who have less are not aware that they are
deprived. Under such conditions, *relative deprivation* may go undetected. To recognize relative deprivation, people must move closer. The more opportunities to
compare themselves with others, the more existing inequalities will be acknowledged. An oasis dweller in the Egyptian desert who gets access to television for
the first time and watches American soap operas is taking a crash course in comparison. What may have been *absolute deprivation* before, becomes relative deprivation with the help of technology.

As discussed before, as long as those who have less believe that inequality is a
natural phenomenon, divinely ordained, they may not develop ill feelings. People
will accept relative deprivation if they see it as legitimate. *Cycles of deprivation*
become entrenched when those who have less develop cultures to explain certain
aspects of their situation as *honorable assets*. It is only when such justifications are
undermined—as they are by the human rights message—that people begin to
question inequality and may move to protect their self-esteem and identity by
attributing their lowly circumstances to powerful enemies who oppress them.[12]
Morton Deutsch summarizes:

> An individual's conception of what he and others are entitled to is determined by at
> least five major kinds of influence: (1) the ideologies and myths about justice that
> are dominant and officially supported in the society, (2) the amount of exposure

to ideologies and myths that conflict with those that are officially supported and are supportive of larger claims for the oppressed, (3) experienced changes in satisfactions-dissatisfactions, (4) knowledge of what others who are viewed as comparable are getting, and (5) perceptions of the bargaining power of the oppressed and oppressors.[13]

Globalization—the coming together of all humankind—provides new opportunities for comparison, turning absolute into relative deprivation. Coupled with the message of human rights, which deems relative deprivation illegitimate, the situation is one that removes all possible justifications for inequality and elicits rage and anger.

In the language of *human rights humiliation,* it is humiliating to be shown the amenities of modern life in Western soap operas and to be invited into the family of equal human beings, while simultaneously being deprived of those very amenities. Ill feelings, including feelings of humiliation, must be expected to increase in such circumstances.

In summary, globalization, by creating superordinate goals that are realistically attainable and that can be tackled in team spirit, is benign. Indeed, globalization may be thought of as a process that provides humankind with common superordinate goals and, through them, the hope that demarcation lines between hostile groups can be transcended.

However, equal dignity must be nurtured to prevent emerging feelings of humiliation from turning these benign tendencies malign.

You Are an Enemy! How Outdated Out-Group Language Can Humiliate

In the global village, all concepts, ideas, and feelings formerly attached to out-group categorizations lose their validity. When there is only *one* in-group left, there can be no out-group. Out-group notions now "hang in thin air" without their former basis in reality. When a tree dies, it no longer bears fruit. People may need time to grasp this, but they cannot escape this new reality.

Words such as "enemies," "wars," "victory," and "soldiers" (as well as the already mentioned word "they," as opposed to "us") stem from times when the human population lived in many separate *villages.* Under the new circumstances *we* are citizens of *one* village, with no imperial enemies threatening from *outside.* There is, indeed, no outside. Likewise, there is no "they" anymore; there is only "us." The only sentence that fits the reality of any village, including the global village, is, *"We are all neighbors; some of us are good neighbors, some are bad neighbors, and in order to safeguard social peace we need police [no longer soldiers to defend against enemies in wars]."*

A village comprises good and bad neighbors, while enemies traditionally have their place outside of the village's boundaries, as have soldiers, wars, and victories.

A village enjoys peace when all inhabitants get along without resorting to violence. Words such as "war," "soldier," or "victory" are anachronistic. The only language that fits the new situation is the language of policing, because safeguarding social peace within a village calls for police sustaining a cohesive social web, not soldiers seeking victory. Currently, we witness many such transitions of language. The traditional notion of the *soldier* is presently changing to connote *peace keepers* and *peace enforcers*.[14] The *warrior-soldier* who left home to reap national and personal glory, fame, and triumph is becoming obsolete. Furthermore, there is movement away from the word *enemy*, toward the word *terrorist*. Terrorists are *inner enemies, very bad neighbors,* the only subgroup of enemy that can exist *inside*.[15]

It is crucial to learn that the use of outdated language may have humiliating effects. Friends from different parts of the non-Western world, among them those who supported the American government when it went to war against Iraq, regularly write to me. I summarize and paraphrase their reactions at the period around April 2003:

> I agree that Iraq must be liberated. But saying Saddam Hussein has to be removed because he threatens the civilized free world is obscene. Does this mean that there is a "civilized" world and "uncivilized" world? Does it mean that Iraqis are uncivilized? Are Indonesians uncivilized? Are only Americans civilized? America is a baby among the great civilizations! Iraq is the successor of Mesopotamia, home of some of the world's greatest civilizations!
>
> If Saddam only threatened the uncivilized world, would he be allowed to stay in power and freely kill uncivilized people? And what is this nonsense about the free world? Everybody is free who has a passport from a rich country. A person from a rich country, even the most awful sloth and parasite, is free. But, all those poor creatures who are born in a poor country, are not free. They are restricted. They may work a hundred times harder than any rich person, but they are not free. Rich countries call them illegal immigrants and send them back home, deeply humiliated.
>
> If President Bush wants to win the hearts and minds of the "uncivilized" and unfree of this world he should never say that dictators threaten the free civilized world! Dictators threaten the whole world! Period! He should never talk about waging *war!* Even not *just war!* Policing is the word that describes what needs to be done. And, he would NEVER pray: "May God continue to bless America!" He would say: "May God continue to bless America and the whole World!" America is only blessed if the entire planet is blessed!

As my friends' comments indicate, *policing* can be just or unjust, but it is never war. Policing is *just,* at least from the point of view of a human rights framework, when the related institutions are democratically legitimized and target only criminals. It is *unjust* when the police force is dominated by an elite to subjugate competitors. Much of Western war language is anachronistic and humiliating, particularly in the ears of those who subscribe to the human rights vision of equal dignity for all. It feels obscene. It violates decency and mocks the courage that inspires these *missions*. The same endeavor, if framed in police language—saying that *criminals* are to be *brought to justice* (not *killed* or *flushed out*) and that *hostages* (including *enemy soldiers*) have to be *freed*—would be more appropriate.

The globalization process proceeds even in the face of resistance. Conservatives around the world may insist, for example, that bad people deserve to be called "enemy." This word, and related words such as "war," "soldier," and "victory," will not disappear because some soft-hearted dreamers wish it. These words are losing their meaning because they no longer describe reality. When a tree dies, it bears no more fruit. Likewise, the reality that bore words such as "enemy," "war," and "victory" is currently dying, through globalization, whether we support this development or not.

The Emergency Is Over! Globalization Brings Humiliation to the Fore

I suggest there are four logics at the core of the human condition:

(1) The question of whether and to what extent resources are expandable (*game theory*, as developed by the discipline of philosophy),

(2) The question of whether the *security dilemma* is weaker or stronger (*international relations theory*, developed by political science),

(3) The question as to what extent long-term or short-term horizons dominate (as described in many academic disciplines, among others *cross-cultural psychology*), and

(4) The question of how the human capacity to tighten or loosen fault lines of identification is calibrated (*social identity theory*, developed by social psychology).

Game theory is well-known and does not need a lengthy explanation here. It is almost common knowledge that win-win situations are more benign than win-lose situations. As discussed before, the global knowledge society offers a win-win environment.[16] This state of affairs provides a rather benign baseline.

Social identity entails the insight that humiliation can create rifts within social relationships at all levels when people get closer and support human rights. Angry outbursts of feelings of humiliation can be so devastating that they lead to violence even in cases where everything else is in place to produce cooperation. Humiliation can introduce devastatingly malign elements into otherwise benign processes.

The other two logics are discussed in a little more detail in the following paragraphs.

The security dilemma

As long as there were plenty of resources and groups of people lived far enough apart so as to remain unaware of each other, there was no problem. However, as soon as people moved geographically close enough for mutual raiding, but psychologically too far away to build good communication and trust, leaders became trapped in the security dilemma and had no choice but to invest in arms. As these villages now coalesce into one global village, the problem disappears again. The security dilemma poses grave problems only as long as villages stay in a medium distance, too close for geopolitical security and too far for human security.

The term security dilemma is described by international relations theory as follows: "I have to amass power, because I am scared. When I amass weapons, you get scared. You amass weapons, I get more scared."[17] Thus, an arms race and finally war are triggered. In such contexts, even the most "benign" sovereigns are compelled to be belligerent because they are victims of the security dilemma.

The security dilemma forces bloody competition to emerge out of mutual distrust, even if nobody is interested in going to war. The threat of preemption is the ultimate and seemingly inevitable outcome of the traditional security dilemma. The term "security dilemma" was coined by John Herz[18] to explain why states that have no intention to harm one another may end up in competition and war. Its very essence is tragic. The security dilemma has been expanded upon by many authors.[19]

Classical and structural realism, two early international relations theories, saw the security dilemma as unavoidable. Yet, history indicates that the dilemma is amenable to being increased or decreased. The security dilemma can be weakened by involving many members of society in policy and decision making. The dilemma also grows more benign as villages become more interdependent and begin to communicate in ways that make it easier to discern the motives of the other—when trust is built between the residents of different villages. Its logic has a chance to totally disappear when there is only one village.

The time horizon

Florence Rockwood Kluckhohn and Fred L. Strodtbeck[20] have developed a six-dimensional system for categorizing cultures. One of their dimensions addresses the orientation towards the flow of time—the future, the past, and the present. In a culture that emphasizes the past, innovation is difficult, while future-oriented societies welcome it. The authors relate the story of an American and a Bahraini meeting at a restaurant where they find a sign saying that the kitchen will be closed for the coming six months. The American reacts with anger, but the Bahraini says, "We have lived without this kitchen for thousands of years, we will survive the next six months without it!"

A long future time horizon seems to be more beneficial for humankind than a short one. An entrepreneur, who cuts down the trees of the rain forest, the lungs of the globe, has the short-term interest of securing shareholder value. He should also, however, be aware that it is in his long-term interest that his grandchildren inherit a world worth living in.

Players in the Palestinian-Israeli conflict may have a short-term interest in retaliation, but they need to bear in mind that they all share a long-term interest in building a world that provides peace and welfare to their children. Many conflicts "dissolve" as soon as people switch to long future time horizons.

Constituent groups normally look to their leaders to address problems and crises in a timely fashion. However, many of the social, economic, and political problems leaders face today are complex matters where information is scarce or overabundant, and often contradictory, requiring considerable time for effective analysis, planning, and implementation. Furthermore, typically an overwhelming host of many problems—which may or may not be related—all demand equal attention at the same time. Thus, leaders are often driven to (and rewarded for) suggesting quick solutions that insufficiently address the root causes of the problem.[21]

In conclusion, long-term orientations, projected into the future, provide common ground and are more benign than short-term orientations or orientations projected into the past. The technological advances that coalesce with and drive globalization may represent a push towards such benign long-term orientations because they help bring long-term processes to public awareness—research on climate is an example. Democracy, with its in-built short-term political horizon, is benign only as long as a strong civil society counteracts short-term outlooks and safeguards long-term future orientations.

Four logics

Table 3.1 displays the four basic *logics* of (1) the pie, (2) the security dilemma, (3) the future time horizon, and (4) social identity that may have guided the development of cultures of (a) *pride*, (b) *honor*, and (c) *dignity*. The table is based on the understanding that, about 10,000 years ago, human communities based on *pristine pride* confronted a dramatic alteration in the core *logics* that define human lives—suddenly abundant pies turned into fixed ones. Humanity responded with a completely new moral ethos and emotional coinage, namely the *honor coinage* that legitimizes the vertical scale of human value and worth. Present changes are inspiring the development of yet another, completely new and initially disruptive ethos and emotional coinage, that of *equal dignity*. As the incipient global knowledge society transforms the fixed pie into an expandable pie, the "second round" of globalization invites humankind into *one single in-group*. The *security dilemma* weakens and long-term thinking becomes the norm. This development delegitimizes practices of *putting and holding down*.

In 2000, I wrote:

> The most benign scenario is a combination of weak Security Dilemma, expandable pie, long time horizon, and an atmosphere of respect. Conversely, the worst scenario brings together a short time horizon, positioned in an environment that represents a

Table 3.1
The Human Condition[22]

		The Future Time Horizon		Social Identity	
		Short (or long past)	Long	Respect	Humiliation
The Pie	Fixed	(b)			(b, honor-h.)
	Expandable		(a, c)	(a, c)	(c, dignity-h.)
The Security Dilemma	Strong	(b)			(b, honor-h.)
	Weak		(a, c)	(a, c)	(c, dignity-h.)

Source: Adapted from Lindner 2001e, p. 439.

fixed pie of resources, combined with a strong Security Dilemma, within which individuals or groups are exposed to humiliating assaults. As already mentioned, feelings of humiliation and their consequences may be so strong that they override and undermine otherwise "benign" scenarios, in a downward spiral. This model of the human condition may be instrumental to analyzing social change over long time stretches and in different world regions, as well as aid future strategy planning for governments and international organizations. It indicates that the destructive nature of the dynamics of humiliation becomes the more visible the more the other parameters veer to the benign side.[23]

Clashes of humiliation

It is likely that we may in the near future experience, not *clashes of civilizations,*[24] but *clashes of humiliation.*

The idea of a *clash of civilizations* assumes that *villages* have developed at considerable distance from one another and that cultural difference has a firm basis in "real" differences in the belief systems of the various cultures. To state this as simply as possible, one culture is seen as adapted to the mountains, others to the lives of fishermen, and still others to the needs of traders. "Cultures" are regarded as "containers" with more-or-less opaque walls. A small allowance for "diffusion" may be made, meaning that cultures are in contact with each other and learn from each other, but this does not alter their basic natures as isolated containers. Postmodern thought uses this view as its foundation, postulating that different cultures are fundamentally impenetrable, unknowable, and enigmatic to one another. As long as we hold this view, there is little we can do to ease culture clash, except protect ourselves by building walls, fences, and defense armor. We may seek to respect diversity and respect difference and hope to minimize potential hostility from "other" cultures. Respect, however, has its limits. When others shoot at us, we are likely to start shooting back.

I propose that the picture is both more complex and more hopeful, with culture differences being much more relational than the diffusion hypothesis and postmodern thought conceives them to be. Perhaps much of observable culture differences are reactions to perceived hostility from others. It is very possible that they are nothing more than *devices* used when relations go sour, allowing one side to justify its actions and decisions.

During my fieldwork in 1998 and 1999 in Somalia and Rwanda I saw this dynamic in action. Ethnic Somalis are united by language, culture, and devotion to Islam; however, the colonial powers had split the Somalian territory into five different regions. When Somalia became independent in 1960, many people dreamed of a united Somalia. However, counterintuitively, homogeneity does not guard against fragmentation. Today Somalia is a deeply divided country, war-torn for more than a decade and full of bitterness and suffering. Self-proclaimed "Somaliland" in the North is not recognized by the international community or by other Somali leaders. In Somaliland I was beleaguered by Somalilanders who urged me to promote their dream of being an internationally recognized independent republic. They argued that they had been humiliated to such a degree by former dictator Siad Barre and his allies, Somali clans from the south, that they no longer can be part of a united Somalia. They insisted that the "cultural differences" between them and the other Somalis were too significant.

Thus, feelings of humiliation on the side of the Somalilanders made them create a cultural rift and a new culture, namely the culture of Somalilanders. Where there was a dream of unification before, and the notion that "we all are brothers," suddenly there are no brothers anymore, but the wish to be apart. Culture difference, and deep rifts justified by this difference, can thus be constructed in response to humiliation.

Soon after my arrival in Rwanda in 1999, I was struck by the fact that the country has no commonly accepted history. People with a strong Tutsi background maintain that their centuries-old minority rule benefited the country. The Tutsis, they say, would never have perpetrated genocide as the Hutus did. The Hutus, in contrast, insist that Tutsi rule was never benevolent—the Tutsi elite just imagines benevolence to justify domination. The Hutus, feeling humiliated, create a "culture"—including a history—of their own, Hutu culture as opposed to Tutsi culture. They do not want to be part of a culture defined by their dominators.

The conflicts in Rwanda and Somalia can be described more accurately as *clashes of humiliation* than as *clashes between cultures*. Countless other examples show how easily feelings of humiliation can lead to divisions. Using the examples of Ethiopia and Eritrea, Liah Greenfeld suggests that resentment plays a central role in nation building.[25] People say, "I do not want to be part of a people and a culture that humiliates me and violates my dignity. I choose to shape a separate identity—personal, cultural, or national."

Humiliation, which generates resentment, helps create rifts and difference, cultural or national. The danger of this occurring is perhaps most pernicious when there has been a dream of unity. Somalia had a dream of unity, and Rwanda still has. The global village needs a dream of unity to nurture cooperation. This dream of unity can be destroyed when protest against humiliation expresses itself through the formation of separate cultures within the global village. We have to guard against this danger.

Come In! Globalization Can Dignify Women

Women and men are not irreconcilably different by nature, although there are undoubtedly hormonal and physical differences between the two sexes. There is strong evidence for the so-called *gender similarities hypothesis*.[26] It is possible for a woman to step into a male role and vice versa. Women are not better people than men. Nor are men better than women. The two gender role templates offer tools for both construction and destruction. Both are deeply influenced by globalization.

For long stretches of the past, males were responsible for short-term emergency and women for long-term maintenance. I define the traditional roles of men and women by renaming what is usually called the *domestic* sphere, the inside sphere, and what is usually called the *public* sphere, the outside sphere. Women are traditionally responsible for nurturing the next generation inside and men for guarding the frontier between inside and outside and keeping the inside safe. Consequently, a woman could move relatively freely inside her house, or her village, but she could not venture much outside her village walls, where all kinds of dangers, from plunderers to bandits, lurked. Globalization, or the coming together of humankind, slowly dissolves "village walls," increasing the inside sphere available to women.

Women are traditionally expected to maintain a household, to wash and clean, to repair what is broken, to plan for long-term maintenance costs, and to consider the interdependence necessary to keep a household going. The same principle applies to the social inside sphere—a woman is expected to care for the well-being of the people around her, to maintain emotional and social family life, to create harmony and console the distressed, and to maintain social cohesion.

However, apart from the nurturing side of female role descriptions, there is also a traditionally "feminine" role—the *cleaning* role[27] that has proven extremely destructive. At the simplest level, cleaning is often ecologically inappropriate—when women wash clothes white with heavily polluting agents, for example. At the social level, cleaning can degenerate into damage, destruction, and even atrocities, as it does when a group dedicates itself to ethnic *cleansing*, for example. The metaphor that something needs to be *thrown out* from inside into an imagined outside can justify environmental and social atrocities.[28] The

German army tried to deny its involvement in ethnic cleansing during World War II, perhaps on the basis of a belief that it was not "male" enough work for soldiers. Killing defenseless people smacks of "female" cleaning, not the kind of activity that wins soldiers medals for bravery. The killing of Jews in concentration camps was equated with having to eradicate "dirt" or "pests," an unavoidable but unpleasant "feminine" task.

The traditional male role entails constructive and destructive elements as well. The traditional man is expected to go out, to reach for the unknown, to be daring in conquering the unfamiliar, and to risk his life to defend the inside sphere. A German saying asserts: "Der Mann geht hinaus in das feindliche Leben" or "The man is to go out into hostile life." Fairy tales tell of heroes who face a series of increasingly difficult tasks in far away universes to prepare to marry the princess and rule and protect his people. "Male" emergency tasks are not holistic. They are characterized by the sword cutting through and the axe destroying the enemy, both highly efficient operations, even when this efficiency means destroying an intricate network. Historically, males covered distances unidirectionally on a horse or a ship, or with an airplane or rocket. Males opened new horizons. This male action bore valuable fruit, leading eventually to modern technology. However, it also created long-term problems, since this mind-set tends to overlook the fragile interdependence of physical laws and the need to maintain balance.

Yet another, perhaps more serious drawback is connected with this traditional male/female division of tasks. Admittedly, a community under the trance of the security dilemma had little choice but to construct its culture in the described way. It is more conducive to survival of groups to let males "do the early dying"; they are "redundant" at an earlier age, seen from the point of population politics. Yet, as soon as a community decided to use males for defense, male dominance was almost inevitable—because emergency trumps maintenance. Even our bodies follow this protocol. When we are in danger, adrenaline pours into the blood stream and pushes the maintenance tasks of the body into the background. However, there is a price to pay. The body breaks down under conditions of constant emergency when essential maintenance is too-long neglected. Heart attacks—the typical emergency troubleshooter disease—result. Similarly, a world under the grip of the necessity of continuous male prowess is bound to live in constant danger of collapse. Such a setting is potentially malign.

Globalization could save the world from "cardiac failure." Emergency, fear, stress, and the need to send people out to defend borders ebb and wane with the strength of the security dilemma—significantly abating when the security dilemma dissolves. The coming into being of one single global village takes away continuous emergency and stress, and instead makes room for proper maintenance. It lessens the need for a culture of male dominance—a culture that neglects proper maintenance—that characterized humanity almost everywhere on the globe for the past 10,000 years. In the global village, females and males alike can concentrate on maintenance and cautiously planned exploration of new horizons, rather than emergency actionism. Both females and males have an opportunity to become mature adults; women can stop huddling under male protection like children; males can release undue self-confidence.

Indeed, there exists right now an urgent need for the more female holistic thinking on the ecological and social levels. We need more female-oriented individuals—people who understand biological cycles and are willing to work for social peace. Traditional "female" services such as negotiation are called for, instead of military attack, mediation instead of dictatorial order, and social maintenance through an intricate network of courts, lawyers, and police, instead of a unidirectional system of sheer military force. But we also need the "male" skill of unidirectional thinking, a tool essential to innovation.

Indeed, good maintenance work is currently acquiring a higher status virtually in all segments of society. Management courses nowadays try to train managers to understand the importance of "soft" human factors such as motivation, job satisfaction, cooperation, and creative problem solving. Well-balanced "female-type" cooperation is advocated today on all levels, from small companies to the United Nations, while the army-like "male" hierarchical order is considered out of date. Wild-West-pioneering style is appropriate for films, but no longer for real life. Traditional female role characteristics are gaining ground on a global scale.

However, cultural change is not quick or homogeneous. The male sphere has dominated the female for centuries, acquiring a tenacity of its own. Male supremacy may lose its anchoring in reality as the security dilemma weakens, but cultures are slow to follow suit. Yet, women no longer cheer men in uniform; many no longer feel protected by supreme males. They feel humiliated by men and women who adhere to the old order of male supremacy, by those who do not yet understand that change is inevitable in this world of changing *logics*.

Egalization or Humiliation

Globalization is powered by technology and our use of it, and egalization by our day-to-day moral sentiments and moral decisions. Egalization is about our relations with others and ourselves, whether we deem it right to look *up* or *down* on others and ourselves or believe we should treat all with equal respect. Egalization is about whether we use fear as the "glue" for coercive hierarchies or prefer to live in creative networks held together by mutual respect. I coined the word egalization to differentiate it from words such as equality, equity, or egalitarianism because the main point is equal dignity. The term egalization avoids claiming that there are no differences among people. *Egality* can coexist with functional hierarchy that regards all participants as possessing equal dignity; egality cannot coexist with hierarchy that defines some people as *more valuable* than others.

Global Democracy or Global Dictatorship? The Wrong Sheriff Can Humiliate

We need *social contracts* to counteract the *anarchic state of nature*. Somalia, after exiling dictator Siad Barre in 1991, remains lawless for more than a decade. Colombia currently has only one objective, instituting "Order! Order! Order!" and the "Rule of Law!" to stem rampant social *chaos* (says Francisco Santos, Colombian vice president, on May 12, 2003[29]).

What kind of social contract do we need? In *Leviathan,* Thomas Hobbes describes *life under conditions of anarchy* as "continual fear, and danger of violent death" where "the life of man [sic]" is "solitary, poor, nasty, brutish, and short."[30] Hobbes characterizes the *state of nature* as an utterly lawless state of affairs that cannot be remedied by a social contract that is merely agreed upon by its users. In Hobbes's view only unlimited political authority, preferably *absolute monarchy,* is strong enough. Citizens should voluntarily bow to a strong hand.

John Locke[31] had doubts. Absolute monarchs are just human beings with all their weaknesses. Ultimate political authority, according to Locke, resides in the *will of the majority.* This majority entrusts political power to governmental officials, under the condition that they work for the common good and can be removed if they violate the public trust.

To use the traffic metaphor, the *anarchy* of the state of nature poses a problem. Under conditions of anarchy, big vehicles push the small ones out of the way at every crossroad. Small vehicles hardly have a chance, and there is much upheaval and continuous fighting.

Hobbes argues for an *absolute authority* to decide how traffic should be regulated and to enforce these rules. He believes that only a very strong hand can control the usurpers of power who undermine calm and order. Locke, on the other hand, trusts the majority to decide. The *majority* has the power to decide on a superordinate set of rules that bind everyone, weak and strong. An abusive traffic police chief could be replaced by the vote of the majority.

Here we have two models for maintaining law and order in the global village of the future, the solutions presented by Hobbes and Locke. One solution recommends *subjugation through an absolute world ruler,* the other recommends *global democracy.* Hobbes's reflections suggest a global village with a top-down pyramid of power, while Locke proposes a global village of equal citizens. Both solutions may guarantee stability and order. If Hobbes's strong man uses enough force, no underling would dare break the law or instigate revolution. There will be quiet, either out of fear or out of lazy contentment. Saddam Hussein's draconian rule provided a certain degree of stability and order, even if his citizens lived in constant fear. Locke's majority vote, carried out sensibly by a citizenry that is not too unruly, will also produce calm. Both a draconian honor code and a successfully applied dignity code can produce calm and order.

How will our future global village be structured? This master question contains many subquestions, such as the following: Is there a chance that the United Nations might be supported by all in common humility? Or will there be an elite ruling from the top? Will today's global champion—the United States—continue to be the only superpower, relegating the rest to a kind of "second league?" Will the human rights message that calls for a combination of egalization and globalization be heard? Emotions run high when these questions are addressed.

If Hobbes could go on TV and promote his ideas of an absolute ruler, the world might acquiesce to his solution and the United States might be the most obvious candidate. However, it appears that Locke's views have won. Even the United States would not want to fill the role of absolute world subjugator, not as long as its people continue to believe in human rights and equal dignity. This means that the only solution is a global village shaped according to Locke's views, a global village of democratically determined superordinate structures that guarantee equal dignity.

Such global superordinate structures are at least rudimentarily present through the United Nations, but confidence in these yet undeveloped structures is easily shaken. The idea of world federalism, for example—see, among others, Baratta[32]—is hotly debated. Democracy and democratically anchored capitalism mean traffic lights and rules selected by majority vote. The democratic ideal is that every driver, independent of the size of the vehicle, has the same right to pass at each traffic light. Large and small vehicles (capitalism allows for such differences) all have to stop for the red light and to start driving when the light turns green (equal dignity despite differences). This system is managed by officials who can be replaced with majority vote where every person, the driver of a Rolls Royce as well as the pedestrian, has a say (democracy). During the current period of transition, when the envisaged superordinate roof of rules and institutions is not yet securely in place at a global level, many ask whether those with large vehicles are genuinely willing to give up their "freedom" in deference to rules set by all. When a large vehicle forces another off the road, doubts arise about the future of the global village.

Western film illustrates this process as well as our much-used traffic metaphor. The story line for most Western films is simple. Gangsters terrorize the city, with different gangs vying for power and control. Raw might, brutality, and gun power, as well as promises of wealth and riches, determine who is at the top at any given moment. There is no peace for the ordinary citizen. All are drawn into this power play. Then the sheriff arrives to represent the interest of common citizens against their tormentors. He symbolizes an impartial superordinate force that protects all citizens against brutal power. He does not yearn for personal glory. Prior to his arrival, each gang had a name. There was the gang of Bloody Jim, Dirty Harry, or Vicious Jack, each calling the other *enemy* and terrorizing everybody else with promises and threats. After the sheriff's victory, there are only *citizens* and *criminals*. Bloody Jim and Dirty Harry are criminals, sitting in prison, with the hope of being rehabilitated into humbled citizens. The common interest has won. The sheriff's victory creates *one single city*, or *one single state*, huddling under *one single roof* of the law and order built by the citizens. Those with ambitions of becoming gang bosses are asked to abandon their dreams and support the sheriff. Even the best-intentioned liberator is asked to invest in the sheriff's efforts instead of behaving like Robin Hood. Nobody defends themselves alone anymore; everybody has to help the sheriff defend and secure everybody.

The sheriff fights in the name of *law and order*, the principle of the state that has the monopoly on the use of force. In the past, citizens were forced and humiliated by state might and brutality. In modern times, citizens voluntarily extend genuine humility to superordinate institutions, as long as they are democratically legitimized, because they understand the benefit.

In our vision of the global village, former *villages*—brutal Iraq and arrogant/benevolent America—coalesce into *one village* under the roof of the superordinate structure of international law and reformed United Nations institutions. Saddam Hussein is a criminal to be brought to justice like any other criminal. The world's citizens are protected by "sheriff" UN secretary general. Nobody acts to defend themselves unilaterally. Everybody helps the sheriff. If the superordinate institution of the sheriff is too weak to cope, it is strengthened. Nobody ridicules and humiliates this institution when it needs support. Nobody bails out, selfishly focusing on their own business. If there is dissent, it is resolved under the common roof, lest the door be opened to anachronistic warlordism. In such a world, *my* security is *common* security.

With this dream in the background, doubts arise when the richest citizens go their own ways. Do they, after all, intend to implement a draconian world rule à la Hobbes? Why do they not help the sheriff do his job and get their own people to implement the law? Will the outcome be global humiliation?

To summarize, at present, Locke seems to have won the competition in theory, but not always in practice. Worries and uncertainties about the future structure of the global village represent malign elements in a situation where strong political commitments towards global superordinate structures anchored in human rights would have benign effects.

What do you mean, "The problem with rhetoric"?

The human rights version of the global village is the one that Western elites and individual advocates and organizations officially support. Human rights ideals are held to be morally right; they feel correct at a gut level. White supremacy received a death blow when Apartheid fell. This does not mean that everybody is "converted"—it just means that white people who want the old order back have to express this desire privately, even secretly.

Official public discourse is no longer dominated by a vocabulary of supremacy. The language of the old honor code is obsolete. Honor killings, until not long ago accepted as cultural traits, are now seen as violations. Offering girls in marriage to relatives of victims, a practice called *vani* in Pakistan, was made illegal in January 2005. The Indian caste system, once "respected" as cultural idiosyncrasy, is now condemned as "Indian Apartheid."[33] The Indian government is not converted yet, and many Indians may agree with white South Africans that "Apartheid" is acceptable and benevolent. Yet, the fact that the term "Indian Apartheid" could emerge as the topic of a large international conference announces the change.

Acceptance of the human rights message is not limited to the world's elites (who in my conceptualization encompass most citizens of the Western world, including many who consider themselves financially burdened), who broadcast the human rights message. The broad majority of have-nots around the world feel attracted to the human rights message and would like to participate in the quality of life the West enjoys. The disadvantaged yearn for clean water, shelter, food, and a future for their children. Today's buzzwords include sustainability, peace, security, stability, freedom, empowerment, and so forth. If we were to live by these words, the transition to a world anchored in human rights would be complete.

However, despite seemingly good intentions to make human rights dignify everybody's lives, the gap between rich and poor widens, and the have-nots watch elites overindulge in luxury goods. Does this mean that our revered buzzwords are empty rhetoric? The problem with these words is that they have two potential meanings, one within the context of the Hobbesian vision of the global village, and another completely different meaning within the concept of the human rights vision. They can be used by tyrants to secure their grip on underlings. Tyrants may call for freedom for their interest groups to "secure" a "pseudodemocratic" system to provide "stability," "peace," and "empowerment" to their constituency. Human rights advocates, on the other hand, hear the very same buzzwords as calls to extend to all humankind, not only to the elites. Words are treacherous. Only deeds show the actual scope of justice such words describe.

Feelings of humiliation emerge in this clash of rhetoric and reality and the struggle between two visions of the global village and its subunits. Underlings feel humiliated by oppressors and by people who raise hopes they do not fulfill. The West broadcasts the message of human rights while maintaining the opposite reality. Human rights are understood as an invitation to the world's disadvantaged to join the West, but when poor suitors from far-flung countries want to move in and get "married" to the rich, they are thrown out. Boats filled with people who seek the promise of equal dignity are turned back, and negotiators who try to achieve fair global rules and regulations are blocked. This gap between human rights rhetoric and human rights reality is a source of disappointment, frustration, and feelings of betrayal and humiliation. Those who want human rights ideals to become realities are frustrated and feel insulted and humiliated by double standards. On the other hand, also those who use human rights vocabulary to hide their desire for supremacy feel humiliated because they reckon that they deserve to be recognized as benevolent patrons.

Elites are often blind to the feelings of humiliation they elicit, aggravating the problem. Marie Antoinette is a telling example. Coleman[34] describes the propensity of the powerful to be blind to the feelings of humiliation they cause in underlings until those feelings reach boiling points. High power holders and members of high-power groups often underestimate low power holders and members of low-power groups. Coleman pinpoints the possibility that *humiliated fury* may accumulate in those with lesser power, a humiliated fury that very well may explode, especially when there is "nothing to lose" anymore, when human life may not count much, even one's own.

Edna Adan is the former wife of the late president of "Somaliland," Mohammad Haji Ibrahim Egal.[35] I interviewed her on December 3, 1998, in Hargeisa, Somaliland. She had the following message to the global village:

> The international community encourages dictators and oppressors. Without mentioning names, there are dictators who have millions and billions of dollars in banks. Those billions of dollars were not generated through a salary or a reward from the people they governed. Those billions came from the money that belongs to the people that was given by the international community.
>
> The international community should act intelligently, fairly and honestly and stop allowing oppressors to accumulate so much of the people's money. They should not give oppressors arms, they should not give them money and they should not help them remain in the power. It is the international world that maintains dictators in power. The bombs that were thrown on my people in Somaliland, were not manufactured by Siad Barre. They came from all corners of the world; they were American, Pakistani, Egyptian, Chinese, Russian, Czechoslovak, Yugoslav. Anybody who made arms, who made tanks, who made ammunition and sold it or gave it to Siad Barre, helped him oppress his own people.
>
> Where was the international community when that power was being used against the weak? It should have said "no," it should have stopped the in-flow of arms to Somalia. It should have prevented the slaughter of the civilians.

Edna Adan concluded that an international community with double standards is humiliating:

> I think the international world has different standards. It preaches human rights, and fairness and so on, in literature! In Europe! But when that humiliation, that aggression, that hurt, takes place in a poor, remote, developing

country like Somaliland, no one wants to be bothered. Let them stew in their own
juice!

These are divided standards, unfair standards.... It is a humiliation! The international community is to blame. I hope you have very strong cupboards in which to
lock up your conscience! Because all the civilians who died here died from bombs
that were manufactured by people in the developed countries.

Edna Adan's message resembles many I heard from Iraq, summarized below:

First you feed Saddam Hussein and then you bomb us to free us from him? What
kind of liberation is this? What kind of help? First you push us into the ditch and
then you try to pull us out? When we were in the ditch, we survived as best as we
could. But now, when you try to pull us out, we drown! Don't you see the hypocrisy?

Don't you see how counterproductive you are? Whoever buys weapons from you
will later be bombed! What kind of world are you creating? You are like a visitor
who congratulates himself for giving the cancer patient pralines while withholding
real medicine! How humiliating! You should apologize that you ever supported
Saddam! Promise you will never support dictators again! And keep your promise!

To conclude, in a global village that is on its way to human rights and caught
in the midst of this transition, at least three groups of people feel victimized by
humiliation—traditionalists who feel that their domination is a blessing, human
rights adherents who feel humiliated when they see human rights terminologies
misused, and individuals who genuinely fight for human rights and feel humiliated by suspicion as to their motives.

Keep Protesting! The Human Rights Movement Is Continuous

Human rights give a voice to those at the bottom of the pyramid of power.
This is in principle nothing new. History has always seen revolts by dissatisfied
underlings. What is special about the human rights movement is that it preaches
the *demise of tyrants,* as well as the *demise of oppressive systems.* Formerly, underlings toppled elites only to replace them with new elites, keeping the hierarchy
in place. The rhetoric of equality was used by revolutionaries and "freedom fighters" until they grabbed the rulers' seats. Even the Russian revolution ended this
way. This may well be the "natural" course of revolutions if nothing intervenes.

However, this course is hampered nowadays by globalization, or more precisely, by global *technology* that makes such hypocrisy more difficult. I suggest
that the technology of mobility and communication that brought people closer
is also a vehicle for the first continuous revolution in human history, the human
rights movement. RAWA, www.rawa.org, was founded by Afghan women who
went out with cameras hidden under their burkhas, taking pictures and publishing them on the Internet. American women and human rights advocates became
aware of this site, forged a coalition, and contributed their resources.[36]

Human rights may never be fully "reachable," and they may have to be striven for in a continuous manner; global networks enable people to do this. It would be a revolution that is kept in motion by and only as long as those who find themselves disadvantaged incessantly protest (and have the material and technological means to do so) whenever hierarchies rigidify.

Even in those regions of the world that have "established" a democratic national culture based on human rights, it was and still is not easy to create and maintain this. It seems to be rather "normal" for elites to keep trying to maintain power (via control of media, for example, or coercion). Elites and the groups they represent do not always surrender power even when they lose the political support of the majority. The human rights movement may be unique in human history insofar as it represents the first permanent revolution.

Our teachers tell us we are being humiliated—then they humiliate us more!

Agnes came to my clinic one lovely spring morning. She had been raped by her psychiatrist, not just once, but regularly. However, this was not her main problem. Her deepest anxieties stemmed from the fact that she had acquiesced for years. She recounted her story:

My father abused me for the first time on my twelfth birthday. Partly, I was proud and flattered, but I also felt ashamed. He told me that I was a lady now and this was part of being a lady. I was not to tell anyone, it was our little secret. A child has to obey her father, he explained to me. I was torn.

He abused me until I left home when I was 18. My mother never interfered, although I think she knew. When I started my studies at university, I did not recognize that I had been abused. I did not see myself as a victim. Then I read a book written by a woman who had lived through very similar experiences. She put clear words to my fuzzy feelings, unclear views, obscure inklings, and vague perceptions. It was amazing, so many of my problems suddenly had a meaning. The puzzle of my existence fell into place.

I knew I needed therapy. I decided to see a psychiatrist in the neighborhood where I lived. He confirmed that I had been abused and my dignity had been violated. The fact that I had internalized this abuse as some kind of compliment had covered the wounds so that I could not see them. The psychiatrist opened my eyes to the wretchedness of my adolescent years.

He had a carpet in a drawer that he would pull out at the end of each session and put on the floor. He explained that I had to regain a healthy relationship with my body and that this intercourse was part of the therapy. I believed him. It took me years to question his behavior. Years that passed in agony. I had problems sleeping, concentrating, and trusting people. I had no friends, no support group. My studies suffered. I needed help and regularly went to my psychiatrist. I took a long time for me to understand that he abused me like my father had done, or worse. My father framed his abuse as a compliment, the psychiatrist as treatment. I think the psychiatrist violated me more, because he knew that I needed help and still he inflicted himself on me.

The realization that the psychiatrist abused me was devastating. Nobody can expect that a child can stand up against her father, particularly when her mother does not help her. I could excuse my victim status as my father's fault and not mine. However, going to this psychiatrist was my free choice. Nobody forced me to consult him. How could I fall for his disgusting explanations? I am in tatters. I had slowly learned, with the help of this psychiatrist, to be proud of myself. Now I detest myself more than ever. I dream of cutting him to pieces, slowly, so that he feels the pain he has inflicted on me.

The story of Agnes resembles the story of our present world community. Let us listen in as Mustafa reflects:

We, the poor of the world hear that poverty is a humiliating violation of our human rights and dignity. We learn that we deserve enabling environments that empower us as human beings. We know how these enabling circumstances should look—access to clean water, health care, a flat, work, a refrigerator, a television set, and, one day, a car, vacation, and university studies for our children. All this is what our local elites and the people of the rich West have. Western tourists and soap operas are an ample source of information for us.

However, our reality, our poverty, gets worse. We are told that our humanity is debased, and then it is debased even more. This is perpetrated by the same people, those from the rich West, who say that they stand for human rights. In our eyes the West is worse than the worst hypocrite. This is the ultimate betrayal.

Stephan Feuchtwang, who is doing a four-year study into how people grieve, wrote me on November 13, 2002, "I am intrigued by two of your contentions. One is that breeches of the promise of human rights create severe humiliation. Why not a sense of betrayal and hypocrisy, which is not the same as humiliation?" I replied:

Absolutely, as far as I can judge, there is a deep sense of betrayal and hypocrisy. But then emerges the next question that those who feel thus ask: 'Why do these people preach empty human rights rhetoric to us? Is it in order to fool us about their wishes to stay at the top and continue exploiting us?'

The motive sensed behind the betrayal is arrogance and the wish to stay at the top. This then is felt to be humiliating.

Feuchtwang responded with an observation that impacted me: "to recognise humanity hypocritically and betray the promise humiliates in the most devastating way by denying the humanity professed" (Feuchtwang, November 14, 2002, in a personal note).

I Am Torn Apart! How People Can Get Caught in Between

A young Tutsi, who I will call Charles, was in Kigali during the 1994 genocide. I talked to him in 1999. He told me how a Hutu friend hid him in his house.

Whenever Hutu militia came to search the house for Tutsi, Charles crawled into a hole in a rubbish heap in the garden. There he stood—only his nose poking out, covered by a plastic sheet—for hours, until the soldiers went away. This procedure continued for weeks, ultimately saving his life. During the same period Charles's Hutu friend had to participate in killing Tutsis outside in the streets, to keep from being killed himself. He took part in the atrocities perpetrated against Tutsis like any other *genocidaire*. Charles's entire family was killed, in the most gruesome ways. (Charles later learned that his 90-year-old grandmother was locked in a room with hungry dogs who ate her.)

This story entails grandeur and horror, kindness and atrocity—all embodied in the same person, Charles's friend. Charles's friend was incarcerated in a reality in which Tutsis were not merely to be killed, but to be "brought down," humiliated to a degree that they would never be able to raise their heads again. At the same time, he adhered privately to a very different framing of the social scenery. It took great courage for the young Hutu to break from his social prison by hiding his Tutsi friend.

I have spoken with several people, in Germany and in Rwanda, who say that the worst suffering, the most painful form of humiliation, is being forced to become a perpetrator because you are too weak to resist, too much of a coward to say no and face death.

In Kenya I heard stories of Hutu genocidaires who were in hiding and needed psychotherapy because they could not eat without seeing the small fingers of children on their plates. Instead of facing punishment, they became "insane." Many Hutus had been forced to kill their own families, their Tutsi spouses and Tutsi-looking children, to show their allegiance to the Hutu cause. The International Panel of Eminent Personalities confirms: "Hutu women married to Tutsi men were sometimes compelled to murder their Tutsi children to demonstrate their commitment to Hutu Power. The effect on these mothers is also beyond imagining."[37]

When the genocide ended and the Hutu government was ousted from power, these people found themselves in a devastating place: Their families had died at their own hands, and they had lost all honor, pride, and self-respect. They were humiliated, not only once, but on many levels and continuously. First, they had been coerced into becoming perpetrators, and the fact that they did not prefer death to succumbing to this pressure was deeply humiliating. Second, after the demise of the Hutu government and the world's moral outcry against the genocide, they were humiliated almost daily for being Hutu, part of the category of genocidaires. Those who had killed family members seem to cry out, consciously, or through psychotic symptoms, "I did not want to kill my family, I was forced! I was told that it was the right thing to do! I wish I were the one dead and not them! I was weak! I deserve to be loathed as a genocidaire!"

In other words, among the most humiliating experiences available to human beings is to be caught in the current transition from the old world of domination/submission to the new universe of human rights. In the first context, you may be hailed as a hero for humiliating and killing underlings; in the second context the very same deeds turn you into an "evil" perpetrator. As important as it is to hold perpetrators of atrocities responsible, all those who are spared such moral dilemmas ought to be thankful and refrain from arrogantly stigmatizing as evil those who were caught. Let us round up this section, and also this chapter, by saying that our task is to jointly dignify globalization by inviting all citizens of the world into realizing egalization.

Summary

- The global village could be structured as a strictly hierarchical entity with absolute rulers at the top and underlings at the bottom. In such a case globalization would exist *without egalization*. Or the global village could be administered in a democratic way, with all citizens enjoying equal dignity, thus wedding globalization to egalization. The latter vision is closer to the current official view in most parts of the world than the former, at least in rhetoric.

- Egalization is a process that is linked to the human rights movement, which perhaps represents the first continuous revolution in human history, a revolution that is, however, advancing in an inhomogeneous manner that causes feelings—particularly feelings of humiliation—to run high.

- Conflict may surface because of shifts in the balance (or imbalance) of power between disputants or because of ambiguity about relative power caused by changing circumstances.[38] This can trigger a deep sense of uncertainty and confusion over rank and power and can motivate two types of aggressive behavior: actions by those previously low in power to claim their rights, and actions by those previously high in power to protect their status.[39]

- The most upsetting humiliation occurs when human rights are promised but withheld, making human rights advocacy appear to be empty rhetoric.

- Words like *sustainability, peace, security, stability, freedom,* and *empowerment* are treacherous, because they are usable by all sides and with opposing meanings.

- The fact that humankind currently lives in the midst of a transition is obscured by the slowness of the transition, with those who lag behind inclined to hang on to old paradigms. Confrontations between adherents of the old and new orders arise, feelings heat up, cooperation is hampered, and trust fails.

- The human rights movement itself is in danger.

We may conclude that the fact that the human rights movement proceeds over many generations in a fragmented and inhomogeneous way—too fast and too slow at the same time—introduces a malign aspect into the project of marrying globalization with egalization. At the same time, the vision of an *egalized global village,* once the transition is successfully mastered by every party, is profoundly benign.

PART II

HUMILIATION AT WORK IN THE WORLD

CHAPTER 4

HUMILIATION AND MISUNDERSTANDING

Many scenarios can be played out with humiliation as the core element. I have outlined 16 scenarios, eight pertaining to the person who inflicts humiliation and eight to the person who suffers humiliation.[1] The first eight cases describe how and why one person might set out to humiliate another person, and an additional eight cases address the situation from the victim's perspective.

We are accustomed to believing that for humiliation to occur there must be—somewhere—a "bad" person, a humiliator, who humiliates others. However, situations of humiliation may also occur when only one party labels them as such, and—as we shall see—these might turn out to be among the most malignant.

Different Interpretations of the Spirit of Human Rights Can Humiliate

When you speak of human rights, you lack passion and caring. To you human rights are dry and abstract concepts. You talk about institutions and theoretical rights. I understand human rights as warm and caring invitations into the family of humanity. Your coldness and aloofness bothers me and your lack of caring humiliates humanity.

This vignette illustrates the fact that the concept of human rights may be interpreted in different ways. Alain Badiou[2] explains the difference between the *Kantian* interpretation of human rights as abstract principle and the *Lévinasian* interpretation, which emphasizes that human rights also mean care and respect for the other. Human rights promoters often speak in the *first* sense; their message, however, is often understood in the *second* sense. The incompatibility between the message that is sent and the message that is heard creates a potential for feelings of humiliation on all sides. A particularly sore point, full of ambiguity, is the notion of dignity.

Kantian or Lévinasian? Positive or negative rights?

The first sentence in Article 1 of the Universal Declaration of Human Rights reads, "All human beings are born free and equal in dignity and rights." This sentence seems to be straightforward; however, the notion of dignity is ambiguous, open to both Kantian and Lévinasian interpretations.[3] There is a Lévinasian connection to equality hidden in the notion of equal dignity. The notion of equal dignity is a Lévinasian "Trojan horse" that "sneaks" into the Kantian view. The "Trojan" connection is implicated in the human rights stipulation that equal chances and enabling environments for all are necessary to protect human dignity.

The Kantian version could be simplified as follows: "Equal dignity means that, although you are poor, you can have full dignity. In order to have dignity you need a societal framework that gives you political rights, such as the right of free speech. You can be poor and at the same time dignified and happy." The Lévinasian version, again simplified, would go as follows: "You are poor and live under circumstances that violate human dignity. To insure your dignity, you must be supported by an enabling environment that gives you the chance to work yourself into a more dignified quality of life." Relevant here is the discussion of so-called negative and positive ("welfare") rights.

Lee D. Ross and John T. Iost[4] carried out experiments on equity to see whether people like to share equally. They found that the myth that "humans are greedy by nature" is inaccurate. Ross and Iost found a strong tendency to share equally *within in-groups,* but not *with out-groups.* The Lévinasian view of human rights is thus surprisingly close to norms that preserve the cohesion of the social fabric within any group, indicating that human rights represent the *inside* ethics of the *global village.*

Globalization as Lévinasian force

In the beginning of the human rights era mainly political rights were equated with human rights.[5] An increasing number of aspects of human rights have since been recognized (beyond civil and political rights, toward economic, social, and cultural rights) and applied to ever wider categories of people, as well as to increasingly widening realms of the biotic and abiotic nature. Honor killings are no longer "respected" as cultural idiosyncrasies, beyond the jurisdiction of human rights workers. The most recent addition to the list of human rights are economic rights. People have begun to experience a gut resonance with the idea that poverty is a violation of a person's basic human rights.[6]

And we are just beginning to understand that animals have rights. Whales, dolphins, and laboratory animals are increasingly regarded as part of us, deserving dignity. The Earth with its biosphere is currently being "dignified" as well, even being named as a living being—"Gaia."

Please read Sir James George Frazer (1854–1941), Professor of Social Anthropology at Liverpool University, who wrote about historic practices, and consider whether his account causes gut feelings of revulsion in you, rather than the joy they produced just a few hundred years ago:

> In the midsummer fires formerly kindled on the Place de Grève at Paris it was the custom to burn a basket, barrel, or sack full of live cats, which was hung from a tall mast in the midst of the bonfire; sometimes a fox was burned. The people collected the embers and ashes of the fire and took them home, believing that they brought good luck. The French kings often witnessed these spectacles and even lit the bonfire with their own hands. In 1648 Louis the Fourteenth, crowned with a wreath of roses and carrying a bunch of roses in his hand, kindled the fire, danced at it and partook of the banquet afterwards in the town hall.[7]

As Sir Frazer's vignette brings home, we increasingly include animals in our circle of empathy. Organizations such as *Animals Angels* protect and help stranded animals or supervise animal transports to ensure dignified treatment. The habit of eating animals is increasingly eschewed; vegetarianism is on the rise. (Media products such as Spaceship Enterprise have managed to introduce even extraterrestrials into human hearts, showing that we are capable of welcoming the entire universe.)

Globalization as love story

My experience is that the coming into being of the global village is a love story that carries the risk of all love stories—it can turn into hatred when betrayed and can be destroyed by rash reactions that may later be regretted.

Elites are typically admired, loved, and envied, and the rich West is not excluded from this phenomenon. What the French court was to Europe, the West is to the global village. Copies of the castle of Versailles can be found everywhere in Europe and copies of the Western style of life over the entire earth's surface. Elites are often quite uninformed about the masses, but the masses always know what the elites are up to. Elites do not realize to what extent their admirers know them, imitate them, emulate their lifestyle, and try to participate in it. Americans are not known as great travelers—there are members of the Congress who have no passports, and Americans can be vague about world geography. However, Somali desert nomads listen attentively to BBC radio every day. Afghans in remote valleys know when a plane crashes in Alaska.

Admiration motivates many to pay huge amounts of money to be smuggled into the "castle," the "court," of the West. America and the entire West is admired and yearned for; they receive declarations of love every day. The recipients of this admiration are not fully aware of this love, however. They tend to believe in a world of independent nation states and assume that everybody is consumed by their own internal affairs. They do not understand that they are the center of the entire world's internal affairs.

Through their media, the rich send Western soap operas around the world that show the poor what life is like inside the palace and how paradise can be experienced on Earth. Then they invite the poor in, as equals, through the message of human rights. The message is heard much more often and much more literally than the rich realize. To say it succinctly, the West sends out powerful love declarations, without realizing that people will respond, hoping to move in and get "married."

Disbelieving love: Penniless suitors are unwelcome

Confronted with uninvited penniless suitors—asylum seekers who are willing to swim through shark-infested seas or climb barbed wire fences—the West is astounded and frightened. The West often sends their suitors away, demonstrating that their messages of love are not to be taken literally. This can generate ugly emotions on the part of the rejected invitees. Their love has been betrayed, and they feel treated as lesser beings, not as the equals the human rights call had led them to believe.

Whenever human rights are understood in a Lévinasian fashion, an additional source of misunderstanding arises. Care is defined differently in collective communities than in Western individualistic societies. Westerners do not understand the degree to which they are charged with responsibility for giving care to the collectivistic rest of the world.

Annegret came to me because she could not stand her Egyptian husband "squandering" their hard-earned money on his brother. She said:

> I love my husband's family. When I arrived from Europe as his wife, I was welcomed so warmly that I never looked back and never got homesick. However, my brother-in-law has financial problems and often sends his wife and children to stay with us. I am not opposed to helping family, but this goes too far. Once, one of his girls liked a picture on our wall and my husband gave it to her. I was shocked and furious, but he told me that it was his duty to open his home to his family and to share everything with them.
>
> My husband accuses me of being heartless and says I disrespect family duties. He explains that in Egypt the family is the only welfare security net. He tells me that the state provides privileges in the West that give their citizens the illusion of self-reliance and thinks I should shed this illusion of individual independence.

I hear his words, but I do not understand his concept of caring. I feel my brother-in-law abuses me and my husband and violates our dignity with his demands. I don't think he has the right to feel humiliated by my lack of caring. I am afraid this will end in divorce!

Annegret's story shows that the Lévinasian view of human rights carries the seeds of another round of misunderstandings. How far must care go? How much of a right do the poor have to be supported by the rich? What does it mean to declare humankind *one family?* Annegret found a way to save her marriage, using her network of European relationships to find a suitable position for her brother-in-law. He can support his family now, without having to send his children to stay with relatives. The feelings of anger and frustration have healed, replaced by those of agency and pride. The marriage is thriving again.

To conclude, global closeness, high expectations, and mutual misunderstanding combined with stress and frustration can generate violent reactions to the West's perceived lack of caring and tendency to inflict humiliation. These mechanisms are rarely understood by Westerners, who, instead of extending enabling care, rebuke the victims for seeking help.

The 2003 Iraq War illustrates the transition from a Kantian to a Lévinasian interpretation of human rights. During the war and discussions preceding it, there was a vacillation among various justifications for the war. Was it to be a war to dismantle Saddam Hussein's regime? Or was the aim only to disarm the regime? Why was disarmament so important? Was it because the Saddam regime killed and tortured its own people or because it might threaten the West? Is it right to support dictators and sell them weapons in the first place? What about global justice? What about sovereignty? Is it a violation of international law to invade other countries and preemptively "take out" regimes?

Different world views drive these questions. In a world of several villages, sovereignty is untouchable, analogous to the old idea that parents have the right to do what they want with their children. Men could beat and rape their wives because these activities occurred within an "untouchable" private sphere. Individuals faced police intervention only when they threatened their neighbors. In contrast, in the single village, national sovereignties are transformed into neighborhood relations subject to common policing.

Some among my American friends adhere to the older philosophy. Their thinking went as follows:

Americans are rich not because we were given help, but because we are industrious! Why are we expected to distribute our wealth to lazy people? Human rights mean democratic institutions and a free press, not the right to lifelong support.

People who envy our riches should emulate our democratic institutions and our industry. If they want tyrants to govern them, it's their problem. If they do not opt for democracy and freedom, it is their own fault if they lag behind.

They accuse us of humiliating them by being arrogant and imperialistic. We find those complaints shameless and humiliating! America has no obligation to "free" Iraqis! The only good reason for us to go to war in Iraq is that Saddam Hussein may be a threat to America. Period. We have a right to defend ourselves!

Other American friends took the second stance:

Parents do not have the right to mistreat their children, nor should husbands abuse their wives. Society has to step in! Neighbors have to send in police, even if the husband protests and feels insulted and humiliated, even if he is no threat to outsiders. In the same vein, we have to step in and depose tyrants like Saddam, even if he has no weapons of mass destruction. We owe it to his people to liberate them!

There is a widespread gut feeling that tyrants who abuse their people have no legitimacy, even if they do not threaten outsiders. The focus of the discussion is how world policing ought best be done and whether the problem could not have been prevented. This state of global discussion marks the degree to which the global village is in the process of being framed as *our village* by its citizens.

The disappointment

Imagine there are no traffic lights. Drivers of small vehicles wait at crossroads until the larger, more powerful vehicles have passed. Then, the owners of the larger vehicles endorse a declaration that all are now one family with equal rights, calling for traffic lights to be installed and insisting that nobody should be treated as lesser because they drive a small vehicle.

There is great joy among those with smaller vehicles. They have admired the big vehicles and envied their owners. Some of the young owners of small vehicles used to fix them up to seem bigger—they even stole big cars. Now they are invited to be equals! They feel elevated, honored, respected, and loved. Finally, their admiration for the powerful has been recognized.

However, most of the drivers of big cars disregard the new traffic lights, continuing their old practices. Great disappointment erupts among those with smaller vehicles—hopes have been created and betrayed. Some begin destroying traffic lights. The owners of larger vehicles react with dismay when faced with such "vandalism"; they preach love and get hatred. They are unaware of how much attention and yearning they have attracted—to what extent they raised hopes they were unprepared to fulfill. The two sides begin to call one another "enemy." It takes generations for the situation to cool down, for both sides to recognize that they misperceived the situation and overreacted.

My Collateral Damage Is Your Evil Intention! Bias Can Humiliate

Currently, the world contains many "camps"; Israelis are pitched against Palestinians in the Middle East, Tamils and Sinhalese in Sri Lanka, Turkish and Greek

Cypriots in Cyprus. "Western" values are often seen to be irreconcilable with "non-Western" values. Usually such controversies are regarded as head-on oppositions. However, research in social psychology suggests that many apparent divisions are based on underlying agreements on values, a congruence that is almost systematically underestimated. The problem is the phenomenon of *biases,* which distort our views and are central to creating feelings of humiliation. *Essentialization, attribution error (fundamental, ultimate), reactive devaluation, false polarization effect,* the list of biases is long. Simplified, we tend to grant ourselves and members of our own group the benefit of the doubt, while we tend to assume the worst from members of other groups. We easily dismiss positive behavior by out-group members, merely because they are out-group members.

We can observe examples everywhere. We see them in the current Middle East conflict, the conflict in Sri Lanka, in the 2003 Iraq War, and in the global *war on terrorism.* We merely have to listen to any spokesperson's statement about the appalling behavior of *others* to understand how this link works. These spokespersons deplore an act of violence committed by the *other* side as "atrocity perpetrated in cold blood," implying that the other side's evil aim is to target innocent civilians. "Look, how we are victimized by deep humiliation that cannot go unanswered, we have to retaliate!" is the message transmitted to the world by both sides. At the same time, each side confirms that civilian casualties that may have been caused by one's own actions to the other side are unintended and unavoidable "side effects" and *collateral damage,* something the other ought to understand and excuse. The Israeli side insists their soldiers do their utmost to protect civilians. Palestinians, the Israelis say, use their compatriots as shields, again proving their moral worthlessness and evil. The Palestinian side explains that suicide bombers do not target civilians, but that as oppressed occupants they have no other weapons than their own bodies.

Bewildered, members of the international community ask, "Don't these adversaries see that all human beings basically want to live in peace and quiet, have some reasonable quality of life and offer their children a future? Don't they see that their distorted mutual perceptions are their biggest enemy? Why don't they change their perceptions?"

"Eastern" versus "Western" values

The "West" is perceived as lacking ethics by many in the "non-West." Anybody traveling in the non-West soon sees that, under the admiration and yearning for Western quality of life, there brews a host of ill feelings. The West, in non-Western eyes, does not sufficiently care for the elderly or for children, has an appallingly high divorce rate, and shows little genuine compassion and insufficient social cohesion. Equally, the West targets the non-West—in Western eyes, non-Western women are abused, individual freedom choked, and self-expression curtailed.

However, the West and the non-West have more in common than is apparent at first glance. Both value social cohesion. For my doctoral dissertation in social-psychological medicine[8] I compared Germany and Egypt and what these two countries regard as core priorities for good quality of life. All yearn for social cohesion balanced with individual freedom. In the West, rifts to social cohesion such as divorce, or lack of compassion, are deeply regretted as unwanted side effects, a price to be paid for the transition towards more personal freedom, authenticity, and flexibility. In the same vein, non-Westerners value individual freedom and regret any need to curtail it as a sad side effect, as a price to be paid for social cohesion.

Again we see that regrettable side effects occurring in our own group are turned into the other's evil essence when observed in the other's camp, while commonalities—such as universality of the appreciation of social cohesion that must be balanced with individual freedom—are underplayed. As I emphasize further down, the significant fault line does therefore not run between the West and the non-West, but between fundamentalists and moderates in all camps. Fundamentalists, throughout the world, have much in common, as do moderates. More so, both fundamentalists and moderates typically have in common that they care for the well-being of the individual within a collective; they differ mainly in the calibrating of space they think collectivistic versus individualistic approaches ought to receive.

Humiliation enters the scene through the self-righteousness that results from *biases*. Each party feels that it is entitled to "help" the other party understand right and wrong, producing often unintended, humiliating effects. This kind of humiliation flows from misunderstanding—misunderstanding oneself, the other, and reality—rooted in the common human tendency to see oneself in a more forgiving light than the other.

Feelings of humiliation stemming from such misunderstandings are typically compounded when the wealthy preach human rights, while being blind to the fact that violations of these very rights may create feelings of humiliation in the victims of such violations. This blindness partly stems from another human weakness, namely the belief in a *just world* that tends to *blame the victim*. The belief in a just world gives the more privileged in the global community an "alibi" to be blind to the sufferings of the less privileged, because "everybody deserves what he gets." The situation is aggravated when wealthy individuals, blind to the injustice and obscenity of poverty, fail to recognize how much they contribute to the suffering of the poor by promoting human rights without assuring that what they promote becomes reality. On the part of the recipients of empty promises, *double standards* quickly become *double humiliation*.

Response to humiliation or evil essence?

The privileged of the planet need to recognize that expressions of discontent are often transparent reactions to perceived humiliation—not unfathomable and opaque actions of unexplainable evil. Terrorism, for example, may in many instances be a response to humiliation and not an expression of evil essence. I return to this point later, but for the moment suffice it to say that this is very good news because feelings of humiliation are much easier to "heal" than "unexplainable evil essence."

Germany after reunification is an example. The Berlin Wall fell in late 1989. East Germans declared "Wir sind ein Volk! [We are one people!]" and danced with West Germans in the streets of Berlin. West and East Germans were reunited. This should have been the beginning of a blissful intracultural communication among this one people. However, things did not develop very well. "I Want My Wall Back!" was the message broadcast on t-shirts only a few years after reunification. Fred Edmund Jandt writes:

> The irony of unification is that it has produced an Eastern identity that decades of Communist propaganda failed to achieve. Products made in the East sector are experiencing a revival as a way to assert a separate identity.... The invisible wall that now exists will take generations to fall because the redevelopment of a homogeneous society takes time.[9]

East Germans explain,[10] almost apologetically, that they did their best to survive in the DDR environment (the former communist German Democratic Republic) and find it humiliating to be expected to confess to "inherent stupidity" in exchange for the help the donors know East Germans cannot do without. To be locked in a situation of degradation, to be pushed to self-degradation by need, fulfils the definition of humiliation. The East Germans respond:

> We are worth something! Our lives in the former DDR were not useless! We would, in fact, be happy if we could do without your help! And, by the way, your help is not as fantastic as you think! Be honest, don't you profit from helping us? Perhaps we would actually prefer to live in a dignified way behind the Wall, than be humiliated without it! We have a valuable and distinct East German culture, which we are proud of! We know what loyalty is, unlike you![11]

Thus, what appears at first to West Germans as "unfathomable" ill will on the East German side is actually an understandable reaction against humiliation. Both overlook that all yearn for respect. West Germans do not understand that their casual display of power may be offensive, and East Germans misinterpret this "accidental" blindness as essentially evil intention.

If we reflect on "Eastern"—especially Islamic—values versus "Western" values, we find a similar dynamic. The rich West exhibits blindness to the fact that its casual display of power may have offensive effects. In the non-Western camp, on the other hand, we see an essentialization, the belief that Western power play proves unbridgeable evil intentions.

In reality all sides are in astonishing concord, both within Germany and between the Islamic world and the West. Just look at people like Osama bin Laden. They speak softly. They present themselves as holy ascetics, not power-hungry bullies. They project an image of brave victims who defend themselves in spite of all hardship. Whether they are authentic and believe what they preach is not the point here. What is important to note is that many of their followers are attracted by this display of humility. My intimate knowledge of the Arab world indicates this. Interestingly, Western human rights activists and Islamic fundamentalists both believe the world needs improvement. Human rights advocates and Islamic fundamentalists share a sense of suffering from a world they perceive as unjust and obscenely materialistic, combined with a vision of how to remedy this sad state of affairs. The difference lies in how the two groups perceive justice and remedy. Western human rights promoters see the way out in the ideals they draw from their social and cultural environment, namely human rights ideals. The Osama bin Ladens grew up in another kind of world and were exposed to a different set of solutions. Not all cultural contexts on the globe have martyrdom on offer. Confucianism in China, for example, does not provide people with a dream of an afterlife that rewards holy warriors for martyrdom. Islam and Arab history, in contrast, provide scripts for heroic martyrdom (see, for example, Saladin). The Arab world has a tradition of "noble warriors." Afghans and Yemenites (this is Osama bin Laden's family background) are noble warriors, as are Somalis. After several years of research on Somalia, I am familiar with people who are intensely proud they never were subjugated. Somalis told me they do not experience humiliation, because "a man would rather die than accept humiliation." Thus, Osama bin Laden and his sympathizers can rely on several cultural "scripts" for bravery and martyrdom, which in a number of ways are anticoncepts to human rights teachings.

What happens to the common ground that could be useful for developing cooperation instead of mayhem? It is squandered by feelings of humiliation that arise when I hear you misattributing my intentions. As long as communities live far away from each other and do not know about other communities misreading them, there is no problem. Everybody feels comfortable whitewashing their in-group and blackening all out-groups. However, this becomes problematic when people learn how biased others' judgments about them are.

It is humiliating to learn about evaluations that place me in a less than advantageous light, particularly when I feel that those who levy such judgments lack any moral authority to do so. Thus, the attribution error, or the human tendency to treat out-groups less leniently than in-groups, can elicit feelings of humiliation in those out-groups who are on their way to becoming part of the in-group. The coming into being of the global village, the merging of out-groups into one in-group, confronts people with humiliating and unwelcome out-group biases that in former times they never would have known. Only when the transition towards one in-group is successfully completed can misreadings and confrontations of this kind be expected to wane.

In an asymmetric situation, when one side fights with the ultimate weapon—the feelings of humiliation that make masses willing to support or even become suicide bombers—to label them "dishonorable," for example, is a sure way to lose. The only way towards mutual respect is to acknowledge common ground and courage, on all sides. Acknowledging this does not mean condoning suicide bombing. On the contrary, it is the first step to halting it. Biases "hide" common ground. In reality, all seek quality of life for their loved ones and are "courageous," nobody is a "coward."

Also Japan helps illustrate this point. If Japan were isolated from the world—as it was when its Tokugawa Shoguns closed it to the outside—Japanese current "inner affairs" would not be known to anybody else. However, in an interdependent world, in 2005, modifications in Japanese school textbooks ("in order to make our children proud of Japan") trigger enraged mass demonstrations in China and Korea, who feel that Japan tries to "gloss over its past." Floyd Rudmin explains what happens (personal message, April 11, 2005): "It is the humiliation of history. Japan's neighbors are furious because Japan has again tried to gloss over its history of humiliating its neighbors, but Japan in turns finds it humiliating that it alone is required to continually account for and atone for its past."

These insights are crucial for building a world without terrorism. It is inherently impossible to win a war on terror with conventional weapons. Admittedly, missiles send powerful messages. Yet, the recipients may not "understand" those messages in the intended way. They may not see them as inducements to humility, but rather as humiliation, reason to react with enraged defiance. Using ever more conventional weapons could mean the eradication of humankind, rather than its rescue. The only way to win this war is to gain trust and turn enmity into neighborliness. The hearts and minds of the masses must be won to take away their incentive to resonate with those few humiliation entrepreneurs who instigate and organize terror. When the masses turn away from the few terrorist leaders, they can safely be policed, without fear that every dead or captured terrorist will be replaced with a new one within minutes.

Sorry! Cross-Cultural Misunderstandings Can Humiliate

That humiliation can be perpetrated by mistake is particularly relevant on the intercultural level, where communication is more prone to produce ambiguities than is communication between individuals with the same cultural background.

It is essential to know how to behave when unintended humiliation occurs—or risk the possibility of setting unnecessary cycles of humiliation in motion.

Arrogant carelessness can humiliate

A German or French citizen may perceive it as humiliating to be addressed with *Du* or *tu* instead of *Sie* or *vous.* A foreigner with an English background, who is used to a simple "you," is unable to fathom the humiliation entailed in the wrong form of address in parts of Europe. A police officer in France or Germany, for example, may use Du or tu with criminals to humiliate them. Thus, a foreigner may humiliate a German or French citizen inadvertently simply by being uninformed. An anonymous reviewer of this text, from America, reacted with the following remark (2002) to the Du and Sie problem:[12] "I would hope that most French and German individuals who are called tu or Du by an obvious foreigner would realize that it's an imperfect command of the language and would not feel humiliated."

This reviewer's hope may meet with sympathy from offended Europeans—however, it may not. His trust that he will be excused could be labeled arrogant and humiliating. What would this reviewer feel if he were entertaining a German intellectual and placed the American flag in the guest room, as a welcome greeting, only to have the visitor put the flag into the wastebasket? Would the reviewer "understand" this? Or would he feel that his national pride had been trampled? The Hitler legacy has besmirched national symbols, especially for German intellectuals, who may find it intolerable to have any such symbols, from any nation, in a room. Even understanding this, the American host might feel irritated, thinking that his German visitor should have taken time to collect some information about Americans. Would it really be sufficient for the visitor to say: "Oh, I didn't know you felt so deeply about your flag! Why make such a fuss, I didn't know! I am a foreigner!"

Cosmopolitan liberal Americans would perhaps react calmly and explain that the flag is the premier symbol of their nation. Those who identify most with their flag may not be so lenient. They may feel deeply humiliated and ridiculed, first by the visitor's throwing their flag into the wastebasket, then the visitor's self-righteous reaction when informed of his faux pas.

Ignorance may have humiliating effects, especially when it is understood to mean "your culture is so unimportant to me that I do not need to be informed, it is your responsibility to excuse my ignorance." The guest's refusal to empathize with the host gives rise to feelings of humiliation. It is not sufficient to merely hope that ignorance will be excused. Expecting excuse for ignorance too lightly, after having been informed of a faux pas, may create the very humiliation that the faux pas itself did not yet cause.

Unwarranted confidence can humiliate

There are a host of seminars and handbooks offering to train individuals to operate in intercultural settings. Thousands of business persons prepare for transactions in other countries by trying to learn what they should do and avoid. They learn long lists of "shoulds" and "should-nots": in some places they should not show the underside of their feet, in others they must refrain from patting children on their heads, in yet others they must be careful not to step on bank notes, and so forth. These seminars aim at minimizing cross-cultural misunderstandings. However, in many cases they may even create them. We now see situations such as the one in which a Japanese bank director reaches out to shake hands with his French counterpart—having learned that this is the French way to behave—while the French bank person only bows and keeps his hands back—because he has learned that this is what his Japanese counterpart expects. This "accidental misunderstanding" can easily be remedied, and both may laugh and feel respected by the other's willingness to adapt to his customs. However, misunderstanding is not always so easily detectable.

During the seven years I worked in Egypt as a clinical psychologist and counselor, I saw countless cases of unintentional humiliation. I caution people against drawing too much confidence from *How-to-Do in X-Land* handbooks or seminars. Many who had relied on such "intercultural training" arrived as clients at my door, shaken by what they called "culture shock." The training handbooks or seminars, which compare "their" behavior to "ours," often damage the cause more than promote it. What such handbooks or seminars should teach is humility, self-control strategies, and the ability to build relationships while tolerating insecurity and fear. It is impossible to learn everything about another culture, especially in one brief training course. Imagine your own homeland and how many seminars would have to be drawn up to cover the whole cultural richness. People in the countryside react differently than people in cosmopolitan cities, one valley may be very different from its nearest neighbor, and so forth. You probably do not really understand your parents, your spouse, your children, and sometimes you wonder about yourself. In short, it is an illusion to believe you ever could learn enough to behave perfectly with all these people at all times.

The illusion of knowing everything is not particularly dangerous as long as one moves in one's own culture, among people who mutually define each other as "us." Under such circumstances, differences are covered by a deep underlying feeling of unity. This commitment to unity makes the illusion of complete mutual understanding viable and perhaps even helpful. However, when you visit "them" the situation is different. It is not so much "their" cultural codes that you have to learn; after all you do not know all the details of the cultural diversity in your own culture and do fine. You need to learn how to negotiate the relationship between "us" and "them." Here is where the potential for mutual humiliation looms largest.

Humble dialogue is the solution

Egalization is of central significance in cross-cultural encounters. Questions about egalization permeate meetings between "cultures" at any level. As discussed earlier, a love story is being played out, with the rest of the world enamored of the freedom and quality of life the West offers. Like all love affairs in their early stages, this one entails a high level of fear, emotional sensitivity, and insecurity that must be negotiated with care.

It is not necessary to learn others' cultural codes by heart. It is crucial, however, to learn to ask questions in a way that signals respect for everybody's dignity and to react with respect when informed of a mistake. Ignorance is no faux pas, but arrogance is. Ignorance can be the starting point for enriching relationships; asking questions can express interest, respect, and recognition and elicit enthusiastic explanations. We may travel through the world and ask questions, respectful questions, humbly admitting our ignorance, and people will open up to us, enjoying our interest. Our blunders and our subsequent apology may deepen our relationships.

However, if we travel through the world comprehensively informed about all cultural codes, and sour our relationships through arrogance, we can do great harm. We may not even notice this dynamic until we find ourselves sabotaged or even hated. This was typically the case with those Western clients who came to me suffering from "culture shock." Also, the following story might illustrate this point:

> Around 1950, a Belgian national (we'll call him Robert) owned a big farm in Mexico. He was proud of his good relations with his Mexican workers, independent people who held their honor dear. One day the workers' foreman, Manuel, asked Robert for a loan. The Belgian felt honored by this trust and granted the loan, which the foreman promised to pay back in three months.
>
> Several months passed and the Belgian was approached by another Mexican who warned him, "Be careful, the foreman is going to kill you!"
>
> The Belgian, astonished, asked, "Why? We have a very good relationship! I even gave him a loan!"
>
> The Mexican explained: "The foreman cannot repay the loan in time and cannot bear to appear untrustworthy. This would be too humiliating to him. He has to kill you."
>
> The Belgian burst out: "Why doesn't Manuel just talk to me? I am no monster!"
>
> The reply was, "His honor does not allow him to do that."

A more oppressive and arrogant master would not have received a warning and would probably have died as a result of his cultural ineptitude. Your very life may depend on being humble when you meet people from other cultures.

Finally, it is important to understand the dynamics of humiliation caused by power differences—including the power differences in the global village—so you can be sensitive to the problems surrounding processes of egalization. If you are a member of the world's elite, you must understand that you are scrutinized carefully by the less privileged who are afraid that you will exploit your superiority. Even the mere suspicion that you may operate by double standards can cause feelings of humiliation. On the other side, if you are a member of the world's less privileged, it would pay to try to understand that some elites may be benevolent and feel humiliated by your mistrust. Both should be prepared to say "I'm sorry, I did not know that I humiliated you."

Love, Help, and Humiliation

Cases of misunderstandings that have humiliating effects are difficult to deal with. Cases of help and love that are "misunderstood" as humiliation are even more difficult. We find benevolent helpers on one side, no evil perpetrators at all, yet help and love sometimes cause deep feelings of humiliation in the recipients. Only *one* participant identifies this event as *humiliation,* the *other* labels it as *help* or *love.* The following vignette may illustrate the case of help and humiliation.

> I have cancer. I have no money for medicine. You come to help me. You bring me chocolate. You feel good. I appreciate your good intentions. However, don't you see that I need medicine? Don't you see that you serve your own interests more than mine by bringing me chocolate? You have proved to yourself and your friends that you are a helpful human being.
>
> But what about me? You buy yourself a good conscience and I pay the price. I feel painfully humiliated by your blindness and ignorance. I am bitter. I understand you do not know better. You are naïve and well-intentioned, but to me, you seem either stupid or evil. A little more effort to understand my situation would really help! And by the way, how much money did you earn with these pesticides that caused my cancer?

Humiliation is an emotional experience that depends upon the relation between at least two parties. It cannot be described through the reactions of one individual or one party. The question is: "If I want to help others, but my arrogant way of behaving humiliates those I want to help, do I then commit a humiliating act?" From my point of view, I do not commit a humiliating act; from the perceiver's point of view I do.

The alleged "perpetrators" may overlook this rift and live in an illusionary world, convinced that good intentions are all that is needed to secure real helpfulness in help and real lovingness in love. The "beneficiaries" will feel humiliated by this blind conviction. Some might overreact and mistrust and reject even those helpers who make every effort to adapt their help and support to the recipients' needs. Whatever the situation, "helpers" and "lovers" typically react with surprise and shock when they encounter lack of gratitude and appreciation. They may develop feelings of humiliation, too, emphasizing their effort and their benign intentions and seeing the lack of recognition as an evil attempt to besmirch and humiliate them.

To avoid such tragic outcomes, helpers and lovers must design their efforts in ways that do not "walk over" recipients, humiliating them. Healthy love is *interdependent,* and not independent and *isolated.* Recipients, on the other hand, need to remember that healthy love is not dependent and engulfed. Both parties in love or help relationships may go too far, either by "walking over" the other or by allowing the other to walk over them. The second case will be addressed in the following section.

You Pretend to Love Me but You Rape Me! Allowing Oneself to Be Seduced into False Love Humiliates

Alice, an educated and intelligent European woman, came to me as a client in 1991 when her relationship collapsed. She said:

> I met Robert ten years ago. He is 18 years older than me. I had just come out of a relationship with an abusive man who could not tolerate an intelligent woman. I yearned for kindness, for not being hurt several times a day. I was touched and happy when Robert said he needed me. My former husband never said such things; he only said I was old and ugly. Robert lifted me up! I was ready to give Robert everything, I was happy to find somebody who loved me, someone who did not feel threatened by my education and intelligence.
>
> Robert lived and worked in Indonesia and I moved there to join him. He was separated from his wife in Europe and he said the laws in his home country would not allow him to get a divorce. However, he said, he considered me his wife now. I accepted. I preferred a happy unmarried relationship to a painful marriage. When I arrived in Indonesia, I was full of plans to do research, get another degree, and have a family.
>
> But none of that happened. I am ten years older now and I have nothing. I wasted all these years on this man. And, I did not even recognize that I was wasting my time. Whenever I wanted to realize one of my goals, there was an existential crisis in his life. He had problems with his job, problems with his family; we lived in emergencies. I hardly ever relaxed. I was always busy helping him with his problems, hoping that we would start "our" life as soon as the current crisis passed. It never started!
>
> I tried to be optimistic! When I felt that I was not optimistic enough, I felt guilty. My mother had taught me that a good woman devotes her life to her man. This is what I did, and it made me feel good! Now I get nauseated thinking about it! Robert hid behind those emergencies, used them to avoid real commitment to me. He was not really interested in my needs, my dreams, and my happiness. He needed my

presence, yes, he enjoyed me being near him. I was a nice object in his apartment and objects do not have needs.

I feel ashamed of myself. I humiliated myself before Alice who once thought highly of herself. I feel exploited by Robert; he manipulated me into helping him and sacrificing my life for him. I feel that he raped me, a slow humiliating rape, which I allowed. Robert raped me and made me believe it was love.

The case of Alice may be placed within the same theoretical framework as the *Hitlerzeit* [*Hitler's era*]. Hitler held one of his manipulative speeches on the Bückeberg, a hill near Hamelin, the city of the *pied piper*. The most popular versions of this tale derive from the poem by Robert Browning and the fairy tale by the Brothers Grimm. "In pretty much all versions, rats infest Hamelin and the town hires a traveling rat catcher to exterminate them. When he does so, the king, mayor, or whoever decides not to pay him, so he extracts his revenge by spiriting away the town's children."[13] On July 22, 2003, a German colleague, Friedrich Flachsbart, wrote to me, "In Hamelin the piper was humiliated and thus transformed from a rat catcher to a child catcher. This has always been a prominent imagery in my mind. My grandfather was on the Bückeberg and there he saw the real rat catcher [Hitler]."

Germany's masses, the so-called *kleine Leute*, or *little people*, previously victims of routine humiliation in the hierarchical German society, felt elevated by Hitler for the first time in their history. Hitler offered the little people, who had never been taken seriously, an elite identity and a clear sense of direction. He even arranged for symphony orchestra music to be played in factories, giving the little people a sense of greatness[14] and ennobled them by including them in the elite Germanic Aryan race with an important national mission. According to a testimonial, which I received during fieldwork in Germany from members of the aristocracy on August 3, 1999, many among the aristocracy in Germany opposed Hitler, calling him "the demon" because of his talent for getting the little people's emotions burning for him. Those among the aristocracy who collaborated with Hitler felt shamefully humiliated: they were forced to work with the demon, because he controlled the feelings of the nation. The masses—busy with daily survival—had paid less attention to the details of the national humiliation inflicted by the Treaty of Versailles after World War I than the aristocracy, until Hitler "explained" the situation to them and gave them a leading role to play.

The little people were also caught up in the other social dynamics Hitler created. It was attractive to share the passions of the group, to be swept up in its enthusiasm. At the same time, it was disagreeable, and increasingly dangerous, to remain isolated from group feeling (to say nothing of the dangers of active opposition). The interpretation proposed here sees the masses not as *willing executioners* but as *willing partners in seduction*. In the course of this seduction, however, they were betrayed and abandoned to a terrible fate by a once-beloved parent or lover. There was no alternative to realizing that they had been "raped."

It took the nation decades to overcome the shock and admit the "rape," the one they suffered themselves and the one they agreed to perpetrate on millions of neighbors.

Alice went for engulfed and dependent love, as did the little people in Germany. Both gave up large parts of their independent selves to immerse themselves in the loved person's world. Robert and Hitler saw themselves as providers of love and salvation. However, they brought destruction (the list of national and ethnic saviors/seducers/rapists is long). Alice was caught in the old definition of love that insists a woman give up herself for her "man." The little people in Germany were led into engulfed love by their lack of experience with "seduction" at a national level. The end was harsh for all.

Alice and Germany's little people gave their lives and souls for their lovers. Both had to realize, at the end, that their lovers had not extended genuinely caring love. Their lovers were isolated people, living in secluded hallucinatory worlds, within which they defined love and help on their own terms. Robert and Hitler ignored the fact that reality did not conform to their hallucinations and misjudged what would be good for the well-being of those they supposedly loved, bringing humiliation to all. Alice and the little people had reason to feel betrayed by their lovers and ashamed at the "stupidity" with which they allowed themselves to be used. Robert and Hitler felt humiliated by the lack of thankfulness they encountered. Hitler, before his death, concluded that Germany deserved to be destroyed.

The lesson here is that providers of love and help, as well as recipients, have a responsibility to engage in active *attunement*. Providers need to make sure that what they provide is meeting its goals, while recipients must verify whether providers indeed are willing and capable.

Do No Harm! Aid Can Support Peace—or War

The Hefter Center at the University of Wisconsin–Milwaukee, called for participants for the Wisconsin Institute 19th Annual Conference in 2003 with the following text:

> Failed and failing states pose perhaps the most dangerous threat to the security of the U.S. and the world community, as well as the millions of inhabitants of those states. However, the international community has not found a reliable way to build sustainable peace and development in many of the world's neediest areas…(quoted from the Wisconsin Institute for Peace and Conflict Studies, UWM Peace Studies Program, and UWM Center for International Education 2003). The keynote speaker is Mary B. Anderson (1999), author of the book *Do No Harm: How Aid Can Support Peace—Or War.*

When I came to Africa in 1998, my motivation to do research was suspect. I encountered the following complaints:

> First you colonize us. Then you leave us with a so-called democratic state that is alien to us. After that you watch us getting dictatorial leaders. Then you give them weapons to kill half of us. Finally you come along to "measure" our suffering and claim that this will help us!? Are you crazy?

How was I to react? Was I to feel humiliated by such aggressive insults hurled at my benevolent intentions? Should I merely shrug my shoulders and label these critics as oversensitive people, clinging to old injuries instead of getting their act together and rising from their lamentable condition? Who was to blame? What is helpful research? How should it be designed to be of benefit and not contribute to humiliation? I tried to listen more.

> You Westerners get a kick out of our problems. You have everything back home, you live in luxury, and you are blind to that. You think you're suffering when you can't take a shower or have to wait for the bus for more than two hours! Your four-wheel drive cars cover our people with dust! You enjoy being a king in our country, but you're just average at home! All you want is to have fun, get a good salary, write empty reports to your organization back home or publish some articles, so you can continue this fraud. You are a hypocrite! You know that we need help—how glad we'd be not to need it! It would be great if you'd really listen to us, not just to the greedy ones among us who exploit your arrogant stupidity for their own good! We feel deeply humiliated by your arrogant and self-congratulating help! (Taken from an interview with an African intellectual, January 2, 1999, in Kenya; however this view was typical of African intellectuals.)

After many years of failed aid programs, many observers agree that it is often the donors' responsibility to ensure that their help meets the needs of the recipients. The recipients are judged "right" in feeling humiliated by ill-considered help. In Africa, I continuously met descriptions of United Nations (UN) or Non-Governmental Organization (NGO) activities that came close to parody (but contained elements of truth):

> You helpers come along, build wells (or some other installations or services liable to be ecologically unsound or unmanageable in the longer run), create a few short-term jobs for chauffeurs, secretaries and security personnel, and then you disappear again![15]

Does this mean that helpers are always responsible when help fails or is insufficient? Are helpers always "wrong" when help goes wrong? No. Help may be well-intentioned and well-designed, but meet recipients who show insufficient appreciation for the effort of the helper. In that case the helper's actions would have to be evaluated as right, while the blame would go to the recipients. Before starting my field work in Somalia in 1998, I talked with NGO personnel who had worked with Somali refugees. They told me that they would not support me in emphasizing Somali victimhood:

> These people are arrogant and unappreciative. You should have seen their behavior in the refugee camps! They regard help as their right and are extremely pushy,

unreasonable and choosy. They cheat us helpers wherever they can. They accuse us of humiliation. But if you want to speak to the people who are really being humiliated, then speak to us, the helpers!

What are we to do in such a situation? Who is right? Perhaps this question is inappropriate. Perhaps it is important to describe the interplay, as well as the complexity of accusations and counteraccusations. What is the role of research and science in this case? Sam Engelstad, the UN's Chief of Humanitarian Affairs (and on several occasions Acting Humanitarian Coordinator in Mogadishu in 1994), wrote to me (personal communication from Sam Engelstad on September 28, 1999, quoted with his permission):

> During my time in Somalia in 1994, humiliation was never far from the surface. Indeed, it pretty much suffused the relationship between members of the UN community and the general Somali population. In the day-to-day interaction between the Somalis and UN relief workers like ourselves, it enveloped our work like a grey cloud. Yet, the process was not well understood, and rarely intended to be malevolent.

Engelstad added that "Among the political and administrative leadership of the UN mission, however, humiliation and its consequences were far better understood and were frequently used as policy tools. Regardless of intent, it was pernicious and offensive to many of us."

The background for Engelstad's remarks was the launching of *Operation Restore Hope* (by the *Unified Task Force, UNITAF*), on December 9, 1992, by the United States, as a response to the failure of the first United Nations operation *UNOSOM*. However, UNITAF also failed, as did *UNOSOM II*. Especially, the hunt for Somali General Aidid was widely seen as undermining UN impartiality and turning the UN and the United States into targets of Somali mistrust and revenge. In 1993 an angry crowd dragged a dead American soldier through the streets of Mogadishu in Somalia. The offer of help to an impoverished and ravaged country, Somalia, was greeted by "disrespect" and "lack of thankfulness," with acts of humiliation perpetrated against the helpers.

On New Year's Eve 1998, I interviewed a Somali warlord (Osman Ato, a former ally of General Aidid), one of many Somali voices who insisted that the UNOSOM operation was a humiliation. This was especially true, he maintained, when a house in which respected elders were meeting was attacked and bombed. He felt even more humiliated by the cynical and humiliating justification for the bombing—that this meetinghouse was a headquarters. He argued that "when the Americans feel humiliated because their soldiers' bodies were shown in the streets, they should ask themselves why this happened. They should be aware of the fact that killing elders, for example, is a deep humiliation in Somali society." The helicopters, the bombing, all this, he maintained, were acts of humiliation that united Somalis against the UN. Osman Ato's views illustrated that he, a warlord and an "organizer of violence," thought in terms of humiliation and "counterhumiliation." Many Somalis united with him under the banner of "necessary" humiliation for humiliation.

An American, who reviewed the foregoing paragraph, reacted as follows (2002):[16]

> For a Somali warlord to attribute the killing of US peacekeepers and the desecration of the body of one of them to the humiliation of some Somali elders being killed by American bombing (although there is no reason to think that the Americans knew that the people in the house were "respected elders") is obviously a more moral-sounding explanation than hatred, bloodlust, or a demonstration of power. Here the problem of researcher bias arises: a more neutral interviewer might have asked this man why the attack on the Americans had been preceded by the killing of dozen or so Pakistani peacekeepers, who presumably had nothing to do with those elders, were fellow Moslems, had not in any way been colonial oppressors of Somalia, etc.

This comment leads us directly to the cycle of humiliation. The American reviewer assumes that ignorance protects people from being taken as humiliators (*they* should assume that *we* did not know, that it was an embarrassing mistake) without realizing that such "misunderstandings" very often lie at the heart of cycles of humiliation. With his remarks, the American reviewer makes himself a party to a potential cycle of humiliation instead of maintaining neutrality. By expecting that ignorance protects against eliciting humiliation, the reviewer clearly is wrong.

However, the reviewer is also right. A warlord may indeed cover up power lust by using *humiliation rhetoric.* Ato may or may not be using humiliation to shield ulterior motives. The situation could be mixed—perhaps he sometimes feels genuinely humiliated and sometimes merely uses the humiliation argument to his political advantage. We do not know. What we know, and what a researcher has to report, is that he uses the humiliation argument, genuinely or not. An impartial researcher must recount this, nothing more and nothing less. A researcher cannot discount a person's claims to feeling humiliated.

Furthermore, the reviewer is wrong in expecting that the Somali view should not be reported because it does not correspond to American views. I did ask Osman Ato and others about the killing of Pakistani troops. This questioning failed, however, to fulfill the American reviewer's expectation that it open up Somali self-criticism and counter their feelings of humiliation, authentic or not.

Even though this book aims at "helping" the world by doing good science, it may be drawn into cycles of humiliation and, unintentionally and inadvertently, have humiliating effects on some readers, who may lash out against it. The American reviewer draws *science* into this cycle of humiliation by condemning as "unscientific" reports of views that are unwelcome to the American party in the conflict. He asks research to represent only one side, despite the need for impartiality to end cycles of humiliation. However, cycles of humiliation can be broken only if data are collected from all sides, without censorship, and initially without regard to "authenticity." It is only in a second step that authenticity should be discussed.

Perhaps it is prudent for an accused party, instead of discounting feelings of humiliation professed by the opponent, to consider that these feelings may be authentic, perhaps even "justified." If professed feelings of humiliation are authentic, even if produced by propaganda, flatly discounting them will only inflame the situation. Furthermore, if these feelings indeed are authentic, if not justified, they may be healed by understanding and apologies. Free-floating self-feeding psychopathic "bloodlust" is much more difficult to tackle than humiliation that is relational and can be mitigated within relations. Bloodlust should therefore be the last "diagnosis" we turn to.

If a cycle of humiliation occurred in Somalia and Somalis truly felt humiliated (whether incited by propaganda or authentically) and responded by inflicting humiliation upon dead American bodies, then we have a situation that cries out for analysis. It would be a scientific and political mistake to suppress reports of humiliation because they may entail unauthentic propaganda.

The humiliating ending of the UN operation in Somalia had profound effects at the global multilateral level for which another country in agony, Rwanda, paid a high price. When the genocide started in Rwanda in 1994, the international community left Rwandans to slaughter each other because nobody wanted a "second Somalia."[17] This is more shocking when we realize that as few as 5000 troops may have saved almost a million lives:

> A modern force of 5,000 troops…sent to Rwanda sometime between April 7 and April 21, 1994, could have significantly altered the outcome of the conflict…forces appropriately trained, equipped and commanded, and introduced in a timely manner, could have stemmed the violence in and around the capital, prevented its spread to the countryside, and created conditions conducive to the cessation of the civil war….[18]

What Is Good Help? Action Research

Helping, loving, caring, liberating, and setting free are all services that, if linked to arrogance, may be perceived as humiliating. A sophisticated realization of *intersubjectivity* and a successful effort at *attunement* are at the core of genuine help and love. Help and love are successful only if carried out in a spirit of humility, from equal to equal, not in a top-down manner. The buzzwords *empowering* and *enabling,* informed by human rights, have a place here. Would-be helpers have a responsibility to empower and enable recipients to voice their views. Merely empowering is not enough. The little people in Germany had been empowered only a short while earlier and used their newly won power to elect a hallucinating seducer, Hitler. Many, especially women with their newly gained suffrage, were not yet *enabled* to make informed choices.

Gergen advocates *participatory action research,* particularly in cross-cultural settings. In the chapter "Sensitivity to the Influences of Diverse Cultural Traditions" in the book *Toward a Cultural Constructionist Psychology,* Gergen writes:

> To assist in this effort new methodologies have emerged attempting to dismantle research hierarchies, and replace the traditional autonomy of the researcher (an invitation to cultural blindness) with more collaborative forms of inquiry. Perhaps the most visible form of collaborative research is that of participatory action research (see for example Reason, ed. 1994, in Gergen and Gergen 2000).

Wherever I went in Africa (1998 and 1999) the *War-torn Societies Project in Somalia*[19] received praise for being different from many projects sponsored by aid agencies. The *War-torn Societies Project* concentrated on *action research* and attempted to work with the communities concerned to develop an agenda for development, enabling and empowering people and transforming them from *recipients* into *coactors.* Empowerment heals humiliation—intellectual and psychological—between the *incoming helpers' perceptions or ideologies of what people need as aid* and the *support that local people really need.* This tailor-made approach seems to be successful primarily because it is nonhumiliating.

Summary

Misunderstandings and humiliation is the topic of this chapter, a topic that seems insignificant at a first glance. However, its effects can be particularly disastrous and indeed create enemies, albeit unwittingly. Unsuspecting "perpetrators" know nothing of the ill-feelings they create—it is the nature of misunderstandings and miscommunication that mutual understanding is missed without anybody planning it—and are unprepared for adverse outcomes. As a result, everybody is a righteous victim. Nobody has done anything hurtful, perhaps all tried to be helpful and loving, and all feel outraged when aggressive "retaliation" is what they reap. This can cause unbridled anger and can lead to exceptionally vicious cycles of humiliation.

To prevent such tragic outcomes, it pays to keep a cautious inner distance. It is important to tolerate not having ready-made interpretations of what is going on. It is crucial to be able to endure feelings of fear and insecurity that accompany such uncertainty. It is essential to learn to ask questions, and ask them with respect before hurrying into biased judgments and righteous rage.[20]

CHAPTER 5

HUMILIATION AND CONFLICT

This chapter is bound to omit some examples of the role played by humiliation that the reader would like to have included. The few selected exemplary cases presented here are meant to give the reader but a taste of what humiliation may entail, and where to find it. Obviously, the list of cases in the world is much longer. Each example can be contested, discussed, and criticized. The examples are meant to contribute to a wider discussion—they are snapshots that take the perspective of humiliation as a starting point to introduce interesting new insights. Other snapshots would render other weightings of factors and would be as valuable to the larger dialogue. In no way is it implied that the presentation further down is the "only truth."

World Wars I and II may be taken to support the proposition that humiliation can lead to war, Holocaust, genocide, and ethnic cleansing, while respect can facilitate peace—the humiliation entailed in the Treaty of Versailles led to war, while the respect entailed in the Marshall Plan led to peace. Those very issues are still all very high on the world's political agenda. In recent years, genocide has occurred in Rwanda and Burundi, ethnic cleansing has occurred in ex-Yugoslavia, atrocities have been committed in East-Timor and many other places, until 9/11 awakened the world to "global terrorism," which in turn led to the "war on terror." Usually local cycles of humiliation do not stay local. They tend to bring insecurity to neighbors and can contaminate the highest international levels. Monty Marshall has written most remarkably on protracted conflict and how *insecurity gets diffused.*[1] Global terror is the ultimate diffusion of insecurity. This book posits that building a sustainable world, both socially and ecologically, is absolutely feasible, if only we manage the transition better.

An Example of Humiliation at the Family Level

It is important to understand that humiliation is as active at the personal level as at the global level (although humiliation, in order to become a group phenomenon, requires additional elements, namely group mobilization and organization). On the basis of many years of international experience, I suggest that it is a universal human experience to feel terrible if put down and humiliated. I believe that humiliation is especially salient if your love is being rejected in the very act of humiliation; even worse, if the wish to be loved back is being denied at the same time.

I had a client whose mother-in-law enjoyed saying, in front of the whole family, with disgust in her voice: "And you want to be part of our family? Who do you think you are?" My client reported to me what she felt when confronted with this behavior for the first time: "I was deeply shocked and petrified; I felt cold, could hardly breathe, and I was unable to answer." She came to me because she felt that she had become addicted to her own pain. She could not distance herself, could not develop any leisure interests or relaxing hobbies. Her entire life was consumed by her relationship with her in-laws, a relationship that was filled with a continuous flow of incidents of humiliation and counterhumiliation, sometimes minute, sometimes overwhelmingly vicious; she was obsessed with imagining all kinds of revenge. After her husband's death her in-laws tried to trick her out of her inheritance, and she was locked in bitter court cases with them for many years. She repeatedly became so desperate that she did "stupid" things (as she called them)—writing "hysterical" letters or shouting at her adversaries in the courtroom—behavior that did not earn her the respect she craved from the judge, her lawyer, and others involved in the case. See Table 5.1.

An Example of Humiliation at the International Level

After Germany's defeat in 1945, the humiliation of 1918 was not repeated. Instead of facing draconian demands for reparations, Germany was given help to rebuild its industrial economy and was brought into NATO and the European

Table 5.1
An Example of Humiliation and its Aftermath at the Intercultural Level

Humiliation	My client is being humiliated by her in-laws.
Consequences of humiliation	• My client is obsessed by dreams of revenge. She occasionally gets "crazy," writes "hysterical" letters, or shouts at her adversaries. • As a consequence, she acquired the reputation of not deserving sympathy or help.
Reconciliation	Yet to be fully achieved.

Community (now the European Union). The Marshall Plan was central to preventing renewed humiliation. See Table 5.2. Willy Brandt, Chancellor of the Federal Republic of Germany, confirmed this when he spoke at Harvard University on June 5, 1972, at the commemoration of George Marshall's speech 25 years earlier. Brandt's speech was entitled: "1945 Different Than 1918." Brandt, with his talent for making historic speeches, declared:

> Victories, too, can be bitter, especially if they carry the seed for future conflicts as in 1918, when the war was won, and peace was lost for want of reason on the part of the winners and the losers, through stubborn mistrust on the one side, through resentment of the humiliated on the other.... George Marshall and others agreed that victory did not relieve his country of its responsibility. The United States did not for a moment claim that responsibility for itself, it shared it with its allies.... With his plan George Marshall roused Europe's stifled self-confidence. He gave many citizens of the old continent a concrete stimulus to bring down from the stars the vision of a Europe united in lasting peace...the Marshall Plan was productive proof that America needs a self-confident Europe capable of forming a common political will...it waits for Europe to grow into an equal partner with whom it can share the burden of responsibility for world affairs...1947 marked the beginning of the Cold War, not because of, but in spite of the Marshall Plan.[2]

Two Examples of Humiliation at the National Level

Rwanda could be added to the list of sad examples illustrating the dynamics of humiliation. Table 5.3 proposes a possible version of these dynamics, this time not between states, as in the case of Germany, but within a single state. This example could also be used to illustrate international and multilateral levels, both being arenas for post hoc guilt for not intervening.

Table 5.2
An Example of Humiliation and its Aftermath at the International Level

Humiliation	The Treaty of Versailles humiliated a defeated Germany and—together with economic hardship—prepared Germany for Hitler.
Consequences of humiliation	• World War and Holocaust. • As a consequence, all Germans acquired the reputation of being perpetrators, "willing executioners," who do not deserve sympathy or help and forfeit any right to mourn own suffering and victimhood (German mourning for the loss of homes in Silesia, Pomerania, or East Prussia, for example, was close to taboo for decades).
Reconciliation	The Marshall Plan provided Germany with new dignity, and instead of an excluded pariah, Germany is a member of NATO and EU.

Table 5.3
An Example of Humiliation and its Aftermath at the National Level

Humiliation	Extremist members of the Hutu ruling class–Hutus being the former "underlings" in the traditional Tutsi kingdom of Rwanda—feared the return of past humiliation if their former Tutsi masters were to regain influence.
Consequences of humiliation	• Genocide. • As a consequence Hutus, guilty or not, acquired the reputation of "genocidaires" who do not deserve sympathy or help.
Reconciliation	Yet to be fully achieved.

As Rwanda, the example of South Africa and Apartheid could also be placed at the global level. Unlike Rwanda, Nelson Mandela transformed humiliation into peace; see Table 5.4.

Two Examples of Humiliation at the Global, Multilateral Level

Somalia offers many examples of local occurrences of humiliation; however, it also illustrates a cycle of humiliation at the highest multilateral level (see Table 5.5). The Somalis felt humiliated (rightly or wrongly) and responded by inflicting humiliation upon dead American bodies. The humiliating ending of the UN operation in Somalia had profound effects at the global multilateral level, as this quote illustrates: "The international community's intervention in Somalia has become synonymous with the prevailing mood in many quarters against international intervention in far-flung civil conflicts, against the broadening of peacekeeping into 'nation-building' operations, and against the United Nations in general."[3]

Rwanda paid a high price for this "mood against international intervention": The international community left Rwandans to slaughter each other, because everybody was afraid of a "second Somalia."[4]

Table 5.4
Another Example of Humiliation and its Aftermath at the National Level

Humiliation	Apartheid represented institutionalized systematic humiliation.
Consequences of humiliation	• Struggle for peace without resorting to genocide—Nelson Mandela could certainly have unleashed genocide on the white elite. • The world was given a hope-inducing example as to how to transform humiliation into social change without resorting to genocidal mayhem.
Reconciliation	Truth and Reconciliation Commissions attempted reconciliation.

Table 5.5
An Example of Humiliation and its Aftermath at the Global, Multilateral Level

Humiliation	Somalis felt humiliated (rightly or wrongly) by certain operations that were part of an international intervention that was intended to help Somalis.
Consequences of humiliation	• Somalis killed UN peacekeepers and publicly humiliated the dead bodies of U.S. pilots. Today, Western tourists risk being kidnapped or killed in some world regions.
	• As a consequence, people in need in other world regions have acquired the reputation of being unthankful recipients who do not deserve sympathy or help. The international community, for example, hesitated to protect Rwandans against genocide.
Reconciliation	Yet to be fully achieved.

The latter phase of this cycle is relevant today to any traveler, especially those from the rich world, as fear of incidents of kidnappings and bombings limits the freedom to move internationally. Not even humanitarian workers such as Red Cross and Red Crescent staff are safe from being kidnapped, as the one that occurred in Somalia in April 1998[5] and currently repeatedly in Iraq. Anti-Western violence in Egypt, for example, Luxor, 1997, or the 1998 bombings of the American embassy in Nairobi, Kenya, and Dar es-Salaam, Tanzania, are examples that have filled the media. The attack of 9/11, the attack on the disco-theque in Bali in 2002, and the 2003 attack on the United Nations headquarters in Baghdad showed that nobody is safe from the overflow of cycles of humiliation and their use by terrorists. The Madrid bombings of March 11, 2004, and the 2005 bombs in London shook the world. Innocent civilians live in fear—not only in the West, but also in Afghanistan, Iraq, the Middle East, African countries, and other world regions. Table 5.6 attempts to place global terrorism into the perspective of humiliation.

Table 5.6
Another Example of Humiliation and its Aftermath at the Global, Multilateral Level

Humiliation	Many feel humiliated (rightly or wrongly) by the West and their "cronies."
Consequences of humiliation	• Terrorists kidnap and kill Westerners and those perceived as their "cronies."
	• As a consequence, fear of terrorism leads to an erosion of human rights all over the world.
Reconciliation	Yet to be fully achieved.

An Example of Humiliation Related to American Relations with the World

No matter what they take from me
They can't take away my dignity[6]

This section is written in recognition of a historic fact—the United States of America is by far the mightiest power on the globe. Its impact on the world carries particular significance. It would be beneficial to invite Americans into global responsibility.

I would like to begin by recounting one story to illustrate how the situation became obvious to me: I remember how disturbing it was to see how some of my American colleagues in Egypt "humiliated" their Egyptian clients without noticing it, believing that their actions were in their clients' best interests. An American colleague, for example, advised young Egyptian girls who sought her advice on how to handle problematic family situations to get their own apartments to "cut the umbilical cord" and "by God, get on their own feet!" My American therapist-colleague was unwilling to understand that in most Egyptian contexts it would be quite harmful for a young girl to move into her own flat, that she would be better advised to move in with her grandmother, aunt, or some other relative. My colleague insisted that Egyptians were disadvantaged because they "had not yet had the chance" to learn enough about the American way of life, and were "deprived" of relevant knowledge about how healthy people should behave. When the girls in question did not move to a flat of their own, the therapist concluded that the girls "did not wish to get better." The therapist told the girls that they were wasting her time and should "come back when they were serious."

This example, systematized in Table 5.7, provides an example for the dynamics of humiliation at the intercultural level.

In 1981, I visited a little town in Minnesota, in the midsection of the United States, where many Norwegians have settled. I accompanied a Norwegian friend,

Table 5.7
An Example of Humiliation and its Aftermath at the Intercultural Level

Humiliation	Some "helpful" interventions by American counselors were not well adapted to Egyptian culture. What was intended as help proved to be humiliating.
Consequences of humiliation	• Some Egyptian clients stopped accepting "help" from their American helpers. • As a consequence, these Egyptian clients acquired the reputation of being unthankful recipients who do not deserve sympathy or help.
Reconciliation	Yet to be fully achieved.

Ragnar, who was visiting his Uncle Thor. Thor had immigrated to the United States about 70 years earlier. He was now 86 years old. Ragnar had never met him. We arrived at the house and rang the doorbell. A woman, the wife of the old man, opened the door. She greeted us kindly and led us to the room where her husband was lying, very frail and near death in a hospital bed. Oxygen bottles, cables, and tubes were everywhere. We carefully approached the bed, afraid to awaken or disturb the old man. Suddenly, there came a deep voice: "You didn't want me!" This was all. There was no more talk. "You didn't want me!" was all he said to us. No "hello" and no "good-bye."

We left his room, almost in shock, needing his wife to explain what had happened. She told us Thor had left Norway with one of his elder brothers when he was 16. In Norway the eldest son inherits the farm. Younger sons get nothing. Before finding oil, Norway was a very poor country, and those without a farm had few prospects. This made Thor feel very unwelcome, and he was bitter all his life. His American wife, who had kept in touch with his family back in Norway, was the one who had invited us to visit him before he died. However, his bitterness lay too deep. There was no closure for him.

Many American clients came to me when I worked as a clinical psychologist and counselor in Egypt. I was stricken by the frequency of sad family biographies that in some way or another resembled Thor's. Those who had left their homes to immigrate to America were not always the happiest people. Many fled—they fled from intolerance, from suppression, from ill-treatment, or from humiliation. The biggest legacy for many American citizens is the suffering of their forefathers. Like adopted children, who often grapple with the question of why their biological parents rejected them, American identity seems to grapple with questions of why their forefathers were rejected by their homelands.

There is a great suffering that lies accumulated in the collective historic memory of the people of the United States, along with a legacy of heroic prevailing. The United States is not just "another country"; it is a country with a specific history and a particular ethos. It is important to understand the cognitive and emotional mind-set of Americans and invite them as key players into the task of building a socially and economically sustainable *global village.*

Americans touched base with their sense of extraordinary courage, sheer will, and heroism after September 11, 2001. Many Americans are deeply moved by the vision of standing together in defiance of evil adversity, as heroic as the legacy their forefathers left them. I paraphrase and summarize what I heard from my clients about this legacy:

> Our forefathers did not emigrate to the United States because they needed a casual summer outing. They escaped from places in which they were unwelcome, misunderstood or even humiliated. By extraordinary bravery and perseverance they built a better world, a world that has become the target of global envy; envy entailing both negative and positive connotations. Anti-Americanism is the negative fall-out

of this envy, while imitating America is its positive aspect. Both reactions confirm American pre-eminence. Our forefathers were once humiliated and victimized, but they prevailed. When we are humiliated and victimized now, we will prevail again. We regard those around the world who are able to appreciate our achievements as our friends, those who can't are weak souls or enemies.

Strikes or preventive strengthening

In medicine, there are two basic strategies. The classical school often places the emphasis on *fighting the enemy of cancer or microbes by surgical or pharmaceutical strikes.* Alternative schools highlight the more preventive approach of *strengthening the entire body system to make disease less likely to find fertile ground.*

Comparing these differences in approach to the 2003 Iraq war produces some interesting observations. Fighting the enemy with courageous strikes (including preemptive strikes) and standing together courageously against the enemy feels right to the American gut, congruent with its national ethos. This resembles the classical medicine approach. Cautious containment combined with balancing and strengthening sustainable global interdependence is what feels "right" in "old" Europe (and other regions). The latter approach equates with alternative and preventive health mind-sets.

Clearly, many Americans stand on the European side of the divide. When the term "America" is used in this text, it is meant to point at a certain tendency among some, not all Americans. The same holds for the use of the term "Europe."

Not all strikes strike well

When I studied medicine in the 1980s, debates were waging between proponents of the two approaches. We learned, however, that patients benefit most when both strategies are used, supporting one another. In the global arena, building a sustainable world based on human rights would be equivalent to the preventive *strengthening* approach. Dissuading, isolating, and marginalizing extremists—such as terrorists—would correspond to *strikes.* Current disagreements seem to focus on how the two should be calibrated.

European hesitation confirms American suspicions that Europeans are not capable of being decisive and courageous and that Americans are the world's most visionary and strong-minded leaders. Americans are good surgeons so to speak, and Europeans are weaklings who cannot stand the sight of blood. From the European point of view, American strategies risk being counterproductive —the wrong strikes at the wrong time—exacerbating the disease instead of healing it.

Humiliating arrogance

Once we decide upon the right bullet (or the appropriate strike) we must administer it in the appropriate way. From the European point of view (a view shared with the Arab World), Americans, particularly their hawks, appear arrogant rather than benevolent. Who is right? Are American hawks arrogant or benevolent? Should Europeans and Arabs work harder to see the benevolence of American motives and forget their allegations of arrogance? Should Americans try harder to explain themselves? Perhaps the only thing that can be agreed upon is that all sides have a problem with communication. Perhaps, as a first step, all sides could accept that their inner belief in their own high ideals is not automatically transmitted to the rest of the world. Even if such an inner conviction is self-evident from *inside,* it can be read as arrogance from *outside.* Such misreadings, when they happen, easily acquire the status of hard facts; people start believing in them. The more people believe in such interpretations, the more these interpretations fuel the very antagonism—including terrorism—that all want to avoid. Under these circumstances, any *bravery* and *courage* invested in either *strikes* or *containment* is counterproductive and wasted. Possibly beneficial strategies will probably be rejected. Misreadings have therefore to be addressed, avoided, and prevented, if we hope "to make the peace worth the war" as British Prime Minister Blair phrased it. All parties need to do more explaining.

We can probably all agree that the appropriate approach is to tailor strategies to situations, assuring that the suitable strategy is implemented for the intended goal. Sometimes, courage is better invested in prevention and containment, and sometimes in strikes. Sometimes strikes are necessary to defend ideals, and sometimes prevention and containment will get the job done more easily and with less loss of life. Strikes, if decided upon, must not be counterproductive. What is counterproductive for global peace, in any case, is automatically misreading one another's motives. Such misreadings may stir up feelings of humiliation on a global scale.

Children, Madmen, Criminals, Enemies, or Subhumans? Which Interpretation Fits Terrorists Best?

The Twin Towers of the World Trade Center collapsed in September 2001. They were hit by two planes piloted by a few men who shook the world. They sent America into mourning and outrage and war planes into Afghanistan and Iraq. They inspired new laws to eliminate terrorism. Nobody wants mad people flying into their neighborhoods and crashing into their homes. The big question is as follows: Are terrorists *abominable subhumans,* or *mad,* or *criminals,* or *enemies?* If criminals, can they be reformed? Are they like children or adolescents, who may mature, if aided, or are they hopeless cases, best killed?

The child paradigm fits best

Conservatives (those who are called *conservative* in the United States of America) look down on people who break the law, including terrorists, with moral disgust. Those who are called *liberal* in the United States of America look down with compassion. Conservatives might say: "*We* draw a stark line separating us from those criminals beneath *us* because we believe that *they* are fundamentally different from us, they have an evil essence." Liberals respond: "*We* draw a permeable line between *us* and *them,* perceiving them as misguided children who could be lifted up to our level of integrity if therapeutic efforts were exerted." Monty Marshall writes about *realist's* and *idealist's* images of human nature: "The Realists see no way out of the present mess except to keep the wolves at bay with sticks and fences; the Idealists see a light at the end of the tunnel but have no clear vision of how to get there from here."[7]

Lee D. Ross at Stanford researched the role of the *situation* and of *framing*. When teachers tell students that a task is difficult, they often experience those predicted difficulties. When teachers explain, however, that the same task usually is quite easily accomplished, students respond accordingly. When teachers ask students to play a game in which they have the choice to cooperate or to cheat (*Prisoner's Dilemma* game) and tell them that this is a *community game,* they cooperate; they cheat when the same game is defined as a *Wall Street game.* Morton Deutsch (1973) lays out what he calls *Deutsch's Crude Law of Social Relations.* This law says that "characteristic processes and effects elicited by a given type of social relationship (cooperative or competitive) tend also to elicit that type of social relationship." In short, "cooperation breeds cooperation, while competition breeds competition."[8]

In other words, our reality is shaped by what we believe—not completely, of course, but to a very large degree. We lock reality in with our expectations and framings.

Maria came to me as a client because she felt utterly worthless. She recounted:

> I come from a family with a fundamentalist Christian orientation. When I was a small child, I tried everything to fit in. When I was five, six, and seven years old, I prayed more than an hour every day. When I was nine, I started to study the Bible intensely. Unfortunately, this was the beginning of the end. I developed "religious doubts." I asked questions such as, "Why do all those people who by mere chance have not heard about Jesus have to go to hell? It's not their fault. This is unfair!" I did not want to be part of what I felt were degrading ways of dealing with God. In my social environment, God was somebody who can be bribed, who needs to be given attention so he doesn't get angry like a jealous lover. I wanted a more ennobled and meaningful religion, not just a cover for human stupidities and projections. In a way I was much more religious and more sincere than my family.
>
> My family was shocked but they knew what to do. I had to pray more. God would send me answers, if He deemed me worth His attention. I prayed and prayed

everyday, until I was about twelve years old, but my doubts only grew. I could not help it and I did not want to pretend. After all, religion is about sincerity. After many years of strife, at the age of about twelve or thirteen, still lacking answers that could bring me into my family's religious world, I had to conclude that God did not consider me worthy of His attention.

My family did not understand that I tried my very best, that I prayed for hours, that I was sincere and honest. They thought I was evil. They decided that I had deliberately and malevolently rejected God—even though I felt rejected by Him! They could have helped me, supported me, and consoled me in my loneliness. Instead they deepened the rift. I learned that I was not part of God's world, and, since my family was part of God's world, I was excluded from my family. I was condemned by God, not worth His attention, an evil enemy of religion, exiled from my family. Everyday I tried to reject this death sentence, but it continuously seeped into my soul. My self-esteem is rock bottom. According to the "true" teachings of my family, there is no hope for me even after death. By calling me an *evil enemy,* my parents turned me into an *enemy,* while I yearned for nothing but to be a *part of my family!*

For years I hardly talked to my family. When I did, I was aggressive. I was so disappointed with them. They created their *enemy.* They felt vindicated in their judgment. But *they* had done it to me and themselves! I only wanted to be united with them!

This vignette suggests, if we wish to bring about a peaceful global village, framing it in the liberal way is more useful, because expectancy helps create reality.

Why Do They Hate Us? The Role of Humiliation

"America exports its fear and meets the humiliation of the Arab world. The historic memory of America is perhaps too short, in the Arab world perhaps too long, particularly in Iraq," says Dominique Moisi, Deputy Director of the *Institut Francais des Relations Internationales* (*Guerre en Irak,* March 30, 2003, Channel France). Moisi's words describe the world after September 11, 2001, when the United States felt an unprecedented vulnerability.

I propose that the United States, and the rest of the West, have been much more threatened for a much longer period of time than we want to believe. Paradoxically, however, the West is also much less threatened than many of us believe. Let me explain.

Global admiration and resentment of power that is too casually displayed

My international experience and research on humiliation has revealed widespread simmering rage. In 2000, in an article entitled *What Every Negotiator Ought To Know: Understanding Humiliation,* I wrote:

Fortunately for the West, human rights-humiliation in the Third World has not yet found its Hitler. It would be disastrous if such a leader created a global following among the humiliated by arguing, for example, that the West's human rights' rhetoric was merely a hypocritical device to divert attention from the fact that the divide between rich and poor is greater than before. In view of the danger that a new Hitler would present, the West is fortunate that the influence and prestige of Nelson Mandela are so great (Lindner 2000d, p. 19).

There were clear signs of imminent threat prior to September 11, 2001. The 1998 bombings of the American embassy in Nairobi, Kenya, and Dar es-Salaam, Tanzania, and the attack on a U.S. battle ship in Yemen were but a few examples. The attacks of September 11 could be regarded as the tip of the iceberg, the result of years of covert rage, a response perhaps to *resentment of power too casually displayed,* not only by the United States, but by the entire West. The United States can be proud of its achievements and can rightly dismiss some criticism as envy. However, even feelings based on misunderstandings are valid and can lead to devastating consequences. Even if the bin Ladens of this world misunderstand America, their hatred is real.

At the very least, the United States has an *image problem.* The "rest" believes that American military might makes the world into a more dangerous place.[9]

The White House announced it would create a permanent Office of Global Communications to enhance America's image around the world. At the same time, the House of Representatives approved spending $225 million on cultural and information programs abroad, mostly targeting Muslim countries, to correct what Rep. Henry Hyde, R-Ill., called a "cacophony of hate and misinformation" about the United States.[10]

The images of the falling Twin Towers symbolize the hatred that exists for America in many parts of the world. However, they did not even begin to embody the mayhem we may expect in the future if we do not respond appropriately to this hatred. Millions could die. A few planes crashed into nuclear plants would have devastating impact. Vast landscapes could be turned into deserts. Every human being on the planet can be transformed into a weapon of mass destruction if he or she sets his or her mind to it.

How can I then suggest that the danger is at the same time much less? Because there is also a great admiration for America and the West to be found around the world. As discussed earlier, there is a great yearning among the less privileged to become members of *one single family* of humankind. Many among the poor and marginalized ache to be invited into dignified lives. America and the entire West are seen as shining examples of the *good life.* A good life includes a job, a home, a television set, a refrigerator, perhaps a car, old age security, health insurance, and good education for the children, in sum, a dignified life. All this seems "normal" in the West, but it is far from normal for the majority of the world's population.

Fear of humiliation. The victory can be gambled away

Two human tendencies—*blindness* and *fear of further humiliation*—threaten efforts to bring the love story between the West and the "rest of the world" to a happy conclusion. Blindness is a typical—and very understandable—characteristic of master elites. Many of us in the West travel the world and meet the poor only as servants in hotels or as vendors of cultural artifacts. They smile at us. They treat us well. They do not tell us what they feel. If they were to tell us, they might say: "Why is it that you can pay for an air ticket and room in this hotel? For this money I could maintain my family for a whole year! Why do your children go to school and university, while my children toil? You preach about human rights, but protect your markets against our products! What do you expect us to feel towards you? Don't you see that your wealth forces us to smile because we depend on you? Don't you see how we humiliate ourselves by smiling? Don't you see that our smiles cannot possibly be born out of 'free' choice?"

From the American point of view it is noble to free other cultures from oppression and to champion civil and political human rights. However, there are also cultural, social, and economic human rights that stipulate that more has to be done. Experts like Philippe Legrain[11] call upon the World Trade Association to work for all aspects of human rights, not just political ones. The term *enabling environment* means more than freedom from political oppression; it also means fair global rules. The lack of Western enthusiasm for fair global rules disappoints those who hear the human rights message. One of the buzzwords is *agrarian subsidies* in the United States and in the European Union: The amount of subsidy a cow in Europe and America receives per day— about US$2.50 per head—is more than twice the average daily income of a small farmer in the rest of the world, or more than the average earnings of half of the population of the world. Such obscene statistics makes the "ugly American" and "ugly European" look like the perpetrators of humiliating double standards. Blindness on the American and European sides exacerbates the problem.

Blindness can be cured. However, a second element recently added to the blend of emotions—fear of yet another humiliation—counteracts attempts to be more clear-sighted. The urgency of emergency, the need to stand up to defend loved ones and country from *them,* the terrorists, draws attention away from the more basic task—the building of long-term trust among all citizens of the planet.

One Global Us! American Security Hinges on Global Security

Perhaps the most significant lesson of September 11 is the lesson of interdependence. In an interdependent world, freedom and security for every single nation, including the United States, hinge on global security and freedom. Humiliation is counterproductive in an interdependent world in which everybody lives in a glass house. Dividing the world into enemies and friends becomes a deadly luxury. It is necessary to turn everyone into a *good—or at least support-able—neighbor.* Rifts have to be mitigated, never deepened.

From the American point of view, inspections did not work in Iraq, and sanctions, surely, had not worked for more than a decade; the international community failed to live up to its tasks. The United States had to step in and rescue the weak United Nations. But, maybe the task is to strengthen our international police force, rather than override it for its failures.

Humanity has succeeded in pacifying increasingly large areas. Cities once needed protective walls. Travelers had to be prepared for marauding bandits. Then, the walls were moved back to protect entire nations. NATO and equivalent organizations around the world have pushed the "city walls" back even farther. When will we be ready to include the entire globe under the protection of *a single police force?* When will we feel safe in strengthening the existing multilateral institutions so that they can *arrest tyrants* for *crimes against humanity?*

When police forces are overwhelmed, there are two choices. Either each citizen takes up arms, in self-defense, or each citizen helps strengthen the police force. The first seems to be a historic step backwards, the latter a historic leap forward, both locally and globally. When police forces are undermanned and incapable of doing their jobs, the individual citizen does not say, "The police are failing." Instead, this citizen says, "We have failed to give the police sufficient resources." The United States might choose to say, "We have failed to give the UN the necessary support and resources." Whenever the United Nations fail, their members have failed; nobody can avoid this responsibility.

United Nations resolutions are not "self-executing;" the political will of members is required to implement them, said Shashi Tharoor, UN Undersecretary of State, on April 15, 2003 (in BBC World *HARDtalk* with Tim Sebastian). Churchill is quoted to have said "Democracy is the worst system devised by the wit of man, except for all the others." The same may well apply to current United Nations institutions that could be seen as forerunners for democratic institutions for the global village.

Action is necessary if we are going to achieve a stable and sustainable world order. Prevention, containment, investment in sustainability—all these activities are forms of action. Action is not limited to post hoc damage control. Trust has to be built, global trust, and this requires the most arduous action of all. The world needs for the United States to invest its great abilities for courageous action into a special kind of internationalism of mutual trust and equal dignity. Charles Kupchan[12] wrote a book entitled *The End of the American Era.* In a BBC World *HARDtalk* interview with Tim Sebastian, March 18, 2003, he predicts that the United States will one day become tired of hearing "Yankee go home" and will retreat into isolationism. He suggests that the United States is well advised to give others more political space, move aside a bit, and let the world grow at its own pace for a while.

I suggest that it is time the United States adopt a new form of internationalism, internationalism married to multilateralism, rather than internationalism combined with unilateralism. *Global* security—not just American security—must be maintained. Indeed, *American security hinges on global security.* There is no exclusive American security without inclusive global security. The United States is invited to abandon an *American war on terror,* and join a *global policing endeavor concerning those who perpetrate terrorist acts,* at the same time working *for* a sustainable future, both socially and ecologically, for the *entire planet*—instead of fighting *against* "enemies."

Apologies from the World! What the World Can Do for America

Anti-American language and shouts of "Yankee go home" have a humiliating effect on citizens of the United States. Even the most open and concerned U.S. citizen is bound to feel a little frightened and defensive when he or she is subjected to a barrage of hostility that he or she may understand intellectually but cannot completely comprehend at an emotional level.

Reconciliation between America and the rest of the world is crucial if the global village is to enjoy peace and prosperity for all its citizens. The United States has the power to facilitate or retard the development of our global society as a culture that nurtures the rights and potentials of all its citizens. We need the people and the government of the United States to work with the international community, not against it, as we go about the business of building a sustainable global village.

I believe that the world owes it to itself, to the United States, and to our shared future, to find a way to help America and Americans release their fear and bitterness and join the rest as wholehearted, full partners. In my search for a way to achieve this seemingly impossible aim, I engaged Kathleen, my American friend from Houston, in a dialogue about how her fellow citizens feel about the hostility they have encountered since 9/11. Like many Americans, Kathleen realizes that the attacks on Afghanistan and Iraq were ugly and unproductive in the eyes of many. Like many of her fellow citizens, she is looking for a better way. And, like many of her fellow citizens, she feels hurt and bewildered by the sheer intensity of the hostility currently directed at her homeland by the other nations of the world. The following paragraphs are adapted from our ongoing conversation:

Kathleen: Americans don't really trust the UN. We don't trust anybody very much. If you think about it, the world hasn't given us much reason to trust. The American experience of the world has not been very pleasant. During the sixteenth, seventeenth, and eighteenth centuries, you used our continent as a dumping ground, a place to send your undesirables. During the twentieth century, you dragged us into two horrific world wars. The UN is a nice place to talk theory, but it's all talk. Its deliberations remind me of a college rap session. Americans have not seen any evidence that the rest of the world really wants peace. But, we've seen plenty of evidence that war and hatred is a way of life in most parts of the world.

Evelin: What kind of evidence?

Kathleen: Almost everybody who lives in the U.S. does so because there was no place else that would take them in. We are a country of exiles—people whose ancestors were not wanted anywhere else. My own great-grandparents came here because they were starving in Ireland, systematically starved to death by their British masters.

Evelin: But, that was a long time ago, Kathleen.

Kathleen: People in Bosnia fight over things that happened a thousand years ago. My family history in America goes back only 100 years. Why should Americans have shorter memories than everyone else? Are you suggesting that we should be more forgiving, more rational, more generous, more perfect than other people? The world has given America nothing but its castoffs, its wars, its problems. But, the world seems to expect the United States to be able to adjust immediately to its problems.

Evelin: Kathleen, statistics show that much of the world's resources are consumed by Americans. Can you see that there are many people who resent this statistic?

Kathleen: I know those statistics. Americans make up something like 10 percent of the world's population and use 80 percent of its resources. Of course, it bothers me. I would like for everyone to have everything they need. But, does the world know how hard we've worked for what we have, Evelin? I work at least 12 hours a day. Does everyone in the world do that? I don't see how they could —or they wouldn't have so much time to think about how much they hate Americans. It's a little hard for me to understand how the people of the world can feel justified doing the terrible things they have done to my fellow citizens and then expect us to turn around and send money, food, whatever else is needed to make things right. All Americans know that their forefathers were not wanted, not considered good enough, by the rest of the world. Sit in any social group in America and, sooner or later, someone will tell a story about what happened to his grandfather before he came to the United States.

Evelin: Would you like the world to apologize?

Kathleen: That's ridiculous. Who can apologize to a nation that calls itself the world's only superpower?

Evelin: Would it make you feel better to know that the world understood the pain that drove your ancestors to North America?

Kathleen: They'll never understand—because they don't WANT to understand. They're having too much fun telling us how evil we are. How could they hate if they really understood?

Evelin: Would you be willing to listen to an apology?

Kathleen: I suppose it would be the polite thing to do. But, it seems like a waste of time.

Evelin: We, the non-Americans of the world, apologize to you Americans for the hardship and rejection your forefathers suffered. We see that you are still afraid of us today....

Kathleen: Yes, we are. Because we never know when you'll turn against us...no matter what we do, it's never right.

Evelin: ...you huddle in your country because the rest of the world seems so alien and hostile. You feel that you must either retreat or dominate. Looking at us as equals seems scary. We would like to apologize for every little incident that contributed to your painful isolation. And we would like to invite you to become part of us. We thank you for bailing out Europe during and after the first and second world wars. We are sorry that we so often behave like ungrateful children. When you act, we accuse you of acting, and when you do not act, we accuse you of nonaction. You can never get it right. We apologize for our inconsistency. We apologize for our envy. It's not easy to acknowledge our powerlessness in comparison with your strength. We applaud your wish to bring a better life to the rest of the world. You have a big heart. You like to act, while the rest of us are prone to sit around wringing our hands. We admire you for this trait, too. There are huge problems to be solved—global terrorism, poverty, and an endangered biosphere. We need you in our midst and in action, engaged as much in long-term strengthening and prevention as in short-term strikes. We understand that right now you are finding it hard to find safety in patience. We know that until recently you were protected by two big oceans. But, please, let September 11 teach you the lesson of global interdependence, a lesson that makes helping others humbly without humiliation more important than ever before. Let us together evoke the spirit of the Marshall Plan and the Mandela path. We promise to try to do the same with our national identities. Please learn to love planet Earth as much as you love America. Please accept our apologies and let them sink deep into your souls. Perhaps then you will be able to adopt the entire planet as your homeland. Please know that we understand how debased and humiliated your country feels. People in trauma need recovery. They need support and care. Let us give you that care. People under stress are not always the best representatives of their own interests. Let us help you. Put down your arms and join the global village.

Kathleen: Thank you, Evelin. I appreciate your sincerity and intelligence. You have taken the first step and I acknowledge you for it.

The in-depth regeneration of relationships that the world needs now probably cannot be achieved with a single conversation or a single apology. It can be achieved, however, if we are all willing to take very small steps toward reconciliation. We cannot expect the softening to be automatic. It has taken a long time for the estrangement between the United States and the rest of the world to reach the point at which it is today. It will not be healed overnight. But every time an individual feels heard and acknowledged, the process of healing moves to a new level.

As the process progresses, we may begin to find pleasure in replacing the shopworn, destructive "I know we did this, but you did something even worse" with new, constructive conversations. There may come a day when we—all the citizens of the world—will feel safe promising to refrain from minimizing one another's suffering, from playing and replaying the hurts we might once have sustained at the other's hand, and to understand that we are all victims and perpetrators because we all suffer from the human condition.

In another conversation, Kathleen shared with me her perception of the strength of the American myth, the deep resonance her fellow citizens feel when they contemplate their history of exclusion by the rest of the world:

> Throughout our history we Americans have jammed newcomers together, forcing them to live as neighbors, even though they would be killing one another if they were still back home. We have neighborhoods filled with Poles and Germans, Sicilians and Northern Italians, Jews and Catholics, Pakistanis and Indians—all kinds of murderous mixtures. These neighborhoods should self-destruct. But, they don't. They survive and thrive, if a little mysteriously, building a new shared identity out of the shreds of their pasts. It doesn't matter here that our parents and grandparents spent their lifetimes killing one another. That sad history has been transcended by the American myth of "unity in isolation"—one that allows us to live together in peace and harmony, to love one another's children, to form communities, corporations, churches, a NATION. Our sense of having overcome the entire world's hostility is not something Americans can give up easily without sacrificing a vital part of ourselves. This myth sings and struts and hums of heroism. Is there another myth so fine and powerful, so productive and joyous, so capable of uniting so many diverse peoples into a new kind of whole? Can the world give us another hymn to move our souls?

In a sense, this entire book was written to provide a response to Kathleen's challenge. I believe that the new myth she and her fellow citizens crave can be found in the emerging global village—a world even younger than Kathleen's America, a world that needs to take the best of her country's devotion to freedom and merge it with the best of the planet's accumulated wisdom to create something that— like her country—represents a new life for humankind as it has never experienced it before.

Summary

The examples presented in this chapter give a taste of the wide range of consequences flowing from humiliation. Incidents of humiliation may lead to extreme reactions such as massacres, but may also be relevant in the more subtle undermining of intercultural relations, or they may lead to Mandela-like breath-taking peacemaking. Moreover, these examples show how humiliation may be played out at all levels, affecting relations between individuals as well as groups.

The case of America was given particular attention in this chapter. America needs to be invited out of isolated bitterness ("You did not want us, why should we cooperate with you?") into participating in the joint task of caring for our planet. This chapter attempts to attenuate the bitterness that lingers in many American hearts and minds, a painful bitterness whose existence is either over-looked or dismissed by the rest of the world, cynically or out of ignorance. For the sake of the world's future, the rest cannot afford to look down on the American mind-set. As we know, victims often become perpetrators and perpetrators are often victims—let us grasp the opportunity for bridge building that is entailed in this insight.

CHAPTER 6

HUMILIATION AND TERRORISM

Nowadays torture is widely rejected. This was not always so. To various extents and for a long time, cruel punishment was a normal part of social life, enshrined in law. The Inquisition comes to mind—in the Middle Ages, the Catholic Church tortured people to save their souls, and this was regarded as both legal and divinely sanctioned. The inquisitors even sprayed their torture tools with holy water. Early Greek and Roman law stipulated that only slaves could be tortured. Freemen were subjected to torture only in cases of treason, a crime through which they forfeited their status at the top of the pyramid of power. In no other period of history has torture been used more than under Queen Elizabeth of England, explains Leonard A. Parry.[1] For a variety of crimes, you could find yourself trapped hanging in a cage displayed in a public place as you slowly died, only to be taken down and quartered right before your death. Lords and high officials were usually spared by Elizabeth, and also she regarded treason as one of the worst crimes.

You Deserve Being Pushed Down: Torture Is "Normal" in the World of Ranked Honor

As we see, elites (who legitimized torture) hesitated to torture their equals. Inferiors were more "eligible," as were traitors, those who were perceived to have lost the status of equals through treason. Thus, torture was a legal and normal part of societies' dealings with their lower power subjects for long periods of humankind's past, deeply embedded into the world of ranked honor. William V. Harris[2] explains how Aristotle describes as "slavish" and "ignoble" a man who fails to get angry at insults to himself and his family. Slaves and women, however, were not entitled to show the same assertiveness—they were at the receiving end.

Nobody Deserves Being Pushed Down: Human Rights Turn Torture into the Worst Humiliation and Humiliation into the Worst Torture

In a human rights framework all humans are entitled to enjoy equal dignity. Nobody is regarded as inferior any more, and nobody is "eligible" for torture any longer. Torture acquires the taste of utter obscenity in human rights contexts. Torturing or humiliating people becomes a deep and hurtful, totally illegitimate lowering of the essence of humanity, no longer a lowering of honor along a legitimate scale. Torture in a moral universe of human rights causes more qualms even than torturing equals in a world of ranked honor; it triggers a profound moral disgust about the desecration of the essence of humanity.

As torture becomes more obscene, the act of humiliating people acquires a new significance. It moves to the core of torture. We look beyond the physical pain inflicted to the humiliation involved. Humiliating people is now worse than physical torture; it hurts more than physical pain, because equal dignity has become the essence of humanity. Making people commit or endure undignified treatment, in a human rights context, demeans and soils both perpetrators and victims. No longer are perpetrators "higher" beings, who are entitled to push inferiors further down. No longer do underlings deserve such treatment. Human rights turn torture into the worst humiliation—a violation of the inviolable equality of dignity for all human beings—and humiliation into the worst torture.

Southern Honor and Torture

At the current historic time, as human rights ideals gain acceptance, honor strategies all over the world, including torture, move out of the category of "natural" or "heroic" into the category of "repulsive." More so, the label "torture" is applied to an increasingly wider field as the human rights movement "dignifies" animals and nature. Many forms of human consumption that were formerly accepted as "normal" are now perceived as repulsive torture by human rights defenders. Future generations will most probably regard presently living generations as barbaric and insensitive, due to our blind treatment of people, animals, and nature as inferiors for whom torture is a normal mode of treatment.

Ranked honor is still strong in two realms: in certain world regions (for example, those regions where women believe that being beaten is justified) and at certain macro levels, namely at the level of powerful international elites dealing with each other. Honor often plays a stronger role in foreign policy matters, in armed services and diplomatic staffs, than among the lower echelons of the average citizen. Thus, a passion to retain a state's "honorable" preeminence, as Donald Kagan[3] proposes, applies in today's world no less than it did earlier, even when "national honor" is partly concealed by human rights rhetoric and no longer invoked as openly as in the past.

The current administration (2005) of the United States of America is deeply embedded in the *Southern Honor* that historian Bertram Wyatt-Brown[4] describes in his book with the same title. Southern inclination toward the "warrior ethic" embraces the following elements, according to Wyatt-Brown, namely "that the world should recognize a state's high distinction; a dread of humiliation if that claim is not provided sufficient respect; a yearning for renown; and, finally, a compulsion for revenge when, in issues of both personal leadership calculations and in collective or national terms, repute for one or another virtue and self-justified power is repudiated."[5] David Hackett Fischer informs us that Southerners "strongly supported every American war no matter what it was about or who it was against."[6] Social psychologists Richard Nisbett and Dov Cohen[7] explain the psychology of violence in the culture of honor in the southern part of the United States.

Conceptualizations such as "'they' want to break our will, but 'we' won't let it happen," or "'they' are cowards," or "*the* enemy" are embedded in gut feelings imbued with masculine norms of honor that thrive on contests of "strength," on "keeping the upper hand," on "victory," and on avoiding appearing to be a "wimp" or a "sissy," in other words, avoiding to appear "female." In such a context, humiliating "*the* enemy" is felt to be legitimate, especially when this enemy does not act "manly" and thus is felt to forfeit the status as equal in honor. Terrorists are "unlawful" in this frame of mind because they "hide behind civilians" and are "cowards," regardless of how much actual courage might be invested (even if misinvested). "Unlawful combatants" commit "treason" against traditional honor norms, which makes them "free" to be tortured. The introduction of categories such as "unlawful combatants" informs us that southern honor, though no longer openly invoked, is still permeating certain policies in the United States of America.

Does Torturing "Enemies" Protect Us?

The argument that torture is necessary in order to gain information that can protect against terrorist acts—if it ever was valid—grows increasingly less so as the human rights message gains mainstream acceptance. This is particularly the case when torture is applied by people who otherwise advocate human rights. As explained earlier, torturing people is intrinsically incompatible with human rights ideals of equal dignity, and employing it while preaching human rights doubly undermines the credibility of the perpetrators—first through the incompatibility itself and second through the perpetrators' blindness to the inconsistency in their stance.

Most authorities on interrogation agree that torture and lesser forms of physical coercion produce confessions. However, these confessions are not necessarily true. The mistreatment at Abu Ghraib, for example, may have done little to further American intelligence; Willie J. Rowell, who served for 36 years as a C.I.D. agent (the Army's Criminal Investigation Division), told Seymour M. Hersh, that the use of force or humiliation with prisoners is invariably counterproductive. "They'll tell you what you want to hear, truth or no truth.... You don't get righteous information."[8] Canadian William Sampson[9] was tortured for three years in Saudi Arabia. He describes in his book that he confessed to what was "beaten into me."

This fact should decide the "ticking-time-bomb" argument, which posits that torture may be justified to prevent mayhem if a prisoner knows the location of a hidden ticking time bomb. How do we know that a prisoner is a ticking-bomb terrorist? Would we not have to torture all suspects to identify the ticking-bomb terrorist? We would end up with many false confessions and miss the right one. And the argument that "terrorists are not abiding by rules, why should we" is intrinsically contradictory. Slavery or Apartheid would never have been abolished with such an attitude—"they have slaves, so why should not we have slaves."

Even worse, such approaches would likely bring about more terrorism, rather than less. In a BBC World *HARDtalk* interview (with Jon Sopel on September 7, 2004), Clive Stafford-Smith, lawyer for detainees at Guantanamo Bay, made the case that torture is not only morally wrong, but also "stupid": "you get bad information and you incense the world." He claims that "we have to keep our system civilized, because otherwise we will have more 9/11s, not less." Stafford-Smith is not alone with this opinion. Abdelbari Atwan, editor of *Al Quds al-Arabi*, a London-based Arabic daily newspaper, informs us of the disastrous effects of American torture practices on many in the Arab world, where this torture is felt to be official strategy, "The torture is not the work of a few American soldiers. It is the result of an official American culture that deliberately insults and humiliates Muslims." However, not only "the world" is incensed. *The Washington Post* writes about alleged secret CIA prisons that allow for harsher treatment of prisoners and reports that "the debate over the wisdom of the program continues among CIA officers, some of whom also argue that the secrecy surrounding the program is not sustainable." An intelligence official is reported as saying, "It's just a horrible burden."[10]

In the widely known Abu Ghraib scandal of 2004, acts of humiliation were perpetrated, with detainees being made to stand naked with women's underwear over the head, laughed at by guards, including female guards, and sometimes photographed in this position. The United States administration's initial response was to say that the President was shocked and disgusted by the

photographs. The word "torture" was avoided. The official position was that prisoners had possibly been the objects of "abuse," eventually of "humiliation," but
nothing more was admitted. Susan Sontag reported on Secretary of Defense
Donald Rumsfeld saying at a press conference, "My impression is that what has
been charged thus far is abuse, which I believe technically is different from torture. And therefore I'm not going to address the 'torture' word."[11]

Again, we see southern honor at work. In a moral world of ranked honor,
humiliation may, indeed, be seen as less significant than physical torture. However, in a moral universe of equal dignity for all human beings, humiliation
moves to the center of torture. It is the very core wound that torture can possibly
inflict. Nils Alte, another Falstad prisoner, explained how he was ordered by the
SS guards to lie straight on the floor with his arms by his side. Then he was
dragged down a flight of concrete stairs in such a way that his head bumped onto
the steps and blood poured from his head. He then was commanded to crawl
back up the stairs and lick up his own blood from the steps. He said: "It was
not so much the physical pain that was excruciating, as bad as it was; it was the
humiliation, the degradation, which was the worst." That it is humiliation that
is felt as the most painful suffering, and not physical pain or material destruction,
is a recurrent phenomenon. This is what I heard from my clients as well as during
the course of my fieldwork.

Observing the calibration of concepts of torture and humiliation in today's
world allows us to gauge where the human rights transition stands and to what
extent it has succeeded in undoing deep-seated gut feelings of ranked honor
(and connected concepts of "justified" humiliation). And there is flux. The
BBC reported that U.S. Secretary of State Condoleezza Rice said on her visit to
the Ukraine that the United States was bound by the UN Convention against
Torture. The BBC point out that her comments appear to contrast with those
of the U.S. Attorney General Alberto Gonzales, who said last year the convention
did not apply to U.S. interrogations of foreigners overseas. However, one aide to
Rice said her remarks were "a clarification of policy, not a shift."[12] If we were
Martians and had to report on the human rights transition on planet Earth, we
might report that such stark phenomena as Apartheid have been abandoned,
but the transition is not yet complete, as this push-pull debate over torture
illustrates.

Torturers Are Like You and Me

The famous Milgram experiments[13] provide a powerful demonstration of the
fact that all of us have the capacity to become torturers if put under appropriate
pressure. Average American citizens were willing to give hurtful electric shocks to
other people merely because the researchers in the laboratory, where the experiments were carried out, told them to.

Martha Huggins tried to get "under the skin" of *violence workers,* and she points out that neither the Greek nor the Brazilian torturers discussed in the study were sadistic or mentally unbalanced from the start. On the contrary, the regime selected "normal" men and shaped them. The "banality of their resulting evil" was made vivid during an interview Huggins and her colleagues had with Jorge, a former Brazilian prison operative. His murder toll for each year was about 80. Huggins asked if that meant he had personally killed 80 people.

> "Oh, no," he replied, "eighty incidents. I am counting a whole family just once!" He then left the interview room only to return soon with one of his paintings and poems as gifts to each of our female researchers. These presents were meant to reassure us that he was not a brutal monster but a sensitive, creative person who just happened to have had an interlude of murdering men, women, and children.[14]

Selected men were shaped into torturers by desensitization and by bestowing honor on them. It began with entry into a special elite unit, in the Greek case the Kentron Ekpedeyssis Stratiotikis (KESA). Huggins reports that the inclusion in a torture unit "automatically enhanced these soldiers' status. They wore distinctive uniforms, held rank over other soldiers with comparable tenure, and enjoyed privileges and resources not usually available to their peers. Being a KESA soldier was an honor."[15]

However, before this honor could be enjoyed, the recruit underwent intensive hazing. For weeks, recruits were humiliated and brutalized. "...[S]uch violent treatment desensitized men to pain and suffering, promoted total obedience to authority, engendered acceptance of the system's ideology, and energized their resolve to destroy designated enemies of the state. Hazing also gave a personal reality to the kind of violence that would be acceptable in the recruit's later career."[16]

Torture Survivors: Treating a Terrible Assault on Human Dignity

Sepp Graessner edited a book entitled *At the Side of Torture Survivors: Treating a Terrible Assault on Human Dignity.*

> One prisoner wrote: "The blows don't just strike your body; they strike much more at your soul, your spirit, your reason. Pain and emotion bore their way through the entire body until they reach your soul, your ego. The torment is not merely perceived, it penetrates consciousness, it is apprehended. You want to scream. The screams come from the gut and push through to the throat, but they are held back by reason, self-consciousness, pride, so that you nearly suffocate. It is a struggle between body and soul, a struggle between body and spirit."[17]

Graessner explains that enduring torture requires a kind of mental peak performance that leads victims to cover their experiences with deep silence even after the torture is over.

Even if the physical scars should heal at some point, the psychic wounds will remain for life in the absence of outside help and treatment. Victims often suffer from intense depression, and they are often pursued by nightmares and anxieties. Amnesia, agitation, delusions, feelings of powerlessness, a constant shift between aggressive overreaction and apathy are among the victims' observable attributes.[18]

In interviews with torture victims (in Somaliland in 1998 and later in Israel, with a Holocaust survivor), I learned about the intricate connections between torture, humiliation, and shame. Humiliation is a complex phenomenon of acts and feelings that can occur with or without shame. Shame is widely regarded as an asset, and torturers can shame victims to attain their goals precisely because shame is a virtue. A human being incapable of shame is seen as a monster. Many people have nightmares of strangers standing above them, laughing and ridiculing them, while they lie naked on the floor in their excrement (not surprisingly, this dream is a script for torture). Torture uses feelings of shame to humiliate its victims and uses humiliation to create shame.

However, as in the case of Nelson Mandela, people who face humiliating treatment may also sternly reject feeling humiliated or ashamed. Even when they feel humiliated, victims of torture and maltreatment recount that part of their success in being resilient was not to feel ashamed while indeed feeling humiliated. A young man—let me call him Ahmed—told me that he felt pure triumph, without any shame, when he was beaten and humiliated by the military—he was almost killed—because this predicament proved that he heroically resisted oppression (personal communication, 2004). As long as he meekly bowed to the humiliation of oppression, he felt unbearable shame and guilt, he said. Feeling shame-free triumphant humiliation liberated him, he explained, made him resilient, and gave him new pride.

How Torture, Humiliation, and Loving Empathy Can Link Up with Terrorism

Torture, humiliation, and loving empathy can link up with terrorism. "Torturous" empathy with the humiliation suffered by loved ones can generate a willingness to engage in terrorist acts. In Egypt, I had Palestinian clients who suffered from depression because they felt they should help their suffering families in Palestine, instead of studying in Cairo, preparing for a happy life.

Farida, a young woman, not yet 20 years old, had a compelling story:

My father wants me to study, get married, and have a normal life. But I cannot smile and laugh and think of happy things, when my aunts and uncles, my nieces and other family members face suffering in Palestine. Their suffering is a heavy burden on me. I feel it in my body. Sometimes I cannot sleep. I feel tortured.

I know Palestinians my age who do not care. They go to the discotheque and dance—they even drink alcohol. I think this is disgusting. Our people are suffering and we should stand by them. If we cannot help them directly, we should at least not mock them by living immoral lives or be heartless and forget them altogether. I feel I have no right to enjoy life as long as my people suffer.

I respect my father and I try to obey him and concentrate on my studies. If it were not for him, I would go to my homeland, get married, have as many sons as possible, and educate them in the right spirit. I would be overjoyed to have a martyr as a son, a son who sacrifices his life for his people.

I feel that suicide bombers are heroes, because it is hard to give your life. I want to give my life. I want to do something. I cannot just sit here in Cairo and watch my people suffer and be humiliated. I feel humiliated in their place, and feel that I humiliate them more by not helping them. I feel so powerless, so heavy; sometimes I can hardly walk.[19]

Farida's involvement and sincerity were intense, pure, deep, and selfless. I was reminded of the sincere young students who had been my clients in Germany some years earlier. I remember a young German woman—she was 19 years old and had bulimia—let me call her Rita.[20] Rita's words, translated from German, follow:

I am appalled by the violence in the world, the destruction of the environment, and the lack of sincerity around me. I am a good student, a very good one. But, I cannot live in a world where men play around with the world, with women, and nature, and bring suffering on all. All men want is to show off their muscles and virility and the rest of the world is their victim. This makes me choke.

I am so nauseated that I do not want to eat. And sometimes I do not eat for a long time. As long as I refrain from eating, I feel pure, ascetic, as if I can escape the pollution around me. But then I get very hungry, and I start eating and because I eat too much, I have to force myself to vomit. This in turn makes me feel extremely guilty, because I waste valuable resources. Here I am, I say to myself, eating too much and vomiting, while millions of people do not have enough to eat. They live lives of humiliation and I add to it by my waste! I am caught in this cycle. What can I do? I want to do something, but I don't know what! I feel so powerless and heavy!

These two young women were very similar. Both were particularly intelligent, with a bright future ahead, but they could not digest the violence, neglect, thoughtlessness, and humiliation they perceived around them. They were strong women, with an acute awareness of justice, whose strength was wasted because they saw no constructive action. The Palestinian woman found solace in dreaming about sacrificing her life as the mother of sons who gave their lives to defend their people. The German woman thought asceticism was a solution, an asceticism that threatened to destroy her health.[21]

I had some male Palestinian students as clients as well who dreamt of giving their lives for Palestine in violent resistance. They condemned, as Farida did, those among their male friends who chose to "forget" their people's suffering, enjoying life by feasting and drinking. None of these young clients was driven by any "will to power" or inherent "hatred." They were driven by despair. They suffered from empathy, a "noble" suffering. However, they suffered also from shortsighted, impatient, and counterproductive strategies to relieve their empathic suffering, similar to the alcoholic who believes that alcohol solves any problem.

In other words, their starting point, empathy for others' sufferings—a *noble, sincere,* and *valuable* suffering—contrasted starkly with their *destructive* strategies for action, destructive for these young people, as well as for the social fabric of a world of nonviolence. I was very aware that these bright young people were vulnerable to being recruited by leaders who could use their empathy for acts of destruction.

Two British citizens carried out a suicide attack on April 30, 2003, at the Mike's Place pub on the Tel Aviv promenade. Asif Muhammad Hanif succeeded in blowing himself up. Omar Khan Sharif had a fault in his explosive device, failed in his suicide attempt, and fled the scene (reported on http://www.mfa.gov.il/ on April 30, 2003). These two British citizens had lived most of their lives far from the Middle East, but they were drawn in, like Farida and her friends.

I tried to support Farida's strengths, speaking with her about how she could contribute to a more just world after finishing her studies. I talked about peaceful strategies and tried to help her understand that these would be more beneficial to her people and the world than giving birth to suicide bombers. She was caught in whether to adhere to or violate honor and dignity codes. In an honor context, "doing nothing" is to appear "weak," while showing strength and readiness to defend oneself with violence means being "strong." As long as all actors adhere to this code, there is no complication; raw might wins and all agree with the outcome. Farida's desire to produce sons as "weapons" has its place within such a code, as have Israeli military muscles. However, the situation grows far more complicated and hurtful when the participants and the audience—or parts of the audience—no longer agree on the ground rules. When people see violent demonstrations of strength as violations of dignity codes, unethical and immoral, adherence to the old code produces violations of the new one, deepening wounds on all sides instead of healing them.

Be Aware of the "Inferiority Complex"! Victims May Become Extreme Perpetrators

Many underlings traditionally admire elites. Human rights ideals, however, turn elite admiration into shameful self-lowering. Shame for elite admiration in underlings may explain why we find such particularly extreme cruelty and humiliation inflicted when risen underlings take revenge. The term *ethnic cleansing* may refer to more than "cleansing" and eradicating another *ethnic group;* it may also describe the rising underlings' need to cleanse and eradicate their own *elite admiration.* The obsession with eradicating even the babies in the wombs of their mothers, to wipe out every trace of the formerly admired elite, may have to do with shame over elite admiration. For long-standing elites, oppression of underlings may be "sufficient," excessively humiliating, with killing them "not worth the bother." But former underlings—risen to power—often seem obsessed with "total cleansing" and may perpetrate extreme forms of humiliation, and genocide on the former elite.

Hitler,[22] in *Mein Kampf,* describes at length the political personalities he most admired in Austria, many of them Jews. While reading his text it becomes obvious that he admired Jews, at least at a very early point in his life. Later, he attempted to wipe out every Jewish trace and perhaps also his admiration for them. Knowing their talent and aptitude, he was convinced that they had the capacity to dominate the world, if not prevented. He tried to exterminate a world elite he feared because he admired their competence.

In Rwanda, the former elite were Tutsis, and those who used to bow in deference were Hutus. The Rwandan genocide may have represented an attempt to "cleanse" Rwanda both from the former Tutsi elite and from Hutu elite admiration. Indeed, people often used the term "inferiority complex" when discussing the Hutu *genocidaires.* In psychology the term *inferiority complex* is connected with Alfred Adler (1870–1937), a psychiatrist born in Vienna. The so-called "inferiority complex" in Rwanda may be an example of what happens when underlings rise to power and are confronted with the effects of their own former acceptance of their lowly state and their admiration for the elites. Scheff (2003) explains that "the concept of an inferiority complex can be seen as a formulation about chronic low self-esteem, i.e., chronic shame."[23]

It seems crucial for underlings and those who feel their dignity violated to be aware of the traps entailed in rising from victimhood. Extreme emotional reactions must be expected. Extreme atrocities may sometimes seem to be the "right answer." If the world is to survive the surge of uprisings that characterizes the globe in the wake of the human rights movement, these atrocities must be avoided. Awareness of the underlying dynamics may be helpful. Victims can contribute to this awareness.

Dangerous temptations are entailed in the diachronic and synchronic transitions of underlings, as they proceed from subservience through admiration and ambitious imitation of elites to a desire to humiliate those elites or even cruelly mistreat them instead of striving for joint empowerment. These dangers are relevant for

- Women as they rise out of humiliating subjugation by males and patriarchal structures.
- Blacks as they struggle out of a humiliating position in relation to whites.
- The poor as they try to cope with the increasing gap between themselves and the rich.
- Promoters of rationality as defined as a long-term holistic approach, as they rise against representatives of rationality defined as shortsighted instrumentalization.

• Advocates of nature who struggle against the shortsighted instrumentalization of nature.

In all cases feelings of humiliation may be expressed in violent and destructive confrontations that compound a difficult transition with avoidable secondary problems. Nelson Mandela did not kill the white masters and bully them out of the country or destroy their symbols. Robert Mugabe in Zimbabwe, sadly enough, seems to perpetrate transgressions on the former white masters that are more likely to hurt his country's interests than benefit them.

Public rape as transgression of traditional limits

One of the most gruesome examples of humiliation as a weapon is rape. William Sampson, a Canadian imprisoned and tortured in Saudi Arabia, professes that he felt violated and degraded by being raped in a way the other brutalities could not achieve. Rape, systematically employed and carried out "efficiently," seems to have as its primary aim to humiliate and thus enfeeble the opponent, with all other "gratifications" such as dominance, masculinity, or sexual pleasure being secondary. Interestingly, employing public rape as a "weapon" seems to be a relatively new tactic, at least with respect to the extent it was recently perpetrated in such places as Somalia, Rwanda, or South Eastern Europe.

Asha Ahmed, Information/Dissemination Officer at Somalia Delegation of the International Committee of the Red Cross, explained to me on January 11, 1999, in Nairobi, that the ICRC invited historians from all Somali clans to do research which resulted in the *Spared from the Spear* booklet.[24] This booklet shows that women and children traditionally were "spared from the spear" and that Somali war code explicitly protects civilians against warrior onslaughts. Women were not to be touched. Women embodied bonds between clans, moving freely, even in wartime. Asha Ahmed pointed out:

> When you look at this booklet, the *Geneva Convention* is all in there! At first the *Geneva Convention* was like Latin to the Somalis! But the Geneva rules are theirs already! Usually, women were not touched; consider the ancient practice of blood feud. Rape may have happened in the chaos of war, but not planned in the way it is today. Today it is orchestrated in order to 'send a message to the enemy.'"[25]

Former Somali Ambassador Hussein Ali Dualeh confirmed the "novelty" of public rape and its reverberations in an interview on January 9, 1999, in Nairobi (see also Lindner 2000a):

> There is one thing which never was part of traditional quarrelling between clans, and this is rape, especially mass rape in front of the family. This is new. It happened for the first time when Siad Barre's dictatorial regime sent soldiers to annihilate us. Soldiers raped our women in front of their husbands and families.
>
> We Somalis are united through our common ethnic background; we speak one language, and are all Muslims. Why are we divided today? Humiliation through

rape and its consequences divides us. The traditional methods of reconciliation are too weak for this. It will take at least one generation to digest these humiliations sufficiently to be able to sit together again…believe me, humiliation, as I told you before, was not known to the Somali before Siad Barre came to power! It is a "tradition" that young men of one clan steal camels from another clan, and sometimes a man gets killed. But women were never touched, never. There might have been a rare case when a girl was alone in the semi-desert guarding her animals, and a young man having spent a long time in the desert lost control and tried to rape her. She would resist violently, and at the end the solution would perhaps be that he had to marry her. But mass rape, especially rape in front of the family, this never happened before, this is new! (Lindner 2000a, p. 343).

Human Rights Watch (1996) confirms the systematic application of rape. In attacks on Tutsis before 1994, women and children were generally spared, but during the genocide—particularly in its later stages—all Tutsis were targeted, regardless of sex or age. The widespread incidence of rape accompanied the increase in overall violence against groups previously immune from attack. "Rape was a strategy," said Bernadette Muhimakazi, a Rwandan women's rights activist. "They chose to rape. There were no mistakes. During this genocide, everything was organized. Traditionally it is not the custom to kill women and children, but this was done everywhere too." Other Rwandans characterized the violence against women as "the humiliation of women" or "the disfigurement of women, to make them undesirable" or "total disrespect for the worth of women."[26]

We might wonder why new forms of atrocities, such as systematic rape, have been increasingly employed in recent ethnic cleansings, genocides, and quasi-genocides. Clearly, traditional confines are being transgressed. Perhaps rape is more humiliating and consequently more hurtful on the background of the human rights message than in a pure honor context. Human rights see every human being as endowed with the same level of inviolable dignity while honor codes define different levels of violability. The hurtfulness of rape might be heightened by the human rights message and thus turn rape into a more wounding tool. Furthermore, also the fact that women gain in status in human rights contexts (since all human beings are treated as equal in dignity) may provide the act of hurting women with a potency that was absent before. Hurting what is valuable has more impact than hurting what is invaluable.

Afterlife as Arena

Humiliated underlings may be tempted to flee beyond Earth when they do not get what they yearn for on Earth—recognition, dignity, respect, and worthiness. Fleeing into visions of worthiness extended by God in an afterlife is sometimes a way out of humiliation. During the years I spent in Egypt, I observed how an increasing number of people turned to Islam and, within Islam, to more conservative forms. Egypt in its recent history went from colonialism to communism and nationalism. No "ism" brought the sought-after respect and welfare. The pharaonic past of Egyptian grandeur remains eerily far away.

Egypt is in a poor shape, a beggar on the world stage, kept alive by American funding. Many young people do not know if they will ever have the means to found and maintain a family. Islam is the latest "candidate" to create hope for a better life within Egypt and to make the country a more respected international player. Egyptians, especially in the Nile Delta, are pragmatic people with a capacity for love that is rarely found anywhere else, who have no "natural" tendency to become zealots, but when there is little hope for a dignified life on Earth, even they may be tempted to turn to an afterlife for consolation.

What we call "pragmatic values" appear to be the values of those who feel respected, while "afterlife values," or "beyond Earth values," become attractive as a response to frustration, deprivation, and humiliation. Following this idea through to its logical conclusion, the current pragmatic "Western values" represent the "default" only for people who have a chance to live full, dignified lives, while afterlife values represent an adaptation to deprivation. An increasing afterlife orientation might signal that people are being pushed into a corner.

Every religion—Islam, Christianity, even Buddhism—lends itself to use as a refuge beyond Earth and death. This can happen in either benign or malign ways. Sinhalese Buddhists, for example, promote a specific and, they say, purer and more authentic version of Buddhism. And long before recent suicide missions in the Middle East, Tamil leader Vellupillai Prabhakaran "designed" innumerable suicide operations. Visions of afterlives can offer limitless promises, balanced by equally limitless atrocities on Earth.

Of course, altruism, care, and love can also be promoted by an afterlife orientation. The problem is that the afterlife, by definition, is remote from direct verification. Do divine forces really appreciate suicide bombings, and will they indeed extend the sought-after dignity after death and beyond Earth? The answer is always provided by mere human beings, prone to the biases and failings of human beings. Promises of a dignified afterlife are easily manipulated by earthly motives. Even though anchoring oneself in fundamentalism beyond Earth and earthly death may bring great serenity and solace, it may also turn life on Earth into something not worth living.

Those who feel victimized would benefit from some critical thinking about their afterworld orientations. Life on Earth may be destroyed unnecessarily for the sake of life beyond Earth. Is this really what we want?

Extremists and Moderates

The defining characteristic of moderates is that they are capable of rising above the level of out-group discrimination and perceive all players as fellow participants in *one single larger in-group*. David Kimche, former Deputy Director of Mossad, and Riad Malki, former spokesman for the Popular Front for the Liberation of Palestine, are two moderates who build bridges over the deep gulf between both parties. "At a time of political stalemate and continued violence, why have two former enemies decided to join forces and fight for peace with words?... Considering that 20 years ago the two were bitter enemies, how can they make peace now when their leaders can't, and do they see any chance for the Middle East roadmap?"[27] Extremists are those most mired in humiliation, both as feelings and retaliating acts, and they deepen the rifts of hatred instead of healing humiliation. Armed conflicts are usually embedded within an angry atmosphere of "We have to stand united against the enemy, we have to protect ourselves, and if you do not agree with us, you are our enemy." This sentence would be interpreted by extremists to mean, "We have to eliminate the enemy." In contrast, a moderate would say, "We protect ourselves best by working towards a larger we in a constructive manner to include among us those we today call enemies." These interpretations usually compete, with the more "hot" and emotional interpretation usually being more extremist and promising fast redemption for painful feelings. Moderation is much more difficult to "sell" and needs the support of a larger group of people to gain weight and credibility.

Nelson Mandela is a moderate. He succeeded in transforming his feelings of humiliation after 27 years of prison into a constructive contribution to social and societal change. He distanced himself from his own urge for revenge. However, someone like Mandela is seldom available. Moderation may then be best assured by third parties who are not involved in the conflict and can therefore easier commit themselves to safeguarding social cohesion in a respectful manner and without humiliating any participant. The involved opponents' feelings are often too hot to be moderate, at least during conflict peaks. Sometimes an overpowering force of moderates may be needed, especially when extremists were allowed to become leaders of political movements.

Mature, moderate, responsible people are called upon to invite young, intelligent people to follow the example of Nelson Mandela, and not to follow promoters of terror who have translated empathy with the suffering of the oppressed into an urge to retaliate with violence. Moderates of all camps and third parties around the world carry the responsibility for curbing extremism, inviting their representatives back into the camp of moderation, of patient change, and of long-term solutions.

Once a situation has been overrun by extremists and their polarizing language, moderates face almost insurmountable problems. Moderate Hutus were killed by extremist Hutus in the 1994 genocide. Extremist tyrants usually eliminate critics from their own camp first. Moderates in such a quandary have only one option, namely to gather as many allies as possible from the global third party, the international community, so as to give weight to moderate positions, to help dampen extremist language, and to forge alliances of moderates across all opposing camps. *Quarantine the Aggressor,* said Franklin Delano Roosevelt in 1937.[28] The coming into being of the *global village* facilitates this process as it becomes increasingly apparent that it is in everybody's interest to extinguish extremist fires wherever they burn, before they engulf the whole global village.

For a third party such as the international community, promoting moderation means supporting and advocating leaders such as Mandela. It means collecting and broadcasting moderate traditions and ancient wisdoms from around the world, including opponents' cultures. And, finally, it means continuously emphasizing our children's future, a future that nobody wishes to be bloody and violent. These crucial elements give weight to moderation and have the potential to outweigh extremist voices.

The protection of my people is best secured by working *for* global social sustainability, not *against* any enemies. As Muriel Lester said: "War is as outmoded as cannibalism, chattel slavery, blood feuds, and dueling, an insult to God and humanity...." All third parties who wish for social peace in the global village are called upon to promote moderation and maturity in the face of the hot feelings that tempt people to lash out against "enemies" instead of working for the social cohesion of humankind as a whole.

We may conclude that the important fault lines in conflicts are not those that separate Israelis from Palestinians, Hutus from Tutsis, Sinhalese from Tamils, or Americans from the rest of the world. There is only one important fault line— the division between extremists and moderates in all camps. If extremists gain access to power, they will polarize and deepen whatever rifts they can feed on. Social peace, locally and globally, is secured only if moderates outweigh extremists. It is important for victims of oppression and humiliation, who rise up, to be aware of the dangers entailed in extremism. Extremist stances do not heal; they exacerbate the problem. It is essential for victims to avoid being drawn into extremist camps. This is what victims can do for a peaceful world.

Moderates like Mandela can curb the hot feelings of extremists and forge alliances of moderates above and across fault lines. Mandela managed to wake up the white ruling class in South Africa to the fact that they had to step down before it was too late. In South Africa it was the victim who was the driving force, not the master. Since the rage and fury that feelings of humiliation are capable of engendering is felt by the victims and those who identify with them, it is the victims and those who help them who are perhaps most responsible for making the process of change a constructive one.

Summary

Currently, we live in a world where people are pitted against each other in deep moral indignation. At one extreme pole we have those who are permeated by gut feelings of ranked honor. They are morally indignant about what they see as human rights defenders' despicable "sissy" fear of a strong hand. Saddam Hussein certainly had no qualms when subduing his fellow citizens with brutality. Zimbabwe, Myanmar, North Korea—the list of extreme examples can be prolonged.

Human rights advocates, on the other side, are morally enraged by what they perceive as their adversaries' abominable insensitivity to the concept of equal dignity, a concept they feel is utterly humiliated by the "strong hand" they feel deserves to be defined as torture. Both sides waste much energy trying to mobilize world opinion for what they consider the "right" moral indignation.

I propose that merely wallowing in moral indignation, competing for "who manages to feel more indignant" does not advance humankind. Moral indignation needs to be harnessed to lead to constructive outcomes. The situation would benefit from being freed from finger-pointing and deep sighs. All sides may be served by engaging in more humility.

Let me differentiate three groups. First, human rights defenders are well advised to be thankful that they are not facing situations that coerce them into becoming perpetrators of torture or terrorist acts. Humility about human weakness could help calm feelings of indignation that are too hot to be constructive. Nobody knows how he or she would react if pushed into inescapable dilemmas. The famous Milgram experiment ought to invoke humility.

Second, those who are feeling that ranked honor ought to be ruling the world are advised to acknowledge that honor strategies backfire when placed in the human rights contexts that currently are spreading around the world. Honor strategies simply no longer work in the old ways in a world that has tasted human rights ideals. Old predictions fail. In a world without human rights ideals, torture, terrorist acts, and humiliation may have had a certain chance to "work" within the confines of their goals. Yet, they surely fail as soon as people have been exposed to human rights ideals. No longer do torture and humiliation safely transform people into humble underlings, who will subserviently and reliably "cooperate."

Third, those people who engage in human rights rhetoric, while employing honor strategies on the ground, may need to recognize that this is an intrinsically self-contradictory strategy that may be so unsuccessful as to be called suicidal. People of southern honor, for example, are among those to stand "in the middle"—strong feelings of honor survive under a cover of an assortment of human rights ideals that seem compatible, for example, the ideal of "freedom." Rebecca Lemov[29] wrote a book on American interrogation techniques and how they have been studied and developed "scientifically." In an article in the *Los Angeles Times,* reports on a recently declassified document from November 27, 2002, techniques are listed such as "the use of stress positions (like standing) for a maximum of four hours within a 24-hour period, as well as the forced shaving of body parts."[30] Defense Secretary Donald H. Rumsfeld, who indeed does advocate human rights and freedom, added a handwritten comment: "However, I stand for 8–10 hours a day. Why is standing limited to 4 hours? D.R."[31]

Human rights ideals have at their core the call for equal dignity for all and the abandonment of ranked honor. Representatives of southern honor need to heed that it is intrinsically impossible to rank human worthiness and at the same time oppose the very same practice. This incompatibility is what is bound to destroy both their honor strategies and their embryonic human rights ideals. Equal dignity is destroyed by ranking human worthiness, and ranked honor is destroyed by ideals of equal dignity.

We live in a world where strong emotions of moral indignation and contempt are fed by ideals of ranked honor on one side and ideals of equal dignity on the other. I propose to discontinue enlisting morally enraged people into "our" camp so as to happily huddle in the group cohesion that can be reaped from strongly shared emotions. We cannot live in a world in which we rank and refuse to rank human worthiness. It would be like living in a world where left-hand and right-hand driving are both practiced at the same time. The mere incompatibly would cause the collapse of all traffic. One has to decide. Either we all drive on the right side or we all drive on the left side. Currently, humankind manages this transition miserably. However, merely fueling moral indignation on all sides falls short. We ought to calmly reflect and help humankind make the transition constructively in an atmosphere of mutual respect. The point is not *victory* for any camp, but all of us *cooperating for sustainable solutions*. Whoever opts for human rights must be aware that applying humiliation in a dignity context is equal to humiliating the humanity of all, victims and perpetrators.

PART III

WHY HUMILIATION DOES NOT WORK

CHAPTER 7

THE HUMILIATION ADDICTION

This chapter will unsettle the usual classification of "pitiable victim" versus "evil perpetrator." Sometimes victimhood is used in evil ways.

> My brother is addicted to humiliation; he is a "professional" victim of humiliation. I was my mother's favorite and my poor brother was systematically degraded and humiliated by her. Now, as an adult, he perpetuates his victim status: if he is not humiliated, he imagines it or provokes it. To provoke them, he has let down and humiliated his wife, children and friends, they are the real victims today; however, when they protest, he accuses them of being the perpetrators.
>
> People who meet him for the first time are taken in by his ability to depict himself as a pitiable victim who heroically stands up against all evil in the world. Many make the mistake of trusting and loving him. They buy into his victim heroism. They end up doubly hurt and humiliated, first let down by him and then accused of having humiliated him.
>
> He maneuvers people into an imagined position as a perpetrator of humiliation. His satisfaction is when he can lament to the world about what a pitiable victim of humiliation he is. To get there, he damages and destroys the lives of his family and friends and his own.

Two processes of humiliation are intertwined in this vignette. The speaker explains how his brother inadvertently provokes and imagines being the victim of humiliation to get recognition for suffering that occurred earlier in his life and probably was never sufficiently acknowledged and healed. Overtly, his brother asks for pity, compassion, support, and admiration for his heroic defiance of evil. Covertly, he cannot escape his feelings of being humiliated and constructs pretexts that enable him to reconstruct those painful experiences. He needs to have his suffering acknowledged. Through this *addiction to humiliation* a second process of humiliation is set in motion by which third parties get hurt and doubly humiliated. Family and friends are first let down and treated in a humiliating manner and then publicized as evil humiliators when they protest. One person's addiction to humiliation causes suffering to many.

Reber (1995) informs us in *The Penguin Dictionary of Psychology* that "an individual is said to have developed dependence on a drug or other substance when there is a strong, compelling desire to continue taking it."[1] Nondrugs such as gambling, eating disorders, compulsive shopping, workaholism, and codependency are often foci of addictive responses as well. In all cases, the core of the addiction is its compelling and intense nature. Smokers, for example, know that their habit represents a health hazard to themselves and others, but they go to great lengths to "protect" their habit. Otherwise perfectly "rational" people distort facts, deny evidence, and lie to themselves and others. Feelings of humiliation may be as significant and consuming as any form of addiction or dependence.

Earlier, we met Barbara who came to my clinic, describing herself as a "nervous wreck." Her mother-in-law had not approved of her son's marriage and did not hesitate to say publicly, "*You* want to be part of our family? Who do you think *you* are?" Barbara felt trapped in her own pain. When her husband died, her in-laws tried to deny her her inheritance. Bitter court cases were the result. Her entire life was consumed by her relationship with her in-laws, a relationship that was filled with a continuous flow of incidents of humiliation and counterhumiliation. Suffering humiliation and responding with humiliation had become an all-consuming lifestyle.

How Rejection-Sensitive Men Thrive on Humiliation

Walter Mischel and Aaron L. De Smet describe the "automatic reaction of anger and abusiveness readily triggered in rejection-sensitive men who are quick to perceive it [rejection] from a romantic partner even if it has not occurred."[2] The authors explain that:

> ...this maladaptive reaction pattern of uncontrolled hostility may be essentially reflexive, by-passing conscious control and preventing purposeful self-intervention effort. In such a case, the person applies encodings even if they do not fit and maintains them regardless of contradictory evidence. The ironic and often tragic result is that the outcome the man most fears and expects—rejection by the romantic partner is precipitated by his own behavior in a self-fulfilling prophecy.[3]

"You always hurt the ones you love"[4] is a saying that Mischel and De Smet remind us of, indicating the common wisdom, which insists that:

> ...the interdependence coming from interpersonal closeness creates the very situation where emotions are strong and the tendency to react impulsively in hurtful,

damaging ways is greatest. Although people may attempt to control the hot, emotional responses that intensify conflict and damage relationships, they often find that their good intentions are not enough to refrain from blowing up, making personal attacks, or otherwise doing things they later regret.[5]

Mischel and De Smet teach that in *rejection-sensitive* men the obsessive aspect of addiction forms the basis of their emotional life. They are "hooked" on situations of debasement where they can feel humiliated. We may want to discount this scenario as marginal, since it applies only to the minority of men who believe they are neglected, not taken seriously, belittled, and humiliated even when they are not, and lash out in retaliation. However, these dynamics may be relevant in all contexts where groups are struggling to rise from lowliness.

In his book *The Ethics of Memory*, Avishai Margalit[6] suggests that it is not only the experience of moral emotions like humiliation that motivates aggressive behavior, but also the memory of such emotions. He writes that the memory of a humiliating event can be akin to reliving it. "Margalit proposes that, under certain conditions, individuals can become attached, or even addicted, to the emotion, thus serving as a constant source of retaliatory action."[7]

Angela told me the following story (August 2002 in New York):

I work in an office with Samuel, or Sam. He is an office clerk and a black American. I do not know how to handle him. He does not do any useful work. He is hooked on a weird kind of slave identity. He looks at us white colleagues with eyes veering to the side in angry suspicion all the time. He never looks directly at us, but through us with an air of anger that signals "I know you, you white racist bastards." Whenever we make the slightest mistake, even mistakes that have nothing to do with him, he feels vindicated and tells us that this proves we are all racists.

He constantly fabricates connections that are not there. It is as if he has a magnifying glass and continuously searches for "evidence" for being the victim of racism. This is his full-time occupation. When we remind him that there is work to be done, we are racists. He brags that he cannot be laid off because then he would let hell loose and accuse the employer of racism!

We do his work and avoid him as much as possible. What else shall we do? This guy reads all available books about slavery and knows all the big names of protesters against slavery. He dreams himself into a world where he is a big hero. He "resists" wherever he sees a chance to "resist" and does not realize that he makes a fool out of himself. He speaks with his black *brothers* and *sisters* on the phone all the time; with solemn voices they *share* the *shit* and *humiliation* they endure. (Or, more precisely, he speaks with brothers *about* sisters, who are either 'hotties' or not; *sisters* are mere sexual prey for him. He and his *brothers* treat their *sisters* in an even more humiliating way than they themselves are being treated by whites!)

Brothers and *sisters,* I ask myself, and who are the *parents?* I assume the *parents* are the "evil" whites? Are there no adult black Americans? Sam and his friends seem like small *children* who do not want to grow up. I am no racist—I am Hispanic myself and know what discrimination means—and I understand that there is racism in America. But this guy turns the maintenance of victimhood into his core identity.

His life is like a film. He has the role of the heroic victim and we are the evil humiliators, whether reality agrees with his script or not. He invests all his energy into this, he is hooked and will never get anywhere in life if he continues.

I hope, one day, he will understand and regret. In reality, he turns *us* into victims of *his* abuse everyday and *he* should apologize! It is *he* who humiliates and victimizes *us!* There are many sensible black Americans; I hope they speak out against the humiliation entrepreneurship perpetrated by some of these *brothers!*

We conclude this section by suggesting that the coming together of humankind is likely to increase situations characterized by *hot* feelings and reactions. The coming together of humankind, by increasing the chances for people forming closer relationships across the globe, is bound to increase the hot and obsessive aspects in the emotional worlds of its participants. Angela's story occurs also at the international level. The coming together of humankind, by increasing the chances for people forming closer relationships across the globe, is bound to increase the *hot* and obsessive aspects in the emotional worlds of its participants when wounds arise. A European businessman laments:

I trusted my Egyptian business partners, but they betrayed me. *They* say that *I* betrayed them. I don't really know what they mean or who is right. In any case, I am furious. I am consumed by rage. Day and night I think about how I can get back at these people. I wish those times back when each country was more or less autonomous. This new requirement to be "international" is terrible. Everybody tries to go international! I am disgusted by that. Please bring me back the good old world where we could stay among *us!*

Can One Love a Spring Knife? How the Passive-Aggressive Personality Disorder May Entail Humiliation

The *passive-aggressive (negativistic) personality disorder (PAPD)* may have at its core addiction to humiliation. A health encyclopedia[8] defines PAPD as follows: "Passive resistance to demands for social and occupational performance beginning in early adulthood." According to the PAPD, "The cause of this disorder is unknown. Biological or genetic factors do not appear to play a role." Sharon C. Eckleberry, a clinical social worker in mental health with a special focus on addiction and personality disorders, explains that the passive aggressive personality disorder:

...was first introduced in a U.S. War Department technical bulletin in 1945. The term was coined by wartime psychiatrists who found themselves dealing with reluctant and uncooperative soldiers who followed orders with chronic, veiled hostility and smoldering resentment. Their style was a mixture of passive resistance and grumbling compliance.[9]

Eckleberry describes the way anger is expressed by people with PAPD:

They may have temper tantrums that release pent-up aggression; if their victim is aggressive in response—so much the better. That response is then used to vindicate the initial attack. Anger expressed by commission is usually justified by laudable motives, e.g. concern for the well-being of the victim. The expression of the anger is dictated by the desire to wound while concealing the intention to wound—even the existence of the anger. This is not to spare the feelings of the victim but to wound them more effectively. The intent is to provoke counter anger with such subtlety that the victim blames himself and believes his anger is not justified. That way, people with PAPD can assume the role of innocent victim.[10]

Eckleberry goes on to explain:

...individuals with PAPD do not frequently seek treatment for relationship issues as they consistently blame others for the problems they have. Even if they do come in for treatment for a marital or parent and child problem, they will uniformly demand that the treatment providers "fix" the other person or persons who are at fault for the problems within the relationship.[11]

They stall, complain, oppose, forget, and feel cheated by life. They experience life as dark and unpleasurable. To these individuals, thwarting the expectations of others is a victory even if they sabotage their own lives. They are difficult, angry and needy. They see compliance as submission and submission as humiliation.[12]

The classic passive-aggressive transference pattern is to comply (sort of) with the therapeutic recommendation, and then to declare triumphantly that it was a very poor suggestion and failed miserably. These individuals are programmed to ask for help and then both to defy it and to suffer from it. Clients with PAPD expect to be injured by a negligent and cruel caregiver.[13]

Emmanuel came to my clinic because he was deeply disappointed and hurt by his former partner, Clara. He told me:

Clara had a sad childhood. Her parents were missionaries and to obey their divine call to convert Indians in the Brazilian rain forest to Christianity, they gave Clara to a children's home run by their religious organization. Clara was three. She was not reunited with her parents until five years later. She waited for them for years, enduring terrible loneliness.

When her parents came back, she felt estranged from them. She never trusted them again. I believe she was deeply enraged by her parents' abandonment. Clara never worked through her feelings; she never went to therapy. Instead, she keeps re-enacting her early fate. When I met her, she was deeply distressed because of her husband, who she said was aggressive. I listened for hours to her tales. I was very patient, admiring her heroic stance against her abusive husband.

She left him quite abruptly, carrying only two suitcases, and moved into my flat. We lived together six years, while I waited for her to get her act together. She had big plans. She wanted to become a writer and earn millions with bestsellers. I was her secretary and helped her where I could. My own work suffered and my life increasingly turned around hers. After all, she was the genius, not me!

After six years, I became impatient. I felt that my help went up in smoke and nothing substantial came out of it. I had gradually come to understand that her genius was not all that brilliant. She had told me about the grand scope of her life experiences and the cultural and linguistic knowledge that she supposedly commanded; however, the more I learned about her, the more I understood that she boasted. More precisely, she did not boast, she believed in her grandness. She merely overlooked reality. She saw herself as a victim who is too noble for the world but heroically stands up anyway. When we first met, she impressed me with all her talk about languages, science and culture. I was not as educated as she was. But six years were enough for me to catch up. And I slowly understood that she exploited my ignorance.

I continued to be calm and kind, but I did not worship her anymore. I did not stop trying to help her, but I did not want to support empty dreams. I wanted her to see reality but she couldn't do this. She quickly found herself a new "Emmanuel." She did the same with me that she had done with her former husband. I became the villain who supposedly victimized and humiliated her, and her new partner patiently listened to her complaints. One afternoon she went out, as if she wanted to buy some small thing, but she never came back. She left all her things behind and moved in with the new man. All our friends were drawn into this story. According to her, I was an aggressive humiliator who belligerently kept her things from her (although she never came to get them) and she was the poor humiliatee who heroically withstood my onslaughts.

I am more than enraged, but also sad, and shocked, and very displeased with myself. I never should have been drawn into all this. I was case number four, I think, when I look back on her life. Four times she has attracted men with her "heroic helplessness." The first man listened to her complaints with regard to her parents; the following three were presented with sad stories about the abuse she supposedly suffered at the hands of her former partners. Every new partner was charmed by her grand personality and her vows to have a great future. Every man was inferior to her in education and life experience and dedicated his life to her great goals. After a few years each of them got exhausted, and she interpreted this as evil and left abruptly for the next round of the same game. Our help was scorned. She was the heroic victim.

I now understand her poor husband who was my predecessor. I sometimes want to phone him and apologize for believing her stories about him. He, like me, was pushed into a corner until he could not take it anymore. And I assisted in this crime! I am disgusted, both at her and at myself.

I have thought a lot about her and me since she elected me to play the role of the most recent baddie in her life. I feel utterly abused by her, but there is no way to make her understand. She does not see how she re-enacts her childhood. When she leaves, it is abruptly, with a suitcase or a little bag, exactly like when she was a child and was brought into the children's home by her father. She seems addicted to this script.

Her ultimate audience is her friends, not her partners. She wants to demonstrate to the world that she is a legitimate victim. Her parents never had any understanding for their daughter's feelings of abandonment. I met them before they died and I can confirm that. They never acknowledged any guilt or showed any empathy with her. On the contrary, they humiliated her—and I witnessed that several times—for her "weakness." It is as if she wants to nail them, finally, as perpetrators. And since they are unwilling—now dead—she takes substitutes. Her game is to produce humiliators. Her victory is to be able to point her finger at someone who does evil to her. She does not see that she creates this evil.

Her reality is not that of "normal" people. Her goal is not the well-being of herself and others. What pains me is that I am blamed as nasty humiliator by her, in front of her friends, but I am a victim. All the rest is irrelevant, all her dreams and plans are merely instrumental to this underlying project. And many of my friends are deluded by her game.

If she were to become interested in politics or lead a religious group, she would make fine people follow her into collective suicide. Like Hitler, she would round up supposed humiliators, enlist everybody to heroically stand up against them, and at the end those "helpers" would be accused of failing. Hitler said at his end of his life that Germany deserved to be destroyed because Germans had not fulfilled his ideals! I wonder how the Germans felt when they learned that!

Emmanuel's story shows that psychiatric labels may not be required to understand the dynamic of addiction to humiliation. Perhaps PAPD is caused by biological factors not yet detected by research. But perhaps it rather describes people who compensate for early experiences of humiliation in rigid ways. They are not interested in changing their predicament; the satisfaction is already entirely theirs. They are obsessed with provoking others into giving them the opportunity to appear as heroic victims of humiliation.[14]

PAPD personality profiles are relatively harmless if well-controlled within a society that does not let them rise to positions of power. However, what happens if they achieve positions that give them the power and influence to forge entire group fantasies in their vein? I[15] analyzed the cases of Hitler, the Somalian dictator Siad Barre, and the Hutu extremist elite that instigated the 1994 genocide in Rwanda. They all ended ousted or dead, leaving behind disaster without seeming remorse. Did they sincerely believe in their own propaganda that killing their "enemies" (Jews, Isaaq, or Tutsis) was a rational plan that would make their countries prosperous? Genocide turned out to be a suicidal path for themselves and their followers. Their addiction to humiliation was lethal for millions.

If such individuals gain power, destruction may be unlimited, since these people do not regard suffering as failure. On the contrary, suffering brings them satisfaction; victimhood is sought, not avoided. As discussed above, a central force in this complex psychical landscape may be that the perpetrators of such strategies suffered humiliation in childhood and were not acknowledged as victims. They may seek this recognition throughout their lives.

Israel W. Charny[16] proposes to include "A Personality Disorder of Excessive Power Strivings" in the *Diagnostic and Statistical Manual of Mental Disorders IV* (*DSM-IV*). He insists that the *DSM-IV* does not address conditions in which a person harms *others*. The author posits that a political leader ought to be deemed disturbed when he defines a target population as "undeserving," "inferior," or "enemies of the people," forces a murderous population transfer, calls on followers or coerces them to commit mass murder–suicide, or is prepared to send people who oppose him to psychiatric hospitals, work camps, concentration camps, and killing fields.[17]

Another label related to this cluster of symptoms is *repetition compulsion.* The concept of the *wounded self* is linked to *malignant narcissism, narcissistic rage,* and to what has been called *sadistic personality disorder.* Jerrold Post, psychiatric expert on Saddam Hussein, suggests that the Iraqi dictator suffered from a childhood trauma of rejection by his mother and that his wounded self turned him into a murderous tyrant. Post identifies malignant narcissism as a vicious outburst of a wounded self. Thomas J. Scheff stipulates that tyrants such as Hitler suffer from three symptoms: first, *unacknowledged shame;* second, a *master obsession* (in the case of Hitler, the belief that Jews planned to conquer the world and had to be preemptively eliminated); and third, *isolation* from a very early age (in the case of Hitler from the age of six).[18]

To summarize, psychiatry addresses *malignant* tendencies that are linked with the phenomenon of humiliation. Victims attempt to attain acknowledgment for their victimhood by victimizing others and manipulating them into the perpetrator role. In this process, humiliation is played out on numerous levels and is almost obsessively pursued. What is usually regarded as "rational self-interest" is not the prevailing goal in these individuals who, like drug addicts, are more concerned with getting their "fix" than with the welfare of themselves or others. If such pathologies occur at the leadership level of larger communities, mayhem may result. It is essential for larger communities to be aware of these psychic disorders in order to be in a better position to contain them.

I "Cleanse" Myself from My Admiration for You by Humiliating and Killing You

Joseph, a young intellectual from a Hutu background, told me the following about Rwandan history (the interview took place in December 1998 in Africa):

> During colonial times Tutsi children were sent to special schools where they learned to rule. The colonialists' theory of Tutsi origin indicated that they had longer faces, their women were beautiful with long nails, and that they came from Arab countries. The whites thought that Tutsis were a mixture of Arab and white blood, therefore nearer to the whites, close relatives of whites [this view is also called the *Hamitic hypothesis*]. When Tutsis were admitted to college, they were prepared to be in power, while Hutus entered Catholic seminars to become teachers and priests. There were also some Hutus intellectuals, but the path to power was blocked for them. In short: rulers = Tutsi, servants = Hutu.

The concept of humiliation is therefore related to tradition and culture: Tutsis are convinced that they are "born to rule," they cannot imagine how they can survive without being in power.[19]

Later, Rwandan history turned the hierarchy of the Tutsi-rulers and Hutu-servants equation upside down. Hutus were helped into the ruling seats by their Belgian colonizers shortly before independence, July 1, 1962. Many of the deposed Tutsis left for exile, while others stayed on within Rwandan borders as a routinely humiliated minority. Ironically, at the same time, something of the past lived on, namely their elite reputation. Tutsi women, for example, were still sought-after trophies for wealthy Hutu men. I heard frequently (in 1999) that a Hutu man who gets rich "buys a house, gets a Mercedes, and marries a Tutsi woman."[20] A certain extent of habitual Hutu admiration for Tutsi superiority lived on after the Tutsis had been deposed.

Before traveling to Rwanda, I was told that I should not ask whether a person was of Hutu or Tutsi origin. I was to proceed indirectly, keeping in mind that ethnic labels such as Hutu and Tutsi are under dispute. I was unofficially informed, however, that hundreds of years of subservience had marked Hutu body language, giving people of Hutu background a tendency to bow humbly, whereas Tutsis stood upright, proudly, sometimes even haughtily. Thus, despite their political demise, Tutsi elitisms seemed to have survived, not only in the former elite's minds, but—and this is more remarkable—even in the minds of the former underlings. This was discussed in the previous chapter under the theme of the *inferiority complex*. Hutu rulers harbored a deep fear of a Tutsi return from exile. Otherwise, there would have been no need to design the 1994 genocide to prevent returning Tutsis from ever again humiliating Hutus. The newly gained Hutu power must have felt very fragile. Although the Tutsis had lost most of their real power, memories of their past domination lived on in the minds of their former underlings/now rulers, compelling them to humiliate and kill their former masters.

This leads to the (at first glance) counterintuitive insight that perpetrators may be *weak*. When I[21] explored the experiential worlds of Hitler, Barre, and the Rwandan elite, I found that they did not always look *down* on those they exterminated. Interestingly, at some point in their biographies, they looked *up* to them. The Jews, the Isaaq, and the Tutsis were regarded as *elites*—intelligent, diligent, and superior—and therefore as potential dangerous humiliators whose plans to humiliate in the future "had" to be averted. Instead of *strong* perpetrators and *weak* victims, we may find *weak* perpetrators.

As discussed in the previous chapter, in Rwanda I was frequently told that Hutus allegedly harbor an *inferiority complex* towards their former masters. Something as unexpected as *admiration* may thus be the inspiration for the "evil" mixture of "cleansing" atrocities. Admiration is something underlings may feel the need to "cleanse" themselves of by putting down the targets of this admiration. Being in power may not be sufficient when the inner life lags behind. Recently risen underlings may need to cleanse themselves of both their former masters and their admiration for them.

Figure 1.1 may thus be adapted to produce Figure 7.1. It may not be long-established elites that are the cruelest, but newly risen underlings who attempt to cleanse themselves of elite admiration by killing the former elite, who is now a minority, but feared as former and future elite. The international community must marginalize leaders with these tendencies. Even democracy does not protect against them. They may find ways to incite followers within democratic settings, as Hitler did. People with profiles such as those presented here may lead whole continents into the abyss. It is essential that they be prevented from gaining power.

At the same time, care must be taken to dignify the masses that otherwise may serve as "fodder" for the *narratives of humiliation* these leaders weave so expertly. Zimbabwean *Green Bombers* are trained to attack the opposition through so-called "state-sponsored" violence. Three young boys who escaped to Johannesburg told the sad tale of how they broke into farms, destroyed fences, let the livestock loose, burned down houses, beat people with sticks and axes, and raped young girls. They were promised jobs, money, land, and a dignified future, but "instead they were given alcohol, drugs and orders" (April 17, 2003, on BBC World news). The commentator called for African neighbors to intervene, criticizing the strategy of quiet diplomacy, which was not working.

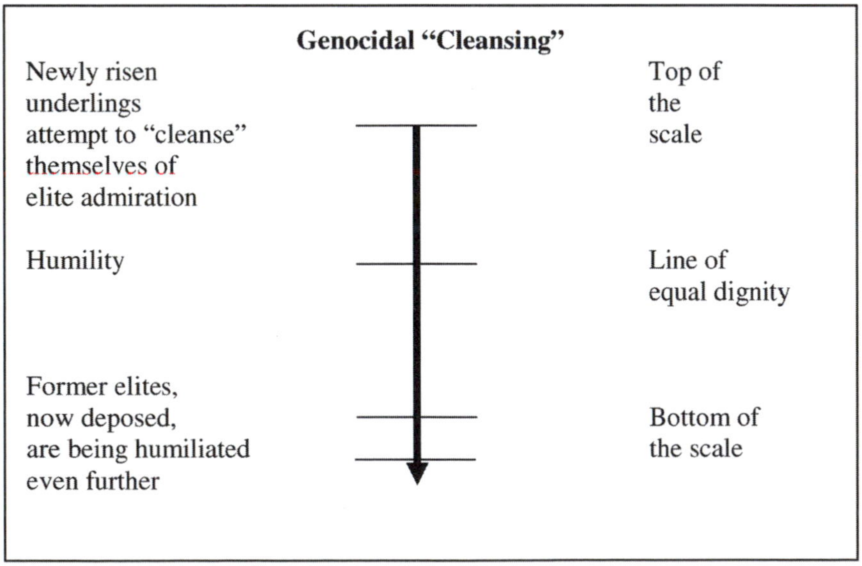

Figure 7.1
Genocidal "Cleansing"

To conclude, genocidal obsessions with "cleansing" may be motivated by *admiration* for the victims of this cleansing. Newly risen underlings may suffer from fragile psychological structures irritated by remnants of admiration for their former elites. These weak individuals attempt to "cleanse" themselves with almost addictive obsession. To humiliate the former elite not merely into power-lessness but into the abyss seemingly "frees" the perpetrators of their own esteem for this elite. When larger populations are drawn into this plot, tragedy may unfold.

Bloody Shoes! Childhood Experiences May Create Humiliation Addicts

Early childhood neglect and humiliation may lead people to perpetrate acts of humiliation inadvertently, through mere *affective blindness*. Bruce D. Perry relates a gruesome story that testifies to the severity of the potential effects of childhood humiliation. It is a story of affective blindness:

> A fifteen year old boy sees some fancy sneakers he wants. Another child is wearing them—so he pulls a gun and demands them. The younger child, at gunpoint, takes off his shoes and surrenders them. The fifteen year old puts the gun to the child's head, smiles and pulls the trigger.
>
> When he is arrested, the officers are chilled by his apparent lack of remorse. Asked whether, if he could turn back the clock, would he do anything differently, he thinks and replies, "I would have cleaned my shoes."
>
> His "bloody shoes" led to his arrest. He exhibits regret for being caught, an intel-lectual, cognitive response. But remorse—an affect—is absent. He feels no connec-tion to the pain of his victim. Neglected and humiliated by his primary caretakers when he was young, this fifteen-year-old murderer is, literally, emotionally retarded. The part of his brain which would have allowed him to feel connected to other human beings—empathy—did not develop. He has affective blindness. Just as the retarded child lacks the capacity to understand abstract cognitive concepts, this young murderer lacks the capacity to be connected to other human beings in a healthy way. Experience, or rather lack of critical experiences, resulted in this affec-tive blindness—this emotional retardation.[22]

George is the son of a British soldier who fought courageously in World War II and was highly decorated. When his father came back from the war, he drank and neglected his family. George was in his late fifties when he came to me, suffering from panic attacks. George explained:

> My mother was alone with the children during the war. I was the smallest. There was no time for friendliness or warmth. When my father came back there was mostly quarrelling between my parents. I am emotionally undernourished, I think. I learned from my father a tough attitude toward weakness. I believe he could not cope with his war trauma and put on a hard face. I seem to have done the same. I

was profoundly alone, lonely, left alone, by my caretakers. I maintained this loneliness later by myself.

By being tough and cynical, I forestalled any warmth that might have reached me. All the women I met, for example, left me because they could not take my constant urge to denigrate them. I am cynical and sarcastic about every shred of warm feeling. At the same time I was a sex maniac. As if something in me wanted to get via my skin what I could not get via my soul. This mixture of sex addiction to women, whom I continuously besmirched with my words and actions, drove women away. No wonder.

I feel that I was destroyed as a child. Nobody taught me to heal my wounds. Worse, I did not even know that I had wounds. Being emotionally neglected felt normal for me. I did not know anything else. Over the past five years I have come to understand that I am a deeply damaged person. Like a baby I have to learn everything about warmth and nurturing and love from scratch. The only thing I know, the only semblance of love that ever reached me, was sexual addiction. I could masturbate without break for hours while watching porno films showing the rape of women. The more humiliating the rape, the more satisfactory for me.

I am sorry that I damaged so many women. Some tried to teach me love. None succeeded. I destroyed a number of them. You could say that indirectly I am a victim of the Second World War and its emotional destruction of my caretakers. These women are indirectly victims of this war, too.

George's story shows that neglected children, emotionally "undernourished," may suffer from affective blindness and later be caught in addiction to humiliation. This emotional neglect may occur in a number of contexts, in George's case through the harshness of war. Elliott Leyton, anthropologist and author of widely known books on serial murder and genocide, underlines the harsh long-term effects of war (on CBC National, March 25, 2003):

I've spent years living in war zones—in Northern Ireland, where Protestants and Catholics have been tearing each other apart for decades, and where nasty boys ran at me with Molotov Cocktails; in Rwanda, where a ruthless Hutu regime exterminated the Tutsi minority, and where we stood in churches stacked floor to ceiling with the bodies of women and children hacked to death with machetes through the eyes; and in Israel, where Christians, Jews and Muslims are joined together in an Unholy Trinity of Hatred, Racism and Murder, and where we were bombed in a fruit market by an enterprising Holy Warrior. Unless you've personally experienced such horror, I hope you'll be cautious about urging it on others.

What's this latest adventure in Iraq *about* anyway? We've all heard the usual theories: Perhaps it's all about controlling the supplies of Iraqi oil and gas; or it's all about some inevitable Christian death struggle with Islam; or it's all about young Bush's Oedipal need to do better than his father; or it's a Jewish plot; or it's evil militant Capitalism out to make some big bucks; or it's about the elimination of an evil dictator; or it's just an elaborate field testing programme for the USA's latest smart bombing Brit-busting military hardware; or it's about punishing Iraqis for what a handful of Saudis did in 9/11?

Who knows? And are any of these reasons enough to justify the human misery—the personal grief, the economic and social chaos, the traumatization of yet another generation of children—that comes with a war?

We know quite a bit about the suffering war leaves in its wake. Everybody loses in a war. Wars kill tens of thousands, and this mass death in turn kills all happiness and hope for the victims' loved ones.

But those who die in war are only the first victims of a much deeper process. The best modern scholarship makes it clear that a major war desensitizes us all to violence, and in so brutalizing us, raises the postwar murder rates for many years. Moreover, most wars generate enough suffering, killing, maiming and hatred to keep us killing, maiming, and hating for generations. Again, the fog of lies that surrounds all wars squanders the credibility of even honorable governments and abandons us to a new generation of cynics who will do nothing if a legitimate call to action is sounded.

And finally, such wars legitimize for decades the deep ethnic, religious and political hatreds from which our ancestors fled, and that we Canadians have been lucky enough to avoid.[23]

History has witnessed many cultures of cruelty and emotional neglect, not the least cultures based on staunch patriarchal honor-based warrior codes. Alice Miller[24] told a wide audience how leading pedagogues in the period that led up to the two World Wars taught that *breaking the will of the child* was essential for child rearing.

Countries such as Somalia provide another example. Somalia, with its semi-desert, which offers extremely difficult living circumstances to wandering nomads, developed unforgiving "warriorhood." This harsh and proud culture fed years of civil unrest, hunger, and death. First came decades of brutal dictatorship by Siad Barre. Even after Barre fell in 1991, Somalia has been unable to achieve peace. Muusa Bihi Cabdi (Somaliland's Interior Minister until 1995) is a man in his fifties, a tough man with a life experience that hardly any Western man or woman could have survived. He explained to me (December 1998 in Hargeisa) how he learned to be "tough" as a small child. A former nomad who trained to survive in one of the harshest environments of the world, he learned by the time he was six years old to never really sleep, to always be alert to danger, and to discern the traces of dangerous animals and "enemy" clans. He left the desert, became a MIG airplane bombardier, and studied in Russia. In the Ogaden War in 1978, he participated in the bombing of Ethiopia. Russia abandoned Somalia during this war and sided with Ethiopia, inflicting a humiliating defeat on Somalia. Somalia was subsequently supported by the United States, and Bihi attended a military academy in that country. When his Isaaq clan was threatened with eradication in the 1980s, he joined the guerrilla forces and became a commander, responsible for the lives and deaths of many. Later he became a minister in the government of "Somaliland." I asked him what he would change if he could live again. He replied that he would change everything, especially his "training to be tough and always ready to fight":

> I was always in war, tribal war; looting each others' camels. I was raised in terror; I was six years old when I saw the first person being killed; when I joined the army, there was always fighting, and I saw a lot of my friends being killed. If I could live again: not all these wars![25]

Summary

There are people who *thrive on humiliation.* They are addicted to feelings of humiliation, provoke them systematically, and perpetrate acts of humiliation to "avenge" the humiliation they feel they have suffered. War and genocide may result when such personalities gain power and tap into a reservoir of frustration and humiliation among potential followers.

The genocidal obsession with "cleansing" may represent another facet of *addiction to humiliation,* insofar as unwelcome elite admiration is "cleansed" away into the abyss along with the formerly elite victims.

Finally, cultures of affective blindness may entail practices of humiliation that become self-perpetuating cultural obsessions. In order to contain them, the wider community needs to become more aware of the dynamics that underlie such malign tendencies.

CHAPTER 8

THE HUMILIATION ANTIDOTE

The Olympic Committee promotes the following *Ideals of Olympism* in the message it sends to all participants:

You are my adversary, but you are not my enemy.
For your resistance gives me strength.
Your will gives me courage.
Your spirit ennobles me.
And though I aim to defeat you, should I succeed, I will not *humiliate* you.
Instead, I will *honor* you.
For without you, I am a lesser man

(Celebrate Humanity campaign 2002; see http://www.olympic.org/. The italic
emphasis is added.)

Olympic ideals are a fitting starting point for this chapter because they link *defeat, humiliation,* and *honor* in a very distinct way and make clear two of the book's aims. First, the message—like this book—is written for people who are highly focused and motivated. Both the Olympic message and this book are written for those who wish to show leadership and make a difference in the world, not for those who are content to wallow in finger-pointing, hand-wringing, or depression. Similarly, the people I am writing for want to win metaphorical medals not only for themselves but for all humankind. This book aims at helping all of us win the Nobel Peace Prize for our world.

The second point highlighted by the *Ideals of Olympism* is the significance of humiliation in human striving. Reflecting on the phenomenon of humiliation and attempting to avoid humiliating people is not a pastime for whining losers, but a noble task for courageous winners, a task worthy of our greatest leaders, those intent on making big changes. I feel compelled to stress this because psychology is often demeaned (particularly by men in power) as a "soft factor," secondary to "hard facts" and "hard thinking." The *Ideals of Olympism* suggest that psychology may be at the heart of success, the hardest fact of all. It is with good reason that top sportsmen and sportswomen are invited as coaches by leaders in the corporate and political sectors. Gold medal winners often know a lot about the psychology of success and failure. Knowing about the psychology of humiliation is crucial for success, not only for successful leadership, but for humankind's survival, particularly in times of globalization when no longer nations, but global citizens, interact. For example, what if global terrorism is about global dynamics of humiliation? What if terrorism is about the humiliation of the loser that the *Ideals of Olympism* warns against? Then including psychology in the analysis is lifesaving.

In former times the *little people* had little to say. The *mob*, the *masses*, or the *crowds* were not worth listening to. In our history books, the players are usually the *rulers*. *Rebels* and *revolutionaries* receive little space. The *media* or *public opinion* are absent. This has changed dramatically in recent times. The individual is among the most influential new forces in the *global village*. The voice of every person has more impact today than ever before. Everybody can, if determined, develop into a Mandela or a Hitler. Individuals can contribute to *peace*, like Mandela, or transform themselves into *weapons of mass destruction*, like Hitler.

This book should not include the word "international" in its title. Conflict is increasingly fueled by global citizens. National governments are losing significance. Osama bin Laden is no head of state, and Mohamed Atta, who flew a plane into one of the Twin Towers, was no diplomat. Times are changing, and words such as "national" or "international" lose their grounding in reality. We need more inclusive terminologies, perhaps "global" instead of "international." (Yet, these thoughts have not sunk in widely enough, and so we have hesitantly included the word "international" in the title of this book.)

Both Mandela and Hitler understood the strength of the feelings stirred up by humiliation and appealed to the deepest wishes of their audiences. However, they used their understanding in different ways. Hitler seduced the Germans into a disastrous strategy for restoring their national honor. Mandela gave the people of South Africa an ambitious strategy for gaining their human rights. In South Africa, the humiliators and the humiliated sat down together and planned a society in which "both black and white" could be "assured of their inalienable right to human dignity."[1]

Mandela's approach resonated with the spirit of *ubuntu*, a traditional African philosophy, a way of life and state of "being," a code of principles for living together, and a strategy for conflict resolution. *Ubuntu* is a way of living together in community in an atmosphere of shared humility. Desmond Tutu's (1999) work of the *Truth and Reconciliation Commission* drew on *ubuntu*.[2] Hitler based his approach on a philosophy of honor and idolization of strength and potency. Hitler's message to Germany was "either you are strong and deserve to rule the world or you are weak and deserve to be crushed."

Hitler's road led to the death of millions, Mandela's to peace. For Hitler, the anguish of German humiliation was a source of destructive energy to be *directed against* targets chosen by the Führer. For Mandela, the task was to *dissipate* the destructive energy engendered by bitterness, to concentrate on implementing human rights rather than victimizing enemies.

As the examples of Hitler and Mandela show, when dealing with humiliation the stakes are high. The twentieth century was fundamentally influenced by Hitler. If the twenty-first century is to be shaped by the example of Mandela, humiliation's role in human relations must be better understood so we can avoid its most negative effects.

How can a person strive for a Mandela mind-set? What does that mind-set entail? What can we learn from Mandela? How do we attain his maturity, balanced calm, and measured sense of direction, even in the face of grave adversity? The following sections attempt to attend to those questions.

Detach! Weak Ties Can Further Social Peace

Mandela's example seems almost unattainable to most of us. How can one turn even one's prison guards into friends? One place to start in our search for personal maturity and social peace is to foster the ability to form *weaker ties* as opposed to too *close* and too *hot* ties—within ourselves and our emotions, with others, and with the world in general.

Having *many weak ties,* instead of *a few strong ones,* seems to offer certain advantages in social relationships. Mark S. Granovetter[3] did research on whether people find jobs through strong or weak social ties. Granovetter builds on Tönnies' differentiation of *Gemeinschaft* versus *Gesellschaft,*[4] explaining that in a *Gemeinschaft* people have strong ties and share norms so thoroughly that little effort is needed to gauge the intentions of others. Such settings do not allow for much individual autonomy and are easily disrupted by even minimal dissent. Granovetter suggests having many weak ties to a number of other people provides more individual autonomy.

Robert came to me as a client because he was unhappy in his work. He had sacrificed 25 years to his company and had always been extremely loyal. Now, older employees like him were being bullied out to cut costs.

> I have put my soul into the company—I *was* the company—and how does the company thank me? My loyalty is trampled on! My whole life's sacrifice is thrown away. I am so enraged I could set the factory on fire! The more I think about it, the more upset I get. The only solace is my brother-in-law. He has an acquaintance, who

has another acquaintance, and they just started a new enterprise and might need me as a consultant. When I imagine an interesting future with this company, I feel better. But, I get upset again whenever I remember what my old company did to me.

Humiliation in the past captures Robert's attention obsessively and only paying attention to a better future releases him. Some of the weak ties in his social environment open the door to that future. On the global level, knowledge, an expandable resource, and numerous weak global ties—rather than belonging to a closed community—may help protect people from clinging in malign ways to local narratives of humiliation.

It is beneficial to loosen links in other realms of life as well, not the least in the emotional realm. Michael Harris Bond, cross-cultural psychologist at Chinese University of Hong Kong, researched the length of time emotions are felt by people in different cultures and how this correlates with the level of homicide in each culture. He writes, "…countries populated by persons who experience emotions for greater lengths of time would, on average, commit more homicide."[5] Bond's findings indicate that it is advantageous for social peace to forge cultures that promote *shorter* and thus *weaker* attachments to emotions. Weaker ties are more supple and flexible, less rigid and obsessive, enabling people to *cool down* faster, to perform calmer evaluations of situations, to choose calmly which emotions to hold on to and which to abandon, and to refrain from uncontrolled eruptions into hot aggression.

Sometimes it is more important to forget than to remember, at least in the sense Miroslav Volf[6] defines forgetting. He is an academician, theologian, and native Croatian, writing from his experience as a teacher in Croatia during the war in former Yugoslavia. He recommends forgetting as an active act of nonremembering. A person who nonremembers, according to Volf, chooses to remember the past, its grievances, and its humiliations, but to forgive and purposively embrace the former enemy in an act of preservation and transformation.

Alistair Little, a former Ulster Loyalist terrorist, murdered a Catholic man on behalf of the Ulster Volunteer Force in Northern Ireland when he was 17, served 12 years in prison, and subsequently renounced violence.[7] Early on, Little felt compelled to devote his life to the plight of his people, to "teach" *the enemy* that he could not perpetrate humiliation and murder without cost. As he matured, he disengaged from this hot attachment, acquired a larger horizon, and *cooled down*. He regrets what he has done and maintains that his degree of maturity—he calls it *tolerance*—is now greater than that of many of his friends. He can, for example, tolerate the shortcomings of the peace process. Many of his friends get enraged by details they perceive as unacceptably humiliating, "compelling" them to want to call the peace process off, he reports. He understands that his greatest contribution is to help *cool* the situation, not heat it up further. He has disengaged from "automatic" identification with history's fault lines and now helps build a new social and psychological contract with the other side to replace the old misunderstood and soured one. He has learned to dismantle psychological mechanisms that facilitate atrocities.

Searching for "roots" may sometimes attach people too tightly to the past, when what we need to focus on is a shared sustainable future. It seems more beneficial to strengthen attachments to constructive visions of the future and to weaken ties to destructive visions of the past, particularly to pasts that call for revenge for bygone humiliations. Peaceful social relations call for weak and flexible bonds with regard to memories, roots, the past, and cultural differences as well as somewhat stronger ties to constructive and common visions of the future. Earth citizens might use the sunflower as a model for constructing their identities —in the middle a large common ground of shared humanity and at the periphery numerous flower petals signifying the diversity of idiosyncratic personal attachments and identifications: I may love Buddhism and cherish this attachment on an equal level with my love for Christianity, or I may hold my love for Asia alongside my attachments to America, all embedded into my core identity as a human being. When asked, "Who are you?" or "Where are you from?" I could reply, "I am a human being from planet Earth, and this is my primary identity. Apart from that I have a great number of emotional ties to different geographical regions on this planet, to different people from everywhere, and to different occupational, intellectual, and spiritual realms; however, all this is secondary to me being a human being." We need to think in layers of identity, with commonalities forming the highest order of identity, and differences the lowest. Universality can contain diversity, but diversity cannot always contain commonality. World peace requires us to stop giving priority to differences. As long as I believe that my culture is separated from yours by an unbridgeable gulf, we are going to have a problem. Only when I make clear that *my* being different does not threaten *us* as human beings who are equal in dignity can I invite *you* to celebrate our diversity together.

By the same token, disagreement can be constrained to the peripheries of identities and identifications and must not be essentialized. Did the Taliban have to blow up two enormous Buddhist statues, dating to the third or early fourth century and sculpted from a cliff overlooking Bamian, in order to introduce "superior Islam" in Afghanistan? Robin Cook disagreed with British Prime Minister Tony Blair on the necessity of the 2003 Iraq War. However, did he demand that Blair step down, or did he plan an assassination? There was no need to destroy Buddhist statues or Tony Blair physically to send the intended message.

Incidentally, war is a minefield for "messages." The incursion of American tanks into Baghdad was designed as a "show of force to send a powerful message to the Iraqi people and their leaders." It seems that "powerful messages of courage and resolve" would benefit from being conveyed without physical and material destruction.

Developing many weaker ties—as opposed to a few dominating ones—allows for a new and stronger "frame" for personal autonomy (a concept not be confused with rugged individualism). Erving Goffman,[8] an "ethnographer of the self," has described how people negotiate and validate identities in face-to-face meetings and establish "frames" within which they evaluate the meaning of their encounters. Developing many weaker ties allows for the installment of strong *personal manager*, or *self-government*, akin to the *third factor* proposed by Eileen Borris.[9] She describes a third factor as an element of strength and faith that can be labeled in a variety of ways, such as closeness to divinity, appreciation of compassion, or faith in shared humanity. *Mindfulness*, a Buddhist concept, carries similar connotations. Victor Frankl's[10] notion of *self-observation* in the framework of *logotherapy* is related, as well.

How did Mandela acquire his unique mixture of *humility* and *pride?* Perhaps there is no recipe, but perhaps we can still learn from his experience. Flexible and weak ties to one's emotions and past experiences and flexible and weak ties to a great number of fellow beings seem to be advantageous for social peace. Robert Jay Lifton calls this kind of personality the flexible *protean self*.[11] Conversely, being tightly integrated into few and homogeneous social bonds, rigidly attached to identities of difference that foreclose common ground appears less propitious for the peaceful maintenance of social cohesion. Little's example shows what it means to grow up. He transformed into a courageous adult who took charge and stepped out of being caught in historic victimhood. His new approach entails humility, warmth, and respect, all of which he uses to form links between himself and fellow human beings and to sustain these relationships in spite of conflicts, misunderstandings, and differing views. Being an adult person means having a *self-government* that treats both self and others with calm respect and warmth. It is the task of all players in the global village to forge stronger ties to common ground and a constructive future and weaken and marginalize those ties that obsessively link up with painful pasts.

Social identity that furthers social peace could be envisaged as layered like a sunflower. The core is a person's belonging to humankind. At the periphery, in a loose fashion, are multiple diverse cultural identities. Thus, in the same individual or group, a strong identity of global human unity may combine with comparably weaker ties to local cultural diversity, enabling diversity to flourish in an inclusive way.

Learn to Communicate! Functioning in a Global Community of Equal Dignity

The emergence of the *one large family* of humankind under the roof of *global village institutions* introduces new challenges to every individual's abilities to function. Or, to be more precise, existing challenges—those generated by life in our current father- and motherlands—are amplified. The *size of the family*, so to speak, keeps increasing—the extended family of hunters and gatherers becomes the tribe, then the nation, and finally the global community. In a hunter-gatherer band, everybody knows everybody quite well. In contrast, a state is quite ignorant of the "children" to which it delivers its services. Cities, urban centers, nations, the global village—all these family-like entities are so large and impersonal that they easily introduce anomie, loneliness, and depression. Therefore, under circumstances of *globalization,* every individual needs to acquire more and new communication skills. Everybody must learn to function as a diplomat, mediator, messenger, envoy, and conflict solver on the national and international parquet. A lot of new learning is necessary to enable a global community to live in dialogue and not be stuck in estranging monologues.

Andrew came to me because he was lonely.

I grew up in a huge traditional family. You were never alone. You were included whether you wanted to be or not. It was difficult to be on your own. You were known to everybody as son of x and grandson of y. You had your place. But now I live alone in an urban center. My social life is no longer automatic. I have to make an effort. I have to talk to people and attract them to me when I want company. This is something I never learned to do, not even in my professional life. I had a very stable job, where everything was formalized. I was the boss of x and the subordinate of y. But now I am retired, suddenly thrown into a completely unstructured and lonesome life. It depends entirely on my initiative whether I wither of loneliness or not.

How do I make friends? I have never had friends in the sense of people who just enjoyed my company. The people I called my friends were attached to my job or to my late wife. I have no skills that enable me to make friends on my own. I am used to structured hierarchical relationships with duties and rights. I know that real friendship should be equal but I have never lived in an equal relationship. I am either too arrogant or too subservient. Nobody likes to be with me.

I get my pension from a state organization and not from my son. Everything is more anonymous and when you are a social illiterate like me, you are lost. I feel like a child that never grew up, I still need father and mother to give me structure. However, they are gone and my family is dispersed.

Andrew was aware of the need to learn new communication skills. However, many people merely descend in depression and anomie, without reflecting on the fact that they may lack knowledge in communication. They may misinterpret their condition as a psychological problem, while in reality it is much simpler: it is a lack of expertise in communication in a changing world. Old communication styles are not sufficient anymore. They are based on each individual *having his or her place* and being included more or less automatically. In the new world, *belonging* requires individual proactive action. Reaching out to the neighbor and creating a relationship that provides the sense of belonging requires skills that our forefathers rarely needed. Humility is a precondition of these new skills.

Nobody likes to be bullied. Arrogance makes no friends, nor does slavish subservience. Since real friendship is a voluntary relationship, force does not work. Warmth, loyalty, solidarity, mutual recognition, dialogue, and humble acknowledgement of equal dignity—this is friendship. People who have these skills will have friends and feel that they *belong* on this planet; those who cannot will be alone. These new skills need to heed and be embedded into the processes of *globalization* and *egalization*.

Stand Upright! Prevent Feelings of Humiliation from Seeping In

Nelson Mandela withstood being invaded by feelings of humiliation, in spite of many attempts to humiliate and break him. As a result, he is admired and revered as a wise man and hero. When arriving as a political prisoner on Robben Island, he "demonstrated a rare talent for conflict management. Meeting the raw brutality of the guards with human dignity, he built a relation of respect."[12]

Nelson Mandela applied a kind of "minimal justice" approach. He did not endlessly lament Apartheid, but firmly demanded justice in a respectful and measured way. After ascending to power, Mandela retained his style of careful measured moderation. He neither bowed when he was a disempowered victim nor did he humiliate his former masters when in power.

In Senegal, the *Tostan-UNICEF program* employs a participatory approach based on dialogue to help end female genital cutting (FGC). *Participatory approach* means that those who support the practice are not confronted in an alienating way, but respectfully invited into a dialogue on new awareness. The Imam of Salémata praised this participatory approach: "The Tostan approach is the best way to proceed, contrary to the approach of the Government which almost created a reaction of resistance and defiance. Dialogue is more effective than force."[13]

To conclude, it is beneficial, in situations of humiliation, to mitigate the heat of feelings of humiliation and thus minimize the potential for violent reactions. The best approach is to confront humiliating situations with measured calls for justice combined with dignifying and respectful behavior towards the humiliators, making it easier for them to step aside without losing face. Indeed, it is necessary to "humble" dictators and tyrants and teach them "lessons." However, the important new point introduced by human rights ideals is that this should be done without humiliation. Mandela did not humiliate his tormentors. He transformed his prison guards into friends.

Lakoff and Johnson describe the *nurturant parent model* of rearing children that combines firmness with respect and helps children to become upright adults. They write:

Nurturant Parent morality is not, in itself, overly permissive. Just as letting children do whatever they want is not good for them, so helping other people to do whatever they please is likewise not proper nurturance. There are limits to what other people should be allowed to do, and genuine nurturance involves setting boundaries and expecting others to act responsibly.[14]

Start with Cooperation! Extend Your Hand in Reciprocal Altruism

Is *Homo sapiens* instinctively an *antisocial* or a *prosocial* animal? Game theorists, whose discipline embraces both biology and sociology, have an answer: populations of people who help others, but refuse to help people who cheat, are more stable than populations in which kindness is unconditional or cheating is the norm. Cooperating is the most intelligently selfish strategy people can employ (when they are involved in long-term relationships with others, meet repeatedly, and know that they may depend on each other in the future). Robert Axelrod[15] explored computer models of the iterated *Prisoner's Dilemma* game (which gives two players the chance to cooperate or betray one another) and formalized the *evolutionary tit-for-tat* strategy. Axelrod's key finding is that the evolutionary tit-for-tat strategy—also known as reciprocal altruism—is remarkably successful and defeats all other strategies, increasing the benefits of cooperation over time and protecting participants from predators. In *Deutsch's Crude Law of Social Relations,* Morton Deutsch stipulates that "cooperation breeds cooperation, while competition breeds competition."[16]

The important point for prosocial results is that the Prisoner's Dilemma game is repeated many times, because people are more tempted to cheat when they know they will never see one another again and are more likely to cooperate when cheating is costly. Peter Singer,[17] who describes himself as a "Darwinian Left," suggests that, in order to create a more peaceful world, we need to set up situations in which people experience long-term relationships in which they do better by cooperating than by exploiting one another. Indeed, *globalization* does just this. Globalization encourages formerly *separate* entities to join *one single unit of interdependent relationships.* It is no longer strategically intelligent to hide behind thick emotional walls, isolated out of fear of being cheated. Entering altruistic and cooperative relationships is the better strategy, even though you may occasionally encounter predators. Carla Helfferich writes:

> For bats, baboons, or barons, cooperating is the most intelligently selfish thing you can do when cheating has swift and obvious costs. From this, Ridley and Low conclude that environmentalism needs healthy cynicism about human motivation. Provide some adequate incentive for cooperating in the work of saving the world, and people will cooperate to save it. Tit-for-tat on a grand scale could mean taxing gas-guzzling cars or boycotting tropical forest wood products. It could mean

government preference in selecting contractors that use recycled materials or low-pollution vehicles. It certainly would mean accepting some very natural aspects of human nature.[18]

Even business relations can be discussed from a standpoint of intelligent cooperation. Chris Nelder explains:

> When we find business viewing its activities in a purely materialistic fashion, and exploiting the environment, bear in mind that we are part of that environment. The successful business of the future will reverse that relationship, moving away from what Jewish theologian Martin Buber calls the "I-It" relationship to an "I-Thou" relationship based on mutual respect. Businesses who value their relationships with their customers will be able to hang onto them, and those who don't, won't. The smart company will hear negative feedback from its environment (including its customers) and respond to it symbiotically.[19]

If we want to contribute to long-term social justice and peace, let our very first approach to other people be cooperation. Let us be nice and not try to win at the expense of others, avoiding unnecessary conflict. Let us learn to enjoy human contact for its own sake. For Martin Buber,[20] meeting a fellow human being in a real dialogue is a reflection of the human meeting with God. Even those of us who are atheists can subscribe to this view and make the world a better place by taking pleasure in the quasidivine nature of human relationships. We can call this religion *philia,* which means "love between friends" in Greek. When we detect somebody cheating, we just stop cooperating—but we do it in a measured way, without overreaction. We discourage predators. We are prepared to forgive to restore cooperation. We are clear, simple, and emphatic in our communication to avoid misunderstandings. We show humility and avoid haughty arrogance as well as submissive subservience. We recognize that all human beings share fundamental existential similarities, among them the need for validation and recognition. We extend our hand.

Creativity Can Be a Trojan Horse for Equal Dignity

Robert M. Solow (1957) used *growth accounting* mathematics to analyze historical gross domestic product data and found that *technological innovation* and *know-how* were much more important for growth than such variables as capital and labor input.[21] These are good news because new ideas are urgently needed for the long-term sustainability of the Earth. Creativity is essential to our future and that of our children.

However, creativity is an extremely tricky phenomenon. It cannot be forced. It must be elicited with care. It is often spontaneous and not easily planned. You can force yourself as hard as you want; the best ideas will still most probably come when you relax in the bathtub. Creativity cannot be increased by oppressing people. Oppressed underlings may very well develop a creativity of their own, but it probably will not benefit the oppressor. More likely it will work to sabotage the oppressor's aims. A corporate manager or a mother who wants her children to succeed in life needs to extend respect to employees or children and open up spaces of relaxation and freedom.

Creativity and creative self-realization represent *pragmatic* calls for equal dignity. Being treated as somebody of equal dignity, as somebody whose views have weight, opens space for creativity. People are much more creative when they feel well-treated than they are when they experience humiliating lowliness. The old practice of ranking human worth resembles Chinese foot binding. Both incapacitate, at least partially. Women with bound feet were reduced to the status of dependent and helpless toys. Likewise, underlings in coercive hierarchies are usually forced into artificial incapacitation. For creativity to flourish, all this has to be undone. Morton Deutsch quotes Lichtenberg (1990) who suggests that dominators must withdraw from processes of domination, re-own and resolve their feelings of vulnerability, guilt, self-hatred, rage, and terror, and undo the projection of these feelings onto the oppressed:

> Psychologists, in their roles as psychotherapists, marriage counselors, organizational consultants, and educators have a role to play in demystifying the psychological processes involved in the dominators. So too, I believe do the oppressed, by not accepting their distorted roles in the distorted relationship of the oppressor and the oppressed.[22]

Indeed, in the early twenty-first century the world finds itself in transition from an ancient *culture of coercion* to a *culture of creativity,* though still in its infancy. In a culture of coercion, underlings are punished simply for being underlings. In contrast, the culture of creativity regards everybody as being fundamentally equal, interdependent, as well as a potential resource. The key to releasing that resource is persuasion, and the basis for persuasion is respect for equal dignity. Cultures today fill less of a preserving function than formerly, acquiring instead a propelling role. Everywhere there is movement towards innovation and towards the creation of new ideas, new theories, new products, and new lifestyles. In the past, change occurred in spite of the efforts of established power elites to stop it, while today the established elites depend on a culture of change. Established elites used to preserve their power by preserving the status quo; now they expect innovation to preserve it.

The effects of the current transition towards a culture of creativity are visible everywhere and permeate all our daily lives, locally and globally. I use the term *custom-tailoring* to capture what is needed, namely a constant *pendulation* movement that includes checking the situation, adapting perceptions, deciding what to do, acting, and beginning again to check and explore. Custom-tailoring describes the effort to interlink abstract concepts (theories, world views) with "reality" in ever more dynamic, flexible, and differentiated ways. "Custom-tailoring" is another term for a method of justification in science, called *reflective*

equilibrium, which means going in circles, again and again, to arrive at ever denser understanding.

In the corporate sector, openness to change, flexibility, and creativity have been
elevated to the status of "official" agendas. Training, learning, openness, flexibility, malleability, and questioning are taught in seminars to prepare modern managers for work in a global world. Terms like rigid system, secure knowledge, and
fixed identity are old-fashioned. Adaptability, not rigidity, is valued in a rapidly
changing environment. Small units are more effective than huge inflexible organizations, too. In the language of economics: Profit in a market economy is
secured only if the clients' needs and wishes are taken seriously and satisfied,
when the right niches for products are found (or created). And since the world
is globalizing, this extends to the global market place.

Democracy is a design that intends in-built mechanisms to ensure that the
overall system stays flexible. One of its primary aims is to *custom-tailor* its
mechanics to its "users," its citizens. *Sustainability for our biosphere and sociosphere*
is nothing but a *custom-tailored* long-term linkage between theory and practice of
this biosphere and sociosphere.

Calm Down, No Stress! How Bystanders Can Stand Up

Staub (1989) argued that the significant element in the atrocities perpetrated
by Hitler's Germany was that bystanders stood idly *by* instead of standing *up*
and getting *involved.*[23] What can the *international community* contribute to the
resolution of today's crises? What can *bystanders* bring to world peace? The
answer to that question may be that the international community can stand up
and forge a relevant *global civil society* and help build *sound global institutions* that
pacify the globe. Since the United Nations is the only truly global institution, it
seems sensible to reform and strengthen it. The United Nations may be embryonic, but we do not cut down a tree because it is still too small to provide shade.

But more can be done, by every individual. Peter Coleman describes how our
hot short-term coping system may be detrimental to our long-term self-interest:

> Many of the coping mechanisms that act to protect and insulate individuals and
> communities from the psychological damage and stress of protracted trauma (such
> as denial, suppression, projection, justification, etc.) impair their capacity to process
> information and function effectively (Lazarus, 1985). Thus, the ability to make
> sound, rational decisions regarding a conflict (such as cost/benefit assessments and
> a thorough consideration of alternatives and consequences) is adversely affected by
> the need to cope with the perceived threats associated with the conflict (through a
> denial of costs, glorification of violent strategies, and dehumanization of the
> other).[24]

All this means that people exposed to traumatic stress are not at their best in
terms of balanced thinking and rational protection of their own interests. Stress,

fatigue, and strain undermine an individual's self-control, increasing the likelihood that he or she will lash out in counterproductive ways. However, all these
factors can be counterbalanced with sufficient personal *maturity*. Mature individuals recognize their limitations under stress and engage in and train for *cooling*. I
spoke with American Muslims during the summer of 2003. Here is a summary
of what I heard, always followed by the advice that America needs to cool
down:

> American feelings after 9/11 run hot. In some people this malignly combines with
> their training in "assertiveness" and a lawyer's style of debate. Lawyers learn to win
> debates; they become indignation entrepreneurs, scoring points at the other party's
> expense. Many Americans seem to have become indignation entrepreneurs since
> 9/11.

Indeed, combative conversational styles, often accompanying the American
ideal of "rugged individualism," can contribute to heating up emotions unnecessarily. If used in the absence of arbiters, the effects can be devastating, rendering
the social atmosphere aggressive and unsafe. Common ground is not sought;
indignation is the goal. If confrontational kinds of discourse are acted out in
the presence of judges and arbiters, or as rituals, they may be harmless, even fascinating. Some television programs—the BBC World's *HARDtalk,* for example
—are built around confrontational discourse styles. But, in these situations, the
adversarial atmosphere is not meant to crush the opponent. The setup resembles
a game.

In contrast, the rifts caused by unabated indignation entrepreneurship are
deep, both within American society and within the global village. Combative
styles such as "concurrence seeking," or "debate" are not helpful.[25] When indignation entrepreneurs abuse and taunt *out-group* members to score points, victims
of such abuse feel insulted and humiliated, making the emergence of a function-
ing global in-group that much more difficult. Thus, current American nervous-
ness, combined with a desire for "assertiveness," can make the world less safe,
both nationally and internationally. A more beneficial approach is "constructive
controversy" or what Aristotle called "deliberate discourse," meaning discussion
of the advantages and disadvantages of proposed actions aiming at synthesizing
novel solutions embedded in creative problem solving.

Third parties—parents, therapists, or the wider community, including the
international community and the United Nations—are called upon to support
a cooling down process. Current world politics are all too often hot reactions that
would very much benefit from cooling down. The participants may be too
involved to do that; therefore, third parties have the responsibility to speak up.
All who have *matured,* as did Nelson Mandela, and who have renounced extremism and embraced moderation need to join in. The first task for these third parties is to extend empathy, compassion, and understanding to all members
of all affected subgroups and facilitate cooling strategies as described by

Mischel and De Smet[26] such as taking time-outs, using better self-regulatory strategies, improving stress management, and reframing goals.

The Middle East, vast stretches of Africa, and several countries in Asia and South America all suffer from continuous stress and strain; help from outside is urgently needed. People are caught in feelings of humiliation and drawn towards self-destructive depression or other destructive violent retaliation, at both the micro and the macro levels. Effective cooling is a precondition for the global village to develop a strong social fabric. At present, such cooling is happening "by chance," unsystematically. Perhaps this process can be hastened by systematic attention from the international community.

Police or physicians who are too close to the "case" are taken off the case. This ought to be valid also for the leaders of our world. People who are *too hot* need to take themselves *off the case* or be taken off the case by their peers. They should not be put into leadership positions. Bystanders have to protect the world against "hot" leaders bringing mayhem. United Nations institutions such as the *World Court* and *International Criminal Court* are instruments that have become available recently to help protect the world from "overheated" leaders.

As discussed in Chapter 7, there are leaders, however, who are more than just overheated. They may be caught in cycles of humiliation from childhood on, perhaps obsessed with humiliation. Global and local bystanders are called upon to *recognize* malignant narcissism personality traits and *prevent* individuals with those traits from entering into leadership positions. People with these traits require therapy, not leadership responsibilities. Bystanders who are aware of this phenomenon need to contribute by campaigning for more public awareness as to the malign influences emanating from people with these traits.

Twenty-to-Two, Women and Men! Coercion and Respect Can Be Combined

How can cycles of humiliation among conflict partners be contained by third parties without inflicting even more humiliation on them?

Colin Powell, former U.S. Secretary of State, recommended a *power strategy* in military conflict. He wanted something like five times as many forces on his side as in the opponent's camp. Donald Rumsfeld, U.S. Defense Secretary, stood for a more mobile, flexible, and inexpensive approach. The two strategies share the element of overpowering—for Powell it is *overpowering with numbers,* and for Rumsfeld *overpowering with speed and the element of surprise.* I agree that coercion and overpowering may be necessary to ensure local and global peace. But this *overpowering coercion should be wedded to respect.*

I was amazed at the low rate of crime and unrest in Cairo, a metropolis of approximately 10 to 15 million people. A high degree of *social control* is part of

Egyptian culture. I frequently witnessed incidents such as the following situation, which gave testimony to this social control:

> An accident occurs in the street in the middle of overcrowded Cairo. The two drivers get out of their cars and angrily survey the damage. They shout and jump at each others necks. They scream, they shove and hit one another.
>
> Around this scene, in the street, in coffee houses, in shops, people watch attentively, their faces reflecting seriousness, urgency, respect and involvement. About ten to twenty men, usually young and strong, slowly approach the two men. They stand in two groups of five to ten men each, with each group assuming responsibility for one of the opponents, restraining and talking to him. The restraint used is enough so that neither opponent can hit or hurt the other, but both can still shout and scream and make brief attacking lunges.
>
> Each group speaks with the man to which it has assigned itself, talking calmly and with respect. They show him that they understand the urgency which forces a man to behave in such a dramatic manner (a person who is *outside* him/herself is almost holy in Egypt). The "facilitators" try to understand the nature of the conflict and propose various compromises to resolve it. They do not focus unduly on the rational side of the conflict, they rather constantly grant respect to the fact that the opponents are psychologically overburdened and that the rupture of social peace has to be healed.
>
> After ten or fifteen minutes the opponents begin to calm down. If it's appropriate, they agree on a compromise. If necessary, some facilitators promise to act as witnesses and/or enforcers of the compromises. The conflict is over. The opponents leave. The facilitators go back to their previous occupations without a lot of fanfare. Patching up conflicts is routine.

The conflict resolution and containment street scenes that I witnessed usually included a ratio of 20 to 2, or at least 10 to 2. Twenty physically powerful men were required to *cool* and *pacify* two clashing opponents. If this scenario is a blueprint for conflict resolution, resources for the prevention, containment, and resolution of conflicts around the world need to be increased. *Overpowering* numbers of blue helmets/global police persons with a credible *overpowering* mandate and well-devised *overpowering* strategies are required. The Powell and Rumsfeld approaches need to be intelligently combined with each other and embedded into *respect for opponents* as underlying orientation.

In many regions—the so-called *failing states*—the absence of good police forces must be remedied. In other regions it is the highjacking of police forces by elite interests that has to be addressed. Resources invested in prevention and containment are well spent; they prevent the much higher investments that are necessary postmayhem.

The international community can develop a wealth of creative ideas based on the 20 to 2 ratio blueprint. Why is it that hundreds of thousands of soldiers are available, but not hundreds of thousands of inspectors? Or, what about human shields preventing atrocities? In the final part of his book *Getting to Peace,*

William Ury (1999) suggests ten roles for Homo negotiator: the provider, the teacher, the bridge builder, the mediator, the arbiter, the equalizer, the healer, the witness, the referee, and the peace-keeper.

It is interesting to observe how the Egyptian approach combines elements of coercion and respect from traditionally male and female roles. The scene combines "female" talking, understanding, empathizing, perspective-taking, and healing on one side, and a "male" potential for overpowering, coercion, force, violence, and aggression on the other. "Male" strength and moderated counteraggression restrain the fighters. "Female" awareness of the cohesion of the social fabric creates an atmosphere in which the fighters feel they are being taken seriously. To combine the "male" aspect of force with female empathy could be the modern recipe of conflict resolution. The old "male" strategy of using destructive force is not appropriate in an interdependent modern *global village,* but the "male" ability to use restraining force continues to be an important tool.

Today's men and women are invited to share roles—men to use more of the traditional female role characteristics and women to become more "visible." Formerly, visibility was connected to the man guarding the frontiers separating *inside* from *outside,* just as clothes protect and hide the *inside* from *outside* viewers. There is an Egyptian saying, "The woman is the neck and the man the head; the woman turns the neck wherever she wants." In other words, Egyptian women feel that they create relevant content inside the home, which is presented to the outside by their men. With the disappearance of an outside sphere in a global village, this "division of labor" loses its significance, letting women and men alike dwell together inside, in intimate privacy, and appear visibly outside.

UNESCO's Culture of Peace Programme urges the strengthening of the "female" aspect in conflict resolution efforts. The list of potential "female" contributions is a long one (adapted from Lindner 1999): using multitrack, "track II," and citizen-based diplomacy; installing early warning institutions; rethinking the notion of state sovereignty; setting up projects to study and understand the history of potential conflict areas, collecting this information, and making it available to decision makers; using psychology on a macro level, taking identity as a bridge; keeping communication going between warring parties; talking behind the scenes; including people besides the warlords in peace negotiations; developing conflict-resolution teams with less hierarchy and more creativity; setting up mediation teams; installing "truth commissions"; allowing warring parties to feel the world community's care, respect, and concern; taking opponents in a conflict out of their usual environment; taking the adversaries' personal feelings and emotions seriously; recognizing the importance of human dignity; introducing sustainable long-term approaches on the social and ecological level; progressing from spending aid money after a disaster to allocating resources to prevent it; and so on.

According to the *Culture of Peace Programme* and conflict resolution experts around the world, these "female" efforts must be combined with a certain amount of "male" coercion to achieve peace. The term "social control" expresses the combination of both aspects. On the national level, police and prisons represent some of the coercive aspects (incidentally more effective if the average citizen does not carry weapons), while institutions like lawyers, courts, and rehabilitation programs have the potential to fulfill the role of social caring and healing. Such a *culture of peace,* merging formerly separate "male" and "female" role descriptions, contains cycles of humiliation among conflict parties without humiliating them.

If we desire world peace, we need to build global awareness and global institutions that are strong enough for the task of social control. On April 17, 2003, Kofi Annan explained that he rejects the idea of the UN taking on a task it cannot fulfill. Annan wants resources and a strong mandate to avoid a UN failure caused by member states withholding support. He says, in short, that you should not send out a boy with a stick to kill a lion, then lament the boy's ineptitude.

Respect the Individual! Recognition Has to Be Carefully Placed

When we speak about intercultural communication, we assume that there are *different cultures* or that there is primary *culture difference* and that culture difference ought to be respected. But where does culture difference come from?

I do not dispute that cultural differences should be respected. I share the stance that ethnocentrism and disrespect for cultural diversity must be overcome. But, how can we judge a situation in which tyrants say to their victims: "*Our* culture is to punish disobedient underlings and the world better accept this punishment because our underlings are part of *our* culture! *Our* culture is hierarchical and our underlings belong at the bottom." Usually masters add, "We are benevolent and our underlings love us and thank us for our efforts to care for them."

Some underlings may agree with their masters and enjoy their patronage. Others will protest vehemently. They may even insist: "*Our* culture is quite different; we are not part of our oppressors' culture!" These underlings will then turn to the international community and ask for respect and protection of *their* culture under the banner of human rights. Their masters will also turn to the international community, calling for respect for their culture, meaning their desire to force their underlings to accept oppression. Oppressed *minorities* fighting for their culture are usually former *underlings.* (As long as underlings are utterly powerless, they are voiceless. It requires a certain amount of resources and ideological support to acquire the label of *minority* and the voice to call for respect for *our* culture.)

Thus, intricate configurations of oppressors and victims unfold in front of the eyes of third party observers. Women may be victims of oppression perpetrated by their families who are victims of oppression perpetrated by their national rulers who are victims of oppression perpetrated by other states. The victims will claim to have different cultures and ask third parties to recognize and respect this, while the oppressors will vehemently urge third parties to keep quiet and not interfere in what they regard as *their culture*. In Gellner's work *Nations and Nationalism* (1983), the central argument is that culture can be a tactic, an instrument, not a primary cause of conflict.[27] According to Gellner, the social chasms of early industrialism brought national cultures and nationalism to the fore. The way to address such conflicts, says Gellner, is to focus not on the culture, but on the socioeconomic circumstances that gave rise to it.

So, in conflicts between members of different cultures, where should recognition and respect be placed—with the other culture or the other person? Third parties, who adhere to human rights values must recognize, acknowledge, and respect the other person, not his or her membership in another culture. Every individual has his or her own personal dignity. The other *culture* may be a cause of *pride* or a *cause* or a *product of humiliation*. Intercultural communication must include an analysis of power relations and probe whether past incidents of humiliation may be the source of supposed culture difference. If this is so, respect and recognition entail an obligation to heal this humiliation. *Respecting culture difference* for its own sake may compound past humiliations by adding further humiliation.

Stop Voluntary Self-Humiliation! How Bystanders Can Help Preserve Cultural Diversity

Walk into any international hotel in the poorer parts of the world, and you will find that indigenous dishes and drinks are hardly available or, if they are, then in some kind of weak imitation, supposedly adapted to the "Western" taste. Ask in Cairo, in international hotels, whether you can get the drinks sold just outside in the street. You will get an embarrassed look and be told that you can have only international drinks in the hotel. Ask for traditional food in Sri Lanka, and people will respond with shame for their delicious heritage, believing that Western visitors cannot be served poor-mans' products in an expensive international hotel. A British friend who was born in Sri Lanka more than 50 years ago told me:

> The last time I went to Sri Lanka, I noticed that the hotel's employees prepared a delicious coconut dish I loved as a child in the kitchen, for themselves, but not for the guests! I made a deal with them and they brought their food to my table in secret, as if it was a crime! They are about to lose their indigenous cuisine out of self-inflicted humiliation!

In the Azores, nine islands in the middle of the Atlantic Ocean, there are still some wonderful old houses, hand-built from the local volcanic stones, some even decorated with the wood from stranded ships. As the islands grow richer, these homes are disappearing, replaced by houses with concrete slabs considered higher status. Modern technology has a quasireligious appeal on the islands. In 1991, I visited a local home and saw a microwave oven in the middle of the sitting room, decorated like an altar with porcelain figures inside. The oven was not in use; it was a shrine. The owners were saving money to tear down their wonderful stone house and replace it with a concrete "box."

A good Egyptian friend filled his Western "container" home with pitiful imitations of Western furniture, Louis XIV or XV styles. He and his family were accustomed to squatting, but he packed the new house with chairs and fauteuils that nobody ever sat on. The only purpose of this furniture was to cater to and impress the Western guest. The new house had a modern kitchen, but no courtyard, where his Egyptian family used to cook their communal meals. The family had no alternative but to huddle in the small, windowless corridor on their carpets to recapture some of the life they were used to living, misplaced in their fine new house. To witness this "voluntary self-humiliation" literally broke my heart. (Incidentally, squatting is a very beneficial exercise, from the anatomical point of view. In recent years gynecologists have admitted that giving birth in bed is convenient for the attending doctor, but not the best position for the woman. Defecating and giving birth are both aided by squatting, as is the overall flexibility of the body. Chairs are not made to promote human health. They produce stiff people with back problems. In this respect, also Western "civilization" does a disservice to itself in a self-humiliating way, without being aware of it. Chairs are like thrones, they give status, the *chairperson,* after all, leads the meeting. However, as soon as everybody is sitting on chairs, we are left with nothing but back pain.)

In 1999, I participated in several field trips in Rwanda with the United Nations Development Programme and with international and national Non-Governmental Organizations. These trips became a series of informal focus groups in which I discussed the topic of humiliation. I monitored not only other people's feelings of humiliation, but mine as well. I shared my shock and humiliation at the way shelter programs were designed and built. To me, many design aspects of these "villages" represented the flagrant humiliation of humanity through an uninformed admiration of outdated concepts of "the state of the art." The design of these artificial villages, corrugated iron sheets on huts set in a military layout, reminded me of the same antihuman philosophy that inspired the *Plattenbauten* (ugly tower blocks) architecture in the socialist East, which today are regarded as a shame by almost everyone, West or East. Obsessive rectangularity and military uniformity is an obsolete concept, and few are proud of having ever admired it. The socialist belief that uniformity (from clothing style to architectural design) would heal past humiliation and promote equal dignity commits the very mistake it aims to remedy.

Difference, a term that is essential to diversity, can and must exist independently of ranking as well as untouched by humiliating pecking hierarchies. Uniformity, meant to promote equality, destroys diversity and introduces a new kind of humiliation, because the loss of diversity is not a small loss. Human beings are diverse, and individual human identity seems to depend, at least partially, on diversity markers. Uniformity ignores this human need, relegating human beings to the status of machines. Those who are forced to live in uniform rectangular blocks or "rabbit boxes," feel humiliated and abased to the level of rabbits, a reaction inadvertently "proven" by the architects who would never live in the blocks they design. I hope that international organizations, accustomed to responding to emergencies and developmental needs, will plan better for the future. Arguments that rectangular military uniformity is efficient and practicable and that poor refugees or returnees should be happy with what they get are not good enough. How is a helpless person, struggling to heal and build a new life, to be expected to improve if his or her basic individuality is removed and humiliated into helpless uniformity?

Blind admiration of outdated concepts of modernity and efficiency is as regrettable as the subaltern elite admiration previously mentioned—the slavish copying of elite lifestyles (usually even outdated concepts of elite lifestyles) that easily progresses into what I call *voluntary self-humiliation.* Both the blind rejection and the blind imitation of whatever elites do, the obsessive humiliation and killing of elites or former elites, and the destruction of elite lifestyle symbols, as much as their slavish veneration, are as wrongheaded. We must step outside of the master-slave dyad and evaluate the lifestyles of elites in a more detached manner. If found to be functional and constructive, elite products and habits may be adopted, if not, not.

Help the United Nations! How the International Community Can Build a Global Roof

The tasks waiting for the international community are daunting, requiring the world to stand together and build sound global institutions to secure social and ecological sustainability. More than ten million children under the age of five die each year, the majority from preventable diseases and malnutrition.[28] An estimated 1.2 billion people worldwide, half of them children, survive on less than $1 per day. Around 40 million children each year are not registered at birth, depriving them of a nationality and a legal name. Children in 87 countries live among 60 million land mines, with as many as 10,000 per year injured or killed by these mines. More than 300,000 youths and girls, many younger than 20 years old, currently serve as child soldiers around the world. Many girl soldiers are forced into sexual slavery.

However, let us not despair. There is also much to celebrate. The global human rights movement is growing. *Apartheid* has been toppled, and problems such as *personnel landmines* and *debt relief* are being addressed. During the 1990s, United Nations global conferences addressed the relationship between the three main goals of the UN Charter: *peace, development,* and *human rights.* Eight Millennium Development Goals have been defined that "form a blueprint agreed to by all the world's countries and all the world's leading development institutions."[29]

Admittedly, all this is not enough. The glass is only half full, and many people, on all sides of the political spectrum, wring their hands and cry that the glass is half empty. Again, let us not despair. Humanity has engaged in *nation building* for ages, and *global village building* is still a very young endeavor. Historically, socioeconomic needs have been met at village, tribe, or clan levels. Building sensible state institutions is a tedious process that can stagnate in what John Stewart Mill in the nineteenth century called *ramshackle states,* or what Robert Jackson describes as *quasi-states.*[30] We currently live in a *ramshackle global village.* In many ways we face the anarchic world that Robert Kaplan describes in *The Coming Anarchy,*[31] where overpopulation, resource scarcity, crime, and disease compound cultural and ethnic differences, rendering us a chaotic, anarchic world. Yet, all these conditions do not justify abandoning efforts to develop *more sturdy local and global institutional structures* that heed principles of *good governance* and *transparency* and include the *subsidiarity* principle to give due room to *diversity* and avoid global tyranny and monoculture (the subsidiarity principle is prominent in the design of the European Union and states that matters ought to be handled by the smallest or lowest competent authority).

I believe that optimism, patience, and long-term thinking are the only choices we have, even when tempted by pessimism or even cynicism. Optimistic patients get well quicker and die in fewer numbers. Pessimism loses what could perhaps be saved. Pessimism drains energy and depletes the gram of force that could save the situation. We must nourish those elements that promote optimism. We cannot naively overlook all those elements that bolster pessimism, but we must not allow them to define our view of the future.

Perhaps there is such a thing as 100 percent neutrality—somewhere, theoretically—but in real life scientists have the leeway to highlight certain aspects more than others. In making this choice, we scientists have an extremely important voice. We do not only describe the world, we also shape it. Any personal psychological leanings towards gloom and depression should be secondary to the strategy of constructive optimism.

The conservative Lord Douglas Hurd, British Foreign Secretary 1989–1995, was in office during the first Gulf War. On April 28, 2003,[32] he spoke about the state of the world after the 2003 Iraq War. Asked about the role of the United Nations, Hurd made the point that military might is good at destruction, but not well-adapted to construction. He added that America is a country that wants to construct, and it will recognize that it needs the United Nations. Perhaps Hurd's message could be projected into the future. Global village building requires support from all world states and citizens for a new global world order, enacted through the United Nations. Perhaps one day we will have a global passport and a global welfare net. Perhaps one day tribal and national identities will be secondary to the core identity of global citizenship everywhere on the globe. The principle of *subsidiarity* could be the blueprint for organizing global power structures, providing a useful frame for personal identities celebrating shared humanity at the core and cultural diversity at the periphery. There will be no need for *enemies;* all will be *neighbors*—"good" as well as "bad" neighbors.

Democratically legitimated police, aided by a global culture of responsible social control and respect, will keep "bad neighbors" in check. A "roof" of super-ordinate global institutions, democratically legitimated, will protect global citizens in the same way democratically legitimated nation states at present attempt to guard the interests of their national citizenry. A *decent global village* could be built, following Margalit's call[33] for a decent society.

Summary

Around the year 1757, a new meaning of the word humiliation emerged, along with a new vision of a *social contract,* based on human rights and the idea of equal dignity for all. This created and still creates what the language of political science calls an *expectation gap,* whereby *grievances* easily emerge. The situation is acerbated by widespread *state failure,* and the preeminence of *short-term interests* that high-jack institutional structures that are meant to protect the common good. In this book's language, these situations mean that newly recognized feelings of humiliation lead to anomie, depression, and simmering rage.

Rising underlings may become humiliation entrepreneurs and use feelings of sullen humiliation brewing in the masses to mobilize collective violent action such as terror or even genocide. Cycles of humiliation destroy the social fabric of communities around the world. The international community, the global bystander, including every citizen, carries a responsibility for counteraction, for building a global culture of peace enshrined in global institutional structures that ensure a *decent* and *dignified* life for all.

CHAPTER 9

THE FUTURE OF HUMILIATION

Michio Kaku, renowned physicist and leading expert in string theory, concludes his book on *Parallel Worlds* with the following paragraph:

> The generation now alive is perhaps the most important generation of humans ever to walk the Earth. Unlike previous generations, we hold in our hands the future destiny of our species, whether we soar into fulfilling our promise as a type I civilization [meaning a civilization that succeeds in building a socially and ecologically sustainable world] or fall into the abyss of chaos, pollution, and war. Decisions made by us will reverberate throughout this century. How we resolve global wars, proliferating nuclear weapons, and sectarian and ethnic strife will either lay or destroy the foundations of a type I civilization. Perhaps the purpose and meaning of the current generation are to make sure that the transition to a type I civilization is a smooth one. The choice is ours. This is the legacy of the generation now alive. This is our destiny.[1]

Give Us Meaning! We Crave Great Narratives

We human beings need narratives that anchor us in the world. Religion often provides such narratives, as do family legends, and clan and national myths. These stories tell us where we come from and where we are going. Such guiding narratives are so important that people are willing to die for them. Serbs risked their lives and waged war from within a narrative that circled around feelings attached to a battle about 700 years ago. In the Arab World, history that reaches hundreds of years back feels as close as daily events and can define life and death decisions. And suicide bombers give their lives for a meaning that reaches beyond their existence on Earth into eternity.

Modern secular Western science does not usually provide us with equivalent long-term narratives and explanations about life's meanings. Concepts such as *democracy, communism, capitalism, modernity, postmodernity,* or *information age* do not tell us where we come from, where we are going, and what our true significance is. Physicists currently have several narratives on offer, all a mixture of "sure" knowledge and so-called "educated hunches." They are still looking for a grand unifying narrative (unifying theory) that connects their subnarratives (theories of subsets of forces). Social scientists on their part wrestle with other questions, for example, whether "man" is aggressive by nature, a question that holds great importance as we begin to realize our responsibility for managing our home planet.

In this book, concepts such as *democracy, communism, capitalism, modernism, postmodernism,* and *modern information age* are treated as *epiphenomena, side effects* of deeper *logics,* which are inscribed in a time frame that reaches back more than 10,000 years.

Psychological mind-sets and emotions, such as *pride, honor, dignity, humiliation,* and *humility,* are regarded as dependent on and intertwined with these logics. Emotions are not viewed as timeless or history-independent. On the contrary, the way emotions are felt, conceptualized, and organized, is interdependent with the overall world view of the community into which people are embedded. People sometimes react with *humiliated fury* when put down, but they may also accept subjugation as "honorable medicine." Underlings even create *cultures of subservience* and transmit them to their children. And sometimes being put down elicits genuine humility and acts as a source of *civilized* behavior.[2]

What about Four Logics? How We May Narrate the Story of the Human Condition

Four logics are stipulated in this book, as described in Table 3.1. These logics are determined by the following: (1) the nature of the pie of resources, whether it is expandable (win-win, win-lose); (2) the strength or weakness of the security dilemma; (3) the nature of a culture's time horizon; and (4) social identity or how a culture handles the issue of of equal dignity.

Homo sapiens—the species that must live within these logics—can be viewed as a "hostage" on Earth, a passive victim. But *Homo sapiens* is also an actor and shaper of the world. *Homo sapiens* is, above all, a social animal with a huge and innate urge for meaning in mutual connection. Furthermore, *Homo sapiens* is extremely curious and very good at making tools and finding solutions.

Let us try to put *Homo sapiens* into the four logics and make the narrative work. Some 30,000 years ago, anatomically modern humans started colonizing

Africa and the rest of the world (except for difficult to reach regions such as the Americas which, as far as we know, were settled later). Population geneticists believe that the ancestral human population was very small—a mere 2,000 breeding individuals, an estimate based on strong archaeological and genetic evidence. It seems plausible that these early people saw the planet as unlimited. For 90 percent of human history, our species was never disappointed by mother Earth. New valleys of abundance could be found by simply wandering a bit farther. The game was a gracious win-win, because the cake of resources could always be expanded. The *security dilemma* was insignificant, because there was plenty of "untouched" abundance, so there was no need to conquer and raid others. The archaeological record shows few crushed skulls or other signs of organized homicide from that period. Under circumstances of abundance, cultures and psychologies of pristine pride—in which members trust and expect to be provided for and in which the idea of subjugating other human beings is hardly existent—are feasible, even probable.

However, the party had to end. Once the easily accessible parts of the world were populated, there were no more known "empty" valleys to populate. The Earth has limits. This is a fact that was bound to make itself known at some point. The populated area began to grow crowded. Although early *Homo sapiens* probably was not consciously aware of Earth's limitations, the growing population felt the indirect consequences of this reality. The anthropological term for this is *circumscription,* meaning that resources have begun to be inadequate. More and more people, more and more often, met circumstances that were not characterized by abundance. We could call this juncture in human history the first "round of *globalization."* Merely by wandering about, *Homo sapiens* had managed to populate the entire planet, at least its habitable areas (see Chapter 3).

Humankind, however, stood up to the challenge of circumscription. Somehow, some people found novel alternative methods to increase faltering resources. They used ideas and skills they were already familiar with, primarily toolmaking, and put those skills to new uses. *Intensification,* or agriculture, was the new game. In this new game, nature, animals, and fellow human beings were instrumentalized and exploited. Hierarchical honor societies were built, with masters routinely subjugating underlings, a practice that was seen as legitimate, a sign of *civilization.* Underlings accepted the pain that came with their lowliness as "honorable medicine." Honor resembles pristine pride, only it operates in a ranked order of human worth and value. There is abundant archaeological proof of this historic development. The pyramids of Gizeh are just one, very impressive, example of masters letting underlings toil for the elevation.

Under the new win-lose conditions introduced by agriculture, raiding neighboring settlements became a widely used method for increasing resources. The security dilemma and a culture of *male dominance* emerged. In other words, the new set of rules made *Homo sapiens* more "aggressive." Eventually, wars were fought by empires, and raids became ingrained as continuous activities in certain cultures and identities, particularly of mobile people in areas unsuitable for agriculture. Mongols were fierce. Somali warriors are feared even today. Archaeological evidence of organized homicide during the past 10,000 years is abundant. Furthermore, raiding introduced short time horizons. Continuous readiness for emergency also created the continuous danger of social "cardiac failure," with male domination resembling malign adrenaline dominance in the body (see Chapter 3).

Today, we find ourselves at the end of the second, much more somber "party" of the last 10,000 years, and at the beginning of the second round of globalization (which Thomas Friedman divides into three phases[3]). There are no "new" continents whose populations can be conquered and exploited. This time, humanity is not only indirectly affected by the limitations of our planet, we are consciously aware of them. Pictures from space of planet Earth cannot be ignored or forgotten. Modern technology powers the current round of globalization, creating a *single global village*—whether we want it or not—eliciting a vision of a future *global village* of diversity, embedded into relationships that are characterized by respect for equal dignity for all.

The security dilemma characterizes a world of several *villages*. The good news is that its basis in reality disappears when there is only *one village*. Humankind can relax in the hope that one village will render a more *benign* reality. Male courage is no longer needed to defend the village's walls; traditional *wars, soldiers,* and *victories* lose their anchoring in reality. Humankind can hope for a more benign future, less prone to "cardiac failure." Since knowledge is a more *expandable* resource than the geographical surface of the Earth, the world regains some of the friendly win-win character that it had among hunters and gatherers. Humankind can devote itself to *maintaining* and *policing* the global village. The past 10,000 years were ferocious, but we may be sailing into more benign times.

Yet there are problems which, if not mitigated, may preempt these benign prospects. The Earth is on the verge of reaching its ultimate limit. The future of the global village hangs in the balance. Will it be a sustainable village where every citizen has equal dignity? Or will it be a pyramid of power with small elites exploiting the rest?

What about Two Transitions? How We May Narrate the Current Historic Juncture

The possibility of a benign future is complicated by the fact that the current transition towards a single global village actually consists of two transitions proceeding at different speeds; see Table 9.1. Modern technology powers globalization, but *egalization* lags behind. Through new awareness of the limits to the planet's biosphere, and through technology's flattening effect (Friedman's

Table 9.1
Transitions Pertaining to Globalization and Egalization

	Past		Future
Globalization	*Many* villages	→	*One* village
Egalization	Hierarchical rankings of human worth and value (honor)	→	Equal dignity or hierarchical rankings?

argument) humility and egalization creep in, but so slowly that we cannot be sure that the global village indeed will develop into a sustainable world of equal dignity fast enough, or at all. Humankind may even choose to make hierarchical rankings of human dignity legitimate, a deeply troubling possibility for those who value human rights.

If we imagine the world as a container with a height and a width, globalization addresses the horizontal dimension, the shrinking width. Egalization, on the other hand, concerns the vertical dimension. Egalization would mean that the container would no longer be a tall one, with masters at the top and underlings at the bottom; instead, we would have a flat container with everybody at about the same height of equal dignity. Globalization and egalization, together, describe a shrinking of our "world," both horizontally and vertically. Globalization occurs "automatically," propelled by technology, but egalization requires deliberate and committed ideological decisions. Globalization can very well occur without egalization. This is precisely what appears to be happening at present when we consider that the gap between the rich at the top and the poor at the bottom is growing, both locally and globally. Globalization without egalization is a story of the container getting narrower and higher instead of flatter.

Globalization moves us from the arrogant belief that the planet has an infinite biosphere to be exploited and that there are always more *villages* to conquer and subjugate to the humble realization that *Homo sapiens* inhabits *one single global village* on a tiny planet. The second transition, egalization, pits those who believe that humiliation is an "honorable duty" against those who see it as a violation of dignity. Both transitions push away from arrogance toward humility—a great source of hope. However, when the transitions do not occur smoothly, especially in situations that place different world views in opposition, humankind experiences great stress. Feelings of humiliation in the less privileged, which elites typically overlook for too long, only to panic when it is too late, heat to the boiling point. The transitions are too slow to put us on guard and too fast for safety. They permeate the relations between all citizens of the earth, international relations, our relationships with our friends and family, and even how we feel about ourselves.

Who Are the Hitlers, Bin Ladens, and Saddam Husseins?

The horrific events that took place in the United States on September 11, 2001, shook the world. By taking down the World Trade Center's Twin Towers, symbols of Western power, Osama bin Laden attempted to send a cruel message of humiliation to the entire Western world. The attacks of 9/11 were terrible, but for years I had feared much worse. I had seen the simmering resentment experienced by the disenfranchised worldwide and dreaded an explosion in which hundreds of thousands—or even millions—would die. I wrote in numerous publications that the world was lucky that no Hitler-like leader had yet seized on the rage boiling around the world and devised grander strategies of destruction. And, indeed, the audacious attack on the Twin Towers spread shock and awe with the same overwhelming effect as if millions had died. I resonate with the fear of Daniel Benjamin and Steven Simon[4] that four years and two wars after the attacks of September 11, 2001, America (and the world) is heading for a repeat of the events of that day, or perhaps worse.

After 9/11, Bin Laden's name was soon joined by the name of Saddam Hussein. He was another rogue, who people feared was planning to humiliate the Western world as cruelly as bin Laden did, or worse. The *war on terror* expanded to include the *war in Iraq*. In other words, the victims of September 11 attempted to send a message to perpetrators (whether involved directly or not) that they did not intend to succumb to attempts of humiliation—that they were (and are) set on resistance.

Many ask, "Why do we find ourselves smothered in violence, war, and terror, and the fear of those threats, when the only thing we yearn for is peace?" As discussed earlier, some scholars and experts identify deprivation and poverty as the main causes of such violence. However, deprivation, poverty, low status, and marginalization do not automatically elicit feelings of suffering and yearnings for retaliation. A religious person may join a monastery, proud of poverty. Low status may be explained as God's will or as just punishment for sins perpetrated in an earlier life. Not all minorities feel oppressed. Poverty may motivate a person to work hard. Parents may sacrifice to give their children an education and a better life, celebrating every small step forward. Allegiance to the *American dream* keeps many of the poor in the United States from rebelling.

Are terrorists driven, then, by pure unexplainable pathological evil? If that were true, there would be hardly any hope for humankind since terrorism can never be controlled by traditional means. Drying out financial resources and access to weapons may help. However, terrorists do not need weapons, they can high-jack planes, and, surely, their minds cannot be controlled by any military or police defense. Worse, sending military "messages" may lead to furious defiance, instead of peace-loving humility.

Perhaps we should ask what transforms deprivation into unbearable suffering and triggers the urge to retaliate with violence. As we know, even where grievances lead to suffering, the probability is high that depression and apathy, rather than highly organized terrorism, will result. What kind of deprivation generates the urge toward violent retaliation, and under what conditions is this retaliation carried out in an organized way?

More than Frustration: Feelings of Humiliation May Be the Missing Link

Why do poverty, deprivation, marginalization, ethnic incompatibilities, or even conflict of interest and struggles over scarce resources sometimes lead to cooperation and innovation, instead of to violence?

Humiliation is presented in this book as the "missing link," explaining this discrepancy. In a globalized and interdependent world, humiliation may work as the *nuclear bomb of the emotions* that instigates extremism and hampers moderate reactions and solutions.

I am convinced that feelings of humiliation are more likely than other forms of deprivation to generate the urge toward violent retaliation. For this urge to be funneled into organized terrorist acts, an additional element is required, namely, leaders who know how to channel the sufferings of their followers into a joint project of retaliation and how to build institutional structures that enforce this project. Hitler engaged Germany in "preventive" extermination of the World Jewry he feared was set to dominate and humiliate the world. Also in Rwanda, Hutus were organized to perpetrate the 1994 genocide against the Tutsis to undo past humiliation and prevent future humiliations.

Humiliation seems to be the catalyst that turns grievances into nuclear bombs of emotions. As noted before, poverty or abuse do not inevitably trigger violence. On the contrary, living under harsh circumstances may lead to apathy, depression, and exhausted submission, on one side, or to constructive cooperation on the other side. They may even produce heroism, as the emergence of someone like Nelson Mandela proves. Yet, as soon as sufferings are translated into overarching narratives of illegitimate humiliation that must be responded to by humiliation for humiliation (something Mandela avoided), the desire for retaliation is on the table. Victims may yearn for and plan acts of humiliation against perceived humiliators (real or imagined), and they may become ruthless perpetrators and humiliation entrepreneurs.

Humiliation: A New Basis for Understanding Conflict and Violence

This book addresses how words and actions can humiliate, how the "victim" perceives humiliating words and actions, what the consequences may be, and how individuals and organizations can work to avoid such instances in the future. From acts of humiliation in Nazi Germany to bloodbaths in Rwanda and Somalia to attacks on the Twin Towers in New York, this book gives vivid examples and unravels events to explain the humiliation at their cores and shows what we can do to avoid unwittingly making enemies.

It is common wisdom that World War II was triggered, at least partly, by the humiliation the Treaty of Versailles inflicted on Germany after World War I. The urge to redress and avert humiliation was the "fuel" that powered Hitler and provided him with followers. Hitler unleashed war on his neighbors to redress these past humiliations. He perpetrated the Holocaust to avert the future humiliation he feared from "World Jewry." The Aryan race, he hallucinated, was to do "good" and "save" the world from past and future humiliation. This, he believed, was the noble task that "providence" had put on his shoulders. Sadly, the German population harbored enough feelings of frustration and humiliation to buy into Hitler's nightmarish vision. Hitler on his own would have been a lone player—he became dangerous through the resonance his *narratives of humiliation* found in the larger population.

Mussolini was quietly deposed in 1943. Hitler's response to humiliation resonated with a large number of German people until as late as 1945, even as it became increasingly obvious that the price of loyalty to this deluded leader was self-destruction—in effect, suicide.

Early in his career, during World War I, Hitler was an isolated human being, scorned for his strange pathetic ramblings. He resembled those disturbed creatures who babble wretched gobbledygook at street corners, believing they are God chosen. Without the simmering rage that humiliation induces, Hitler may have remained a marginal figure, unable to gather the following that made World War II and the Holocaust possible.

This hypothesis has been taken seriously by politicians and historians at the highest international level. After World War II, the Marshall Plan (whatever ulterior motives it may have had) assured that Germany did not experience another round of soul-wounding humiliation. Germany became a respected member of the European family, no longer investing in war, but in peace. What this teaches us is that humiliation may lead to war, while avoiding humiliation may be the road to peace.

Recently, Hitler's Germany has been invoked to explain Saddam Hussein's Iraq, with many insisting that the Iraq War was necessary, just as the allied intervention in World War II was necessary to "take out" evil. I suggest that the similarities between Germany and Iraq are not about evil, but rather about humiliation. The lesson of the Marshall Plan teaches us that long-term prevention through the peaceful "weapons" of respect and dignity may be more effective in handling human affairs than emergency policing of the backlash that looms after humiliation. The lesson of twentieth century history is that humiliation

has to be avoided if we are to drain the murky waters in which tyrants and insti-
gators of terror swim. Hitler's regime could possibly have been prevented if there
had been a Marshall Plan after World War I. Then there would have been no
tyrant and no need to bring him down.

Humiliated hearts and minds may represent the only "real" weapons of mass
destruction. Europe was a hotbed of war and death. The Marshall Plan introduced respect and dignity. Implementing it—against strong political forces that
wanted to humiliate Germany again—required courage and vision. Who would
have predicted the emergence of a European Union, "a union of arch enemies"?
The Marshall Plan teaches us important lessons about courage, serenity, and
resolve, about what these terms really mean for the safety of our loved ones and
where the will to act and stand firm has to focus.

In 1996, when I designed a doctoral research project to focus on the concept of
humiliation, a literature search had shown that the term "humiliation" was seldom researched distinctly, not even in social psychology. An implicit awareness
of the phenomenon permeates virtually all research on trauma, violence, or
aggression. However, despite this awareness, humiliation has hardly ever been
researched as a separately definable dynamic, except by a handful of particularly
insightful researchers, some of whom include humiliation in the category of
shame. I, on my part, do not regard humiliation merely as a variant of shame,
but as a highly toxic and powerful human experience to be studied on its own.

Since 1997, I have concentrated on building a *theory of humiliation* (at all levels, from the macro to the micro). I see the theory of humiliation as a beginning
for our search for ways to prevent violence, war, holocaust, and terror, believing
with David Hamburg, that "An ounce of prevention is worth many pounds of
cure."[5] In this book, I am an educator, advocate, social scientist, and therapist.
The therapeutic aim is not to make everybody love everybody else, but to begin
to move us all toward "a minimum standard for human relations" as formulated
by the Coexistence Initiative.[6] The reader is invited to contribute to, reflect
upon, and draw up research on the questions that form the core of our research
on humiliation.

What Is Humiliation?

Based on many years of research on humiliation, I would suggest that feelings
of humiliation come about when deprivation is perceived as an illegitimate
imposition of lowering or degradation, a degradation that cannot be explained
in constructive terms. All human beings basically yearn for recognition and
respect. When they perceive that recognition and respect are withdrawn or
denied they may feel humiliation, the strongest force for creating rifts and
destroying relationships. (It does not matter for the result whether this with-
drawal of recognition is real or misread.) The desire for recognition unites us
human beings and therefore provides us with a platform for contact and

cooperation. Ethnic, religious, or cultural differences or conflicts of interests can lead to creative cooperation and problem solving, and diversity can be a source of mutual enrichment, but only within relationships characterized by respect. When respect and recognition fail, those who feel victimized are prone to highlight differences to "justify" rifts caused by humiliation. *Clashes of civilizations* are not the problem, but *clashes of humiliation* are.

I define humiliation as enforced lowering of a person or group, a process of subjugation that damages or strips away pride, honor, or dignity. To be humiliated is to be placed, mostly against one's will and often in a deeply hurtful way, in a situation that is greatly inferior to what one feels one should expect. Humiliation entails demeaning treatment that transgresses established expectations. The victim is forced into passivity, acted upon, and made helpless.

Cycles of humiliation occur when feelings of humiliation are translated into acts of humiliation. In cases of collectively perpetrated mayhem, "humiliation entrepreneurs" "invite" followers to pour their frustrations into a grander narrative of humiliation that uses retaliatory acts of humiliation as "remedy." Only "Mandelas," individuals who know how to build dignified relationships, can avoid this. Massacres, for example, typically are not just "efficient" slaughter, but generally more cruel. Rape, torture, and mutilation often precede killing. Many soldiers engage in these actions, even though nothing suggests that they are rapists in civilian life or are drawn to sexual sadism or sadistic violence. The extreme cruelty is therefore hard to explain with average forensic theories. In the Rwandan genocide, for example, killing was not enough. The victims were humiliated before they died. Why else would an old woman be paraded naked through the streets before being locked up with hungry dogs to be eaten alive?

Humiliation is a complex phenomenon. Humiliation is a word that is used for the act of humiliation perpetrated by a perpetrator; it is also used as a word for the feeling of humiliation felt by a victim (in this book the word humiliation is used for both, the feeling and the act, and the reader is expected to discern the difference from the context; otherwise language becomes too awkward). However, the perpetrator may just want to help; still the receiver of this help may feel humiliated. Thus, help may humiliate—a situation where the receiver of help defines a situation as humiliation, not the actor. Or, neither actor nor victim may define a situation as humiliating, but a third party does. The social worker wants to rescue the battered wife, but she insists that beating her is her husband's way of loving her! Marx talked about false consciousness when workers did not feel humiliated and did not want to rise. Then, there are "legitimate" and "illegitimate" feelings of humiliation, depending on the larger moral frame. In the case of honor killings, for example, a father may feel that family honor is humiliated when his daughter is raped and that this humiliation must be repaired by killing her. A human rights advocate will posit that rather than repairing humiliation, killing the girl cruelly compounds humiliation and that the mere thought humiliates humanity in general. The latter view, in turn, will humiliate the father. He will accuse the human rights defender of arrogantly disrespecting his culture. To further add to this complexity, you may expect that humiliation is always avoided, but some people seek it, for example, in sadomasochism or religious rites, where people whip and humiliate themselves to praise God.

I deconstruct the concept of humiliation into seven layers, including (a) a core that expresses the universal idea of "putting down," (b) a middle layer that contains two opposed orientations towards putting down, treating it as, respectively, legitimate and routine or illegitimate and traumatizing, and (c) a periphery whose distinctive layers include one pertaining to cultural differences between groups and another four peripheral layers that relate to differences in individual personalities and variations in patterns of individual experience of humiliation.

So, humiliation is an act, an emotional state, and a social mechanism, which is relevant for many fields, such as anthropology, sociology, philosophy, social and clinical psychology, or political science. Its multidisciplinarity may be one reason why the notion of humiliation has almost never, until recently, been studied on its own account. The other reason for humiliation forcefully entering the stage of public attention at the current point in history is globalization in its connection with the human rights movement. When people come closer, expectations rise, and when these expectations are defined by the human rights call for equal dignity for everybody, any lowering is likely to be felt as deep humiliation, not only by the immediate victims, but by millions or billions of global citizens who learn about such incidents and empathize with the victims.

Interestingly, while humiliation is painful, a closely related word, namely humility, points at healing, particularly in a normative context that is defined by human rights. Inclusive and shared humility, embedded in relationships of mutual respectful connection, can heal wounds of humiliation and prevent future mayhem. Arrogant dominators need to be met with respect and not subjected to humiliation—they need to be humbled into adopting shared humility and mutual recognition of equal dignity. Victims, who feel humiliated, do not undo this humiliation by brutal arrogation of superiority over their perceived humiliators, but by inviting everybody into mutuality, into connecting in shared, wise humility.

This book does not begin the analysis of humiliation with the question of who is "right" or "wrong" or whether feelings are legitimate or illegitimate. Feelings are feelings. Prematurely narrowed-down judgments cannot help build an inclusive and lasting peace for what we have come to call the global village. Our questions in this book are broader, less personal, and more focused on finding solutions than on placing blame. Engaging in the blame game does no good while the ship is sinking. We need mutual support and cooperation to rescue our global ship. Included among our questions are: "What are the tendencies we can observe in past and current ways of organizing human existence and which of them should we strengthen to achieve lasting peace?" and "Which strategies work best in today's unprecedented set of circumstances?"

This last question is based on the conviction that strategies can be right in some contexts and wrong in others. This book invites adherents of "old" contexts and "old" solutions to enter the "new" context of the emerging global village and the novel solutions that are suitable in this new situation. This book's framing of the human condition is very hopeful. It stipulates that there may be a *benign future* in store for the global village, not the least through various beneficial effects flowing from globalization (the coming together of humankind), if we *steer clear* of the mine fields that loom in the short term from the destructive effects of humiliation. We need to "marry" globalization with egalization.

We Live in a World that Elicits Humiliation

We—members of communities around the world today—do not live in contexts that encourage people to accept inequality and deprivation as God's will, as part of the natural order, or as punishment for past failings. We live in a world that invites humankind into the embrace of the human rights message. This message represents an invitation to a dignified quality of life for all. Poverty, under this new paradigm, is no longer fate or bad luck or "one's own fault"; poverty acquires the status of a violation of human rights, perpetrated by the rich on the poor. Disabling environments are no longer accepted, but seen as massive acts of humiliation. Thus, human rights ideals introduce a new link between poverty and humiliation. The disadvantaged of the world hear the invitation, but they fear that the invitation is not genuine. They feel humiliated by suspected hypocrisy, double standards, and unilateralism emanating from the world's elites. Confronted with such accusations, elites in turn feel humiliated by what they perceive as ingratitude.

The terror attacks of September 11, 2001 indicate that the entire world community is caught in cycles of humiliation. Men such as Osama bin Laden would find no followers if there were not a pool of feelings of humiliation, feelings that are so intense that intelligent young men are willing to sacrifice promising futures to follow such leaders by perpetrating suicide attacks. The rich and powerful West has long been blind to the fact that its superiority may have humiliating effects on those who are less privileged and that neglecting this phenomenon may be dangerous, especially when the West simultaneously teaches the ideals of human rights, ideals that heighten feelings of humiliation.

The conceptualization of history presented in this book has been criticized. I am using a Weberian *ideal-type* approach that allows for mutual respect between adherents of "old" honor codes and "new" human rights ideals. The past is not denigrated but appreciated as a solution that emerged in a certain set of circumstances. Attributes such as "old" and "new," in this book, do not connote "better" or "worse," but "good for where it fits." Since we need "new" solutions today, as we face "new" circumstances, "new" is not meant to carry arrogant connotations of "a priori better" but of "better adapted to a new situation."

This is important because it helps human rights advocates stand up for human rights in a respectful, but firm, way. I feel personally humiliated, on behalf of human rights defenders around the world who risk their lives, when people in safety, in the West, opt for "soft" justifications for human rights. I hear people in the West say, out of fear of humiliating other cultures, "I am against honor killings, of course, but for me human rights are merely an expression of my culture, and other cultures have other expressions." People who take this line, do not understand that those who risk their lives for human rights need more substantial support and that attributes such as "old" and "new" do not have to entail disrespect. The soft approach is too weak to face human rights violators with both strong respect and strong critique. This book, through its historic analysis, shows a way to firmly reject human rights violators' deeds, while respecting them as human beings—in the spirit of human rights ideals no human being is "evil."

I wish to encourage readers to abandon "we" and "them" differentiations and define themselves as "we" and "we humanity," where we *together* search for the best ways to provide our children with a livable world. Western individualist societies have a tendency to deify confrontational debate. Readers with that proclivity shy away from identifying with *all* humankind, from sharing the blame for *our* shortcomings and taking the responsibility for our joint way out. They engage in finger-pointing ("you have faults too!") and blaming the victim ("you brought it upon yourself!"). This book invites all its readers into the family of humankind. It proposes that we all need to learn skills that enhance cooperation. We need to learn *constructive controversy* (*deliberate discourse* in Aristotle's terminology) enshrined in a spirit of *cooperation,* rather than *debate.* Not *victory* over *opponents* must be our aim, but *joint search for better solution* and *united building a better future.*

So, this is not a book for anger entrepreneurs or indignation entrepreneurs, not from or for elites and not from or for victims. This book does not condone the instrumentalization of dissent to create rifts. Quite the opposite, we call for disagreement to be embedded into inclusive respect and search for mutual connection. To say it bluntly, reciprocal finger-pointing and lamenting while the Titanic goes down is counterproductive.

Be Aware of Misreadings

A host of misreadings typically occurs when we speak about humiliation, misreadings that in themselves often have a humiliating effect. Humiliation is used as a neutral word in this book. Understanding humiliation is not to be confused with condoning mayhem. Feelings of humiliation do not render a "license" to commit atrocities. Feelings of humiliation do not automatically lead to violence.

Nelson Mandela did not unleash genocide on the white elite in South Africa. After 27 years of humiliation in prison, he emerged as a wise peacemaker, not as a humiliation entrepreneur like Hitler.

Moreover, not all feelings of humiliation are caused by oppression. Some people feel humiliated—due to a haughty lack of humility—when asked to give up privileges that are no longer tenable. To say it crudely, some feel humiliated by the call of red traffic lights to stop. The differentiation between humbling and humiliating or humility and humiliation is important. Tyrants and dominators need to be humbled. Humbling is an experience that liberates human beings from baseless pride that keeps them from connecting fully with their social and ecological environment. Humbling may be painful—who likes to recognize that their pride has no basis?—but it is not soul scorching, as humiliation usually is. It is not unusual, however, for a haughty person to misperceive humbling as humiliation and react with the rage that humiliation often entails.

Another misreading is to believe that only the downtrodden themselves have a "right" to feel humiliated. Often those with education and resources identify with others' sufferings, feeling humiliated on their behalf, frequently expressing very strongly their feelings of humiliation. Feelings of humiliation are not less authentic or less "justified" because they are arrived at through identification. Those who identify with others may not speak about humiliation but about solidarity, empathy, or love, love for those who suffer. Human rights defenders like me deliberately choose to stand *up,* and not stand *by,* in the face of the suffering of the downtrodden in this world. We dedicate our lives to bettering the world, despite the fact that we could close our eyes and live "normal" lives in the "palace" of the global village. I feel personally humiliated by being part of a humanity that chooses to neglect the ailments of our world, ailments that would be relatively easy to fix. Therefore I write this book.

However, not all "identifiers" choose the "Mandela way" as remedy; some, sadly, go the "Hitler way." Destructive and counterproductive as the "Hitler solution" is, feeling humiliated on behalf of others can still be as deep a feeling as feeling humiliated on behalf of oneself. Farida, the young Palestinian woman I presented in Chapter 6, lived a safe life in Egypt when I met her—still she empathized with the humiliation of her family back home, and out of love and empathy she wished to go down the path of violence. The impulsive "solution" she envisaged was destructive; however, her motives were noble and merited respect. She was thankful for being invited into a more constructive concept of a remedy. I could rescue her from being enlisted by humiliation entrepreneurs with their often ulterior motives.

Another misreading is that good intentions protect against the perpetration of humiliation. Even the most benevolent help can humiliate without the helper being aware of it. International aid is a prime example. Resentment and violent backlashes typically shock those who thought they were doing good. This book proposes that we all need to cool down, take a step back, and engage in dialogue in such situations instead of setting in motion cycles of humiliation.

This book, though well-intentioned, cannot avoid humiliating some readers, those who are too "hot." The reason is that this book takes people's subjective framings seriously. If people profess that they feel humiliated on behalf of themselves or others, their case is included in the field of humiliation studies. The risk for misreading is related to the status of a case of humiliation as factual or not. When I kill your child unintentionally, you scream, "You killed my child!" I might scream back, "I did not kill your child! I did not intend to kill it!" Still, the child is dead. A week later, I might concede, "I am deeply sorry, I did not intend to kill your child; however, I know, I did." In other words, if a person accuses me, screaming "You humiliated me!" this case of humiliation is to be included in humiliation studies, even though it occurred unintentionally. And even those cases are eligible for discussion in humiliation studies which emanate solely from the "victim's" psychological problems or ulterior agenda, for example, when people abuse the humiliation argument to frame others as perpetrators.

A related complexity that leads to misreadings is that subjective and objective elements are confounded in the phenomenon of humiliation. My American friends explain to me that 9/11 feels like their Pearl Harbor and al Qaeda like their Hitler. They feel humiliated by being told that they struggle because they were humiliated by an attack on their buildings. This feels to them like suggesting that their parents fought World War II because they were humiliated by an attack on their battleships. Let us disentangle this situation. Mandela did not struggle to discontinue Apartheid because feelings of humiliation were a personal problem of his. However, this does not mean that humiliation was not what he felt. Both are intertwined. Mandela found himself in a humiliating situation that needed redress, not because of some neurotic symptoms. Still, he felt humiliated, at numerous times, as he professes in his biography.[7] The solution is to acknowledge feelings of humiliation in ourselves (Mandela, people in America), to deal with them constructively and with resilience, without blindly retaliating and lashing out in response (Mandela could have lashed out in a genocide on the white elite in South Africa), so as to be able to redress situations such as Apartheid or terrorism in ways that promise a better future instead of merely rendering new cycles of humiliation.

Last, accepting a case as an object of attention in humiliation studies does not mean that we, as researchers or the third party, "agree" with the underlying conceptualizations that give rise to this case. Students of my work have accused me of "legitimizing" certain perspectives by including them. People say, "I feel my opponent is wrong in feeling humiliated by me, and if his perspective is included in your book, his view receives legitimacy. Only I am entitled to feel humiliated by my opponent, only my case merits inclusion." Some even count the length of the sentences I dedicate to describing examples or they weigh the visual strength of pictures I use in my lectures and accuse me of humiliating them by making longer sentences or using more vivid imagery for their "enemies." I have been shouted at aggressively and thrown out by an audience because of a picture whose strength they felt elicited undue sympathy with their "enemy," thus, to their view, exposing my covert intention to humiliate them. Indeed, feelings of humiliation can be explosive!

The Tasks Facing Us in the Coming Years

The *United Nations Millennium Declaration* of September 2000 calls on the world to unite to achieve the following tasks:

- eradication of extreme poverty and hunger
- improvement in maternal health
- achievement of universal primary education
- control of HIV/AIDS, malaria, and other diseases
- promotion of gender equality and the empowerment of women
- promotion of environmental sustainability
- reduction of child mortality
- creation of a global partnership for development

The *World Summit on Sustainable Development* (also known as the *WSSD, Earth Summit III,* or *Rio +10*), which took place from August 26–September 4, 2002, in Johannesburg, South Africa, lists the following *successfully agreed upon goals.*
By 2015, agreements are set to

- halve the number of people living without clean water and sanitation
- reduce the loss of biodiversity
- restore depleted fish stocks
- reduce infant mortality rates and the prevalence of HIV

No concrete targets or tangible goals, however, were set for numerous other issues. The Summit *disappointments* concern the inadequacy of programs to

- plan for renewable energy sources
- phase out agricultural subsidies
- lay the foundations for good governance
- encourage corporate responsibility

Many voices, academic and political, call for fair global trade. According to Sergio Cobo:

People who live in rich countries account for only 20 per cent of the world's population, yet they get most of the fruits from globalisation. The world's poor, who count for 80 per cent, receive nothing. Is this really the type of globalisation we want? Let's globalise the struggle; let's globalise hope. We want to make trade work for all.[8]

Web sites devoted to the promotion of fair trade include *Fairtrade Foundation, Fairtrade Labelling Organizations International,* and *Oxfam's fair trade site.*[9] Philippe Legrain, in his book *Open World: The Truth About Globalisation*[10] delineates the responsibility that has to be shouldered by the *World Trade Organization* to create fairer global trade. Jeffrey Sachs explains, how world poverty can be ended.[11]

We live in a *World Risk Society,*[12] and we must tackle it constructively. Fortunately, we also live in an *Information Age,*[13] in which knowledge and creativity are available to save us. With this creativity we may manage to build a global village with fair rules (Legrain) and *good* and *transparent governance.* The solutions are on the table, and we now need to muster the political will to implement them.

How the Road Map to the New World Order Might Look

Is there another planet to move to after divorce?

The first step to a sustainable global village is the acknowledgement of new realities. Global interdependence is an inescapable component of those new realities. Global terror, new computer and biological viruses, and global climate change all bring this fact dramatically home. These are *problems without passports,* as Kofi Annan is reported to have said.

Old concepts of *Realpolitik* are no longer appropriate and undermine constructive change. Everybody on the globe is "married" to everybody else *and there will be no possibility of moving out of the neighborhood after divorce.* In many societies, married people who fall out with one another can get a divorce. If, after many rounds of humiliation and humiliation-for-humiliation they hate one another's guts, they can move to different neighborhoods and never see each other again. However, this is not possible for humankind in a global village. The maximum distance people can create under such circumstances is that of *neighbors.* The United States cannot move to another planet when it has enough of China. Nor can people who fear terror or climate collapse find an alternative galaxy to call home. The only solution is to strive to create a *good neighborhood* on planet Earth—or at least a *supportable neighborhood*—a neighborhood that remains livable even in the event of a divorce.

The obligatory aim for humankind is to prepare for minimum damage in worst case scenarios. This world will never be a place where everybody loves and forgives everybody else. We certainly all hope for a world that takes maximal strides towards constructive social and ecological futures, yet humankind does not have to reach its highest dreams to survive. We must simply avoid pushing the planet over the edge, both socially and ecologically. This is the mandatory minimum requirement.

In many countries parents increasingly receive joint custody for their children after divorce. Humankind has *joint custody for the planet*—irrespective of any interpersonal or international falling out. For divorcing parents joint custody is only one among several alternatives—a family judge may decide for it or against it. However, for humankind this arrangement is compulsory. Our global challenges—from fair trade to pollution control and disease containment—must be tackled even in the face of mutual antipathy. Societies that understand that couples will have to continue living as good neighbors and parents after divorce will prepare their citizens in profoundly new ways for marriage and cohabitation. It is not sufficient to merely hope for the best, allowing lovers to throw themselves blindly into hot passion and high mutual expectations. Society has to be more *proactive* and insert some *sensible security valves*. Society needs to encourage prospective lovers and spouses to forge new relational cultures and interaction skills. A new type of calm maturity has to be created that allows individuals to enjoy the richness of human contact in a the-glass-is-half-full fashion, rather than immaturely smashing the glass whenever it appears to be half empty. Many in the corporate sector understand this and are aware of the negative effects private problems can have on corporate interests. Some companies offer family courses to teach communication skills and prevent the breakdown of families.

In the same vein, it is in the interest of humankind, for the sake of a sustainable future of the global village, to be better prepared for the maintenance of good global and international neighborhood relations. The call for the promotion of a *culture of peace* (UNESCO) is not a rosy idea, not a dream; it is the Realpolitik for the future. If humankind fails this new Realpolitik, unprecedented mayhem may befall us. The downing of the Twin Towers could very well be the first taste of unimaginable disasters.

On April 1, 2003, Egyptian President Hosni Mubarak said he fears that 100 Osama bin Ladens will emerge as a result of the Iraq War. Subsequent attacks in many parts of the world tend to substantiate this dire prediction. It is not sufficient to round up a few individual terrorists. We must also work to diminish the widespread feelings of humiliation that provide the background for terrorist action.

Clients often see psychotherapists because they want to get rid of a problem—smoking, alcohol, or some other obsession. They expect the therapist to "cut out" this problem like a surgeon. However, in many cases the superficial problem is only an expression of an underlying imbalance, and the entire personality must be considered and restructured to effect a cure. Likewise, we cannot hope to save the world by surgically removing a few terrorists from the flesh of humankind.

We cannot afford to fuel the fires of local and global family fallings out and "divorces." Overheated calls for revenge have no place in such a limited space as the global village. Constructive neighborhood relations must remain paramount, however deep the rifts. Psychologists, sociologists, teachers, and others trained in relationships should be enlisted by global society to teach better *communication skills,* especially cross-cultural skills. Learning and teaching these skills is a new, but necessary, local and global task. Not least, the global community of scientists also has a central responsibility.[14]

To begin with, the world must *calm down.* Every individual must strive for a degree of detachment that makes sensible reflection and action possible. Taking time out, improving self-regulatory strategies and stress management, and reframing goals are essential skills.[15] Global society must provide efficient third-party intervention to promote composure when potentially destructive emotions are aroused. Every individual needs a *personal manager* to help the self sustain uncertainty, avert the urge to jump to premature conclusions or rigid attachments, and maintain respectful and warm relationships with self and others. New communication skills that embrace the Buberian dialogical *I-Thou* relationship and the Lévinasian caring for *the other* can be learned once individuals have the self-control and composure of a personal manager. In effective communication, the interlocutors achieve good *attunement* with one another.

Mandela's approach to justice is the only path adapted to a viable future for the global village. Mandela focuses on constructive solutions for the future instead of being caught in bitterness over past humiliation.[16] Glass-half-full thinking, decency over justice, avoiding the acts and feelings of humiliation—these are all aspects of the new need to be proactive and train for constructive "divorce" in case love fails.

And we must remember that misunderstandings and help can lead to feelings of humiliation even in the absence of the intention to humiliate, setting in motion bitter cycles of humiliation. It is essential for helpers to understand that even the most well-intentioned display of help may elicit feelings of humiliation.

There is currently an upsurge of literature on forgiveness and reconciliation. However, forgiveness is complex, and reconciliation may sometimes be too much to ask and not always necessary. A Tutsi genocide survivor told me (1999 in Kigali), "I cannot forgive the killers of my mother. That would arrogate a right that only she has. But, I can curb my urge for revenge and contribute my share to make sure my children will live in a friendlier world."[17]

The Medical Foundation for the Care of Victims of Torture, established by Helen Bamber in Britain, deals with 5,500 new cases every year. An excerpt from a report on the 1999 Forgiveness Conference recalls the following incident from Bamber's work:

One man, whose story Helen Bamber described movingly, had been forced to witness his own son's execution, and to applaud. He had also been badly tortured himself. He did not talk of forgiveness, but neither did he seek revenge. He felt anger, extreme grief and a lack of purpose in his life. 'The battle he had been prepared for had been lost. How do you help a man who has suffered this kind of loss and abuse, to grieve appropriately?' What he needed was validation and recognition. He was able to talk about his son, to re-live his relationship with his son and to make him present enough that he was finally able to release him and symbolically bury him.[18]

Third party intervention

The human rights movement has been called in this book the *first continuous revolution in human history* because underlings are constantly rising up in different parts of the world. Masters (dictators and other supremacists) are asked, by the human rights call, to step down from their illegitimate positions of superiority and underlings (the poor, low castes, and underprivileged individuals in general) are encouraged to view themselves as illegitimately humiliated and entitled to better circumstances. Both former masters and former underlings are invited to meet and connect at the line of equal dignity and humility. Feelings of humiliation—the fuel that drives this continuous revolution—might be thought of as the "red thread" that binds all *rising underlings* together, be they *the colonized, people of color, women, or advocates for nature, feelings, creativity, or individual freedom.* Fragmented movements of underlings would benefit from greater awareness of what they share and what binds them together—the experience of humiliation.[19]

As hope-inducing as the *continuous human rights movement* may be, minefields loom ahead. Morton Deutsch writes:

> … any attempt to end long-enduring oppressive relations will have to address the psychodynamic issues which lead people to resist changing unhappy but familiar relationships. Some of the anxieties and fears that have to be addressed for the oppressed and oppressor are listed below:
>
> 1. Both feel anxious in the face of the unknown. They believe that they will be foolish, humiliated, or helpless, in a new unclear relationship;
> 2. Both fear the guilt and self-contempt for their roles in maintaining the oppressive relationship;
> 3. The oppressed fears that their rage will be unleashed; the oppressor is in terror of this rage;
> 4. Both fear punishment, if they change; the oppressed from the oppressor, the oppressor from the oppressed and other oppressors; and,
> 5. Both anticipate loss from the change: the oppressed will lose their sense of moral superiority and the excuses of victimhood; the oppressor will lose the respect and material benefits associated with being more powerful.[20]

Underlings, rising towards equal dignity, may not understand that humiliating their former masters is as much a violation as the humiliation they once had to endure. During the process of change, care must be taken to discourage rising underlings from surpassing the line of humility. Former masters and former underlings should be encouraged to meet at the line of humility in a respectful Mandela-like way. Whereas in former times masters were replaced by revolting underlings and the hierarchical structure remained unchanged, the new strategy is to dismantle tyranny together with the very oppressive hierarchy that produces tyranny.

Feelings of humiliation emerging around the world can ironically be interpreted as a success of human rights teachings because feelings of humiliation are sharpened when ideals create new expectations, and they are sharpened even more when these new expectations are subsequently disappointed. And heightened feelings of humiliation have profound effects on people, as I observed in my clients and during my social psychological research. Human rights advocates need to be aware that these intensified feelings of humiliation represent the *nuclear bomb of feelings*. We must work diligently to teach individuals and groups dignified ways out of humiliation. The international community's aim must be to contain situations that involve humiliation dynamics and prevent new situations from developing. Hurtful acts of humiliation must be avoided, at all levels, at the family, organizational, national, international, and global levels. Humiliating people is no longer a prosocial way to obtain humble cooperation. Feelings of humiliation can probably never be eradicated totally; these feelings can occur over simple and honest misunderstandings. However, we can strive to eliminate acts of humiliation that are knowingly inflicted on others, either through individual or through institutional actions, and we can work to acquire the skills required to process feelings of humiliation without descending into mayhem and cycles of humiliation. It is essential, at the national and global levels, to drain the waters in which despotic humiliation entrepreneurs, those who spread global terror, swim. As an Arab friend told me (May 1, 2003), "Why do you first feed dictators, sell them arms,[21] and then you bomb us to liberate us? Stop feeding dictators in the first place! Why is global trade still not fair and poverty abject in so many world regions? Invest in a fairer world and not in dictators that you first nurture in and then bomb out!"

Global village building

Global village building is not an affair to be left to *laissez faire* strategies or appeasement. It requires firm and courageous resolve. The question, however, is which kind of firm and courageous resolve is suitable. Courageous action can be invested into global institution building, containment, and policing, or it can be invested into self-appointed law enforcement aiming to protect one's own family and interests only. The first application of courage is the one fitting in a global interdependent world, and the second one is appropriate in an unsafe frontier region at preglobal times.

Wars that employ surgical strikes to liberate peoples from tyrants certainly have laudable advantages. *Surgical strikes* surely are preferable to *carpet bombing* because they attend to the problem in a more tailor-made fashion. However, even in medicine, surgeons—even the most skilled—risk failure. We need to develop new healing skills for human encounters. Prevention is preferable to post hoc intervention. Prevention of disease can make surgery superfluous. However, even when prevention fails, surgeons usually operate with painstaking meticulousness. Surgery is not a hit and run remedy. We need to stop thinking in terms of surgical strikes. To minimize damage, we had better learn to appreciate *prevention* and, as last resort, *surgical art.*

Building sustainable global village institutions is tedious. It is a long-term operation that requires meticulous surgical art. Building a constructive future for the global village means it is no longer practical to round up *friends* and *enemies* for short-term operations. It is not useful to ask "are you with us or against us" because this insinuates that there is space for enemies or those against *us* in *our* neighborhood. Humankind huddling on a tiny planet does not have this option, as difficult as it may be to let go of familiar friend or enemy notions. What is needed, are superordinate global institutional structures that include all.

There will always be unpleasant people around on the globe, and dangerously disturbed or psychotic individuals will never go away. Yet, the maximal negative label we may apply to such people is something like *bad neighbors,* never enemies. Bad neighbors have to be attended to by police, courts, or psychiatry. Only in this way can the damage done by such individuals be limited. The majority of the global community has to be protected from being drawn into standoffs steered by immature and unwise people.

Courageous fighting and decisive resolve—these virtues have to be invested in fighting *for* global social and ecological sustainability and not *against* enemies. Everyone, of course, has the right to self-defense; however, defending oneself by *striking back* can be counterproductive. As long as self-defense does not include all opponents and satisfy all sides, it represents not *self-defense,* but *self-damage.* This is inescapable reality on a limited, interdependent globe, at least for those who listen to the human rights message and wish for a pacified global village.

Security, stability, freedom, peace—these words have an old and a new meaning. The old meaning advocates the infliction of humiliation, the new meaning the abstaining from humiliation. Only the new meaning is adapted to new realities of globalization embracing egalization. Furthermore, for global security, stability, freedom, and peace it is not sufficient anymore to wait until problems arise; it is mandatory that we work to *prevent* them.[22] It is, for example, no longer adequate to foresee that country X may become a threat to country Y's interests in the coming years and prepare for defense *against* this threat. It is not sufficient to ally with country Z to counterbalance the threat, overlooking that nation's human rights violations. This kind of action was—perhaps—good enough in the old world, but no longer.

In the new world of global interdependence, it is indispensable to include everybody in our neighborhood—nobody can escape from it in any case—in at least a minimal constructive way. Old *enmity* is no longer an option. Protecting *against* is no longer on the table. Fighting *for* inclusive neighborhood is the only choice. *Everybody's security hinges on everybody else's security.* Global terror has brought this home to everybody.

The core approach to a new *inclusive world order* is to implement the rule of law at the global level. Present United Nations institutions are the beginnings of such superordinate roofs of law for the entire global village.[23] *Might-is-right* muscle power loses significance when interdependence increasingly dictates the terms. One of Tony Blair's closest foreign political allies has warned that Britain and America may regret unleashing the "law of the jungle" in international relations when China becomes the dominant world power later this century. The Labour prime minister of New Zealand, Helen Clark, told the *Guardian* that Washington and its allies had created a dangerous precedent by going to war without a UN resolution. She said:

> This is a century which is going to see China emerge as the largest economy, and usually with economic power comes military clout.... In the world we are constructing, we want to know [that the system] will work whoever is the biggest and the most powerful.... It would be very easy for a country like New Zealand to make excuses and think of justifications for what its friends were doing, but we would have to be mindful that we were creating precedents for others also to exit from multilateral decision making. I don't want precedents set, regardless of who is seen as the biggest kid on the block.

Helen Clark said the damage to the UN must be repaired to prevent a return to nineteenth century style anarchy in international relations, leaving countries like New Zealand at the mercy of the great powers.

> New Zealand has always argued for the rights of small states.... We saw the UN as a fresh start for a world trying to work out its problems together rather than a return to a 19th world where the great powers carved it up.... Who wants to go back to the jungle? The multilateral system had been damaged by the rifts over Iraq, but countries were now redoubling their efforts to cooperate in the Doha round of global trade talks.[24]

As important as the global rule of law may be, humankind's efforts must reach beyond it. Mere *justice* is inadequate, *decency* has to be achieved. Avishai Margalit wrote *The Decent Society,*[25] in which he calls for institutions that no longer humiliate citizens—*just* societies no longer suffice; the goal should be *decent* societies that transcend humiliation. Decency reigns when dignity for all is made possible. Decency calls for a joint effort to attain the goals of the *United Nations Millennium Declaration* of September 2000. Margalit's call for decency is

Table 9.2
Road Map of Transition from the Old to the New World Order

	Old Honor Order	New Dignity Order
Architecture	• We observe many *villages* (not *one single global village*) based on a hierarchical honor code that legitimizes humiliation as a strategy (ranking of human worthiness; *humbling* and *humiliating* are not differentiated in the current way, in English, until 1757). • Feelings of humiliation are "locked" by the honor code (ranking human worthiness is legitimate). • We see the world as divided into *friends* and *enemies, in-* and *out-groups* (because there are many *villages*), *higher* and *lesser* beings (because ranking human worthiness is legitimate).	• We observe *one single global village* (*globalization*) based on a code of equal dignity that delegitimizes humiliation (*egalization* of human worthiness). • Feelings of humiliation are being "unlocked" by the human rights message (stratification of human worthiness is illegitimate). • We see *one single* global family, *One single in-group* (*globalization*), within which feelings get hotter, especially when equal dignity (*egalization*) is seen to be violated.
Toolbox for strategy	• Humiliating others may at times protect my self-interest, both *inside* and *outside* my group. • Protecting freedom and security *against* adversaries is feasible, since walls, bulwarks, and war indeed may protect me. Furthermore, "empty" regions such as Australia still are available to send enemies into exile; moreover, global environmental interconnectedness is still limited.	• Humbling tyrants serves my self-interest only if it is done without humiliation. Bullies are not to be met by *war*, but by *policing*, and they are not *enemies*, but *misguided family members* or *bad neighbors*. Words such as "enemy" and "war" are obsolete in the new order. Defending the old honor order is increasingly self-defeating. In the corporate world, humiliation as a tool to increase effectiveness of team work is increasingly counterproductive. • Freedom and security are only feasible *together with* everybody else because even my next-door neighbor may turn his body into a missile or environmental hazard if I do not secure our relationship by ways of mutual trust. Freedom and security furthermore hinge on the achievement of global dignity through attaining the goals of the *United Nations Millennium Declaration* of September 2000.

essential if we are to prevent neighborhood deterioration and keep the globe from slipping over the edge. See Table 9.2.

This book presents a novel perspective on the human condition and issues an invitation to the reader to contribute with his or her research. The questions asked are not "who is right or who is wrong?" but "what is beneficial?" or "how can humankind tailor-make solutions for new circumstances?" or "which social tendencies should we strengthen and which should we allow to go by the wayside?"

A central question of our times is whether the deplorable state of the global village is an expression of the *essence* of globalization or a *side effect* that can be remedied? My position is that this obscene condition is a side effect. A core problem is that *unifying tendencies* transgress *national borders in a way* that hampers egalization. The building of global institutions to curb Hobbesian anarchy lags. I believe that a benign future lies ahead for the global village, if we manage to *steer clear* of the *malignancies* threatening in the short term. Those threats are linked to the phenomenon of humiliation. If not curbed, the dynamics of humiliation could undermine all the benign tendencies. Our hope lies in the fact that many countries have learned to tame their internal tendencies toward Hobbesian anarchy, and in the process have created models that can be followed at the global level. These models operate from the benign belief that the existence of *one single interdependent in-group* is feasible, where differences are not divisive but diversity is embedded into mutual respect. We need to realize such models on the global level. And we need to imbue them with a worldwide commitment to overcoming the lack of egalization that currently humiliates humanity. To capitalize on the benign tendencies of the global village, we must call for a *moratorium on humiliation.*[26]

NOTES

Introduction

1. I thank Dagfinn Føllesdal for helping me to draw up these questions in 1996.
2. See for Lindner's publications

- A.C. Hudnall and E.G. Lindner, "Crisis and Gender: Addressing the Psychosocial Needs of Women," in *Handbook of International Disaster Psychology,* Vol. 4, *Interventions With Special Needs Populations,* ed. G. Reyes and G.A. Jacobs (Westport, CT: Praeger, 2005).

- E.G. Lindner, "Humiliation and Reactions to Hitler's Seductiveness in Post-War Germany: Personal Reflections," in "History and Humiliation," Special issue "Humiliation and History in Global Perspectives," *Social Alternatives* 25, no. 1, first quarter (2006).

- E.G. Lindner, Judy Kuriansky, and Neil Ryan Walsh, "Humiliation or Dignity in the Israeli-Palestinian Conflict," *Psychosocial Approaches to the Israeli/Palestinian Conflict,* ed. J. Kuriansky (Westport, CT: Praeger, 2006).

- E.G. Lindner, "Humiliation, Killing, War, and Gender," *The Psychology of Resolving Global Conflicts: From War to Peace,* Vol. 1, *Nature Vs. Nurture,* ed. M. Fitzduff and C.E. Stout (Westport, CT, London: Praeger Security International, 2006), 137–174.

- E.G. Lindner, "Emotion and Conflict," in *The Handbook of Conflict Resolution: Theory and Practice,* ed. M. Deutsch, P.T. Coleman, and E.C. Marcus, 2nd ed. (San Francisco, CA: Jossey-Bass, 2006).

- E.G. Lindner, "Mature Differentiation as Response to Terrorism and Humiliation: Refrain from the Language of 'War' and 'Evil'" (Transnational Foundation for Peace and Future Research, 2005), http://www.transnational.org/tff/people/e_lindner.html

- E. G. Lindner, "Human Rights, Humiliation, and Globalization," *Symbolik, Gesellschaftliche Irrationalität und Psychohistorie, Jahrbuch für psychohistorische Forschung, Vol. 5, 2004*, ed. L. Janus, F. Galler, and W. Kurth (Heidelberg: Mattes Verlag, 2005), 143–172.

- E. G. Lindner, "Die Psychologie der Demütigung," *Punktum, Fach- und Verbandszeitschrift des Schweizerischen Berufsverbandes für Angewandte Psychologie SBAP* (März 3–8, 2005).

- E. G. Lindner, "Gendercide and Humiliation in Honor and Human-Rights Societies," *Gendercide and Genocide,* ed. A. Jones (Nashville, TN: Vanderbilt University Press, 2004).

- E. G. Lindner, "Humiliation in a Globalizing World: Does Humiliation Become the Most Disruptive Force?" (paper, "Workshop on Humiliation and Violent Conflict," Columbia University, New York, NY, November 18–19, 2004), http:// www.humiliationstudies.org/whoweare/evelin13.php

- E. G. Lindner, "Humiliation or Dignity: Regional Conflicts in the *Global Village*," *The International Journal of Mental Health, Psychosocial Work and Counselling in Areas of Armed Conflict* 1, no. 1 (January 2003): 48–63; see also http://www.transnational.org/ forum/meet/2002/Lindner_RegionalConflicts.html.

- E. G. Lindner, "Healing the Cycles of Humiliation: How to Attend to the Emotional Aspects of 'Unsolvable' Conflicts and the Use of 'Humiliation Entrepreneurship,'" *Peace and Conflict: Journal of Peace Psychology* 8, no. 2 (2002): 125–138.

- E. G. Lindner, "Humiliation as the Source of Terrorism: A New Paradigm," *Peace Research* 33, no. 2 (2001): 59–68.

- E. G. Lindner, "How Research Can Humiliate: Critical Reflections on Method," *Journal for the Study of Peace and Conflict,* Annual Edition 2001–2002, 16–36; see also http://jspc.library.wisc.edu/.

- E. G. Lindner, "Women and Terrorism: The Lessons of Humiliation," *New Routes: A Journal for Peace Research and Action.Special Issue: Targeting Women* 6, no. 3 (2001): 10–12; see full text at www.life-peace.org under http://www.life-peace.org/newroutes/ newroutes2001/nr200103/lessonsofhum0301.htm, or in *RBSE* 1 (1):76–92, João Pessoa, GREM, abril de 2002, on http://www.rbse.rg3.net as artigo ISSN 1676-8965.

- E. G. Lindner, "Humiliation—Trauma That Has Been Overlooked: An Analysis Based on Fieldwork in Germany, Rwanda/Burundi, and Somalia." *TRAUMATOLOGYe* 7, no. 1 (2001): Article 3 (32 pages); see http://www.fsu.edu/%7Etrauma/v7/ Humiliation.pdf.

- E. G. Lindner, "Humiliation and the Human Condition: Mapping a Minefield," *Human Rights Review* 2, no. 2 (2001): 46–63.

- E. G. Lindner, *What Every Negotiator Ought to Know: Understanding Humiliation* (Oslo: Coalition for Global Solidarity and Social Development, Peace and Conflicts, 2000), http://globalsolidarity.transcend.org/articles/what.pdf.

- E. G. Lindner, "Were Ordinary Germans Hitler's 'Willing Executioners'? Or Were They Victims of Humiliating Seduction and Abandonment? The Case of Germany and Somalia," *IDEA: A Journal of Social Issues* 5, no. 1 (2000); see http://www.ideajournal. com/lindner-willing-executioners.html.

- E. G. Lindner, "The Psychology of Humiliation: Somalia, Rwanda/Burundi, and Hitler's Germany" (Doctoral dissertation in psychology, Department of Psychology, University of Oslo, Oslo, 2000).
- E. G. Lindner, "Women in the Global Village: Increasing Demand for Traditional Communication Patterns," *Towards a Women's Agenda for a Culture of Peace,* ed. I. Breines, D. Gierycz, and B. Reardon (Paris: UNESCO, 1999), 89–98.

3. L. M. Hartling, "Humiliation: Real Pain, a Pathway to Violence" (preliminary draft of paper, "Round Table 2 of the 2005 Workshop on Humiliation and Violent Conflict," Columbia University, New York, December 15–16, 2005), www.humiliationstudies.org/documents/HartlingNY05meetingRT2.pdf.
4. V. D. Volkan, *Blind Trust: Large Groups and Their Leaders in Times of Crisis and Terror* (Charlottesville, VA: Pitchstone Publishing, 2004).
5. Marshall McLuhan is credited with having coined the phrase "global village" in 1959, after borrowing it from Wyndham Lewis; the term appeared in H. M. McLuhan, *The Gutenberg Galaxy: The Making of Typographic Man* (Toronto: University of Toronto Press, 1962).
6. Quoted from http://www.fni.no/christ.htm.

Chapter 1: The Mental Landscape

1. Initially developed in E. G. Lindner, "Humiliation and the Human Condition: Mapping a Minefield," *Human Rights Review* 2, no. 2 (2001): 46–63.
2. D. G. Dutton, E. O. Boyanowsky, and M. H. Bond, "Extreme Mass Homicide: From Military Massacre to Genocide," *Aggression and Violent Behavior* 10 (2005): 437–473.
3. Elliott Leyton (2000) in his report on *Médecins sans Frontières.* E. Leyton, *Touched by Fire. Doctors Without Borders in a Third World Crisis* (Toronto: McClelland and Stewart, 2000), 3.
4. Human Rights Watch/FIDH interview, Brussels, February 26, 1997.
5. Human Rights Watch/FIDH interviews, Kigali, September 9, 1995.
6. A. L. Des Forges and Human Rights Watch, *Leave None to Tell the Story. Genocide in Rwanda* (New York, NY: Human Rights Watch, 1999), 119.

Chapter 2: Once the Cure, Now the Disease

1. Please read in Coser, "Weber's three kinds of *ideal types* are distinguished by their levels of abstraction. First are the *ideal types* rooted in historical particularities, such as the 'western city,' 'the Protestant Ethic,' or 'modern capitalism,' which refer to phenomena that appear only in specific historical periods and in particular cultural areas. A second kind involves abstract elements of social reality—such concepts as 'bureaucracy' or 'feudalism'—that may be found in a variety of historical and cultural contexts. Finally, there is a third kind of *ideal type,* which Raymond Aron calls 'rationalizing reconstructions of a particular kind of behavior.' According to Weber, all propositions in economic theory, for example, fall into this category. They all refer to the ways in which men would behave were they actuated by purely economic motives, were they purely economic men" [L. A. Coser, *Masters of Sociological Thought: Ideas in Historical and Social Context,* 2nd ed. (Fort Worth, TX: Harcourt Brace Jovanovich, 1977), 224].
2. W. Ury, *Getting to Peace. Transforming Conflict at Home, at Work, and in the World* (New York, NY: Viking, 1999).

3. J. Haas, "Warfare and the Evolution of Culture" (Working Papers 98-11-088, Santa Fe Institute, Santa Fe, NM, 1998), 8, http://www.santafe.edu/sfi/publications/Working-Papers/98-10-088.pdf (accessed November 15, 2002).

4. Latin *circum* means around, *scribere* means to write, and "circumscription" means limitation, enclosure, or confinement. The terms "territorial" or "social circumscription" address limitations in these respective areas.

5. P.J. Richerson, R. Boyd, and R.L. Bettinger, *The Origins of Agriculture as a Natural Experiment in Cultural Evolution* (Davis, CA: University of California, Center for Agricultural History, 1999), 2, http://www.des.ucdavis.edu/faculty/Richerson/Origins_Ag_IV3.htm (accessed November 2002).

6. Z. Bauman, *Intimations of Postmodernity* (London: Routledge, 1992), x–xi.

7. G.H. Hofstede, *Culture's Consequences: International Differences in Work-Related Values* (Beverly Hills, CA: Sage, 1980).

8. M. Harris, *Culture, People, Nature: An Introduction to General Anthropology* (London and New York, NY: Longman, 1997), 299.

9. Ibid., 299–300.

10. M. Deutsch, "Oppression and Conflict" (Plenary address given at the annual meetings of the International Society of Justice Research, Skovde, Sweden, June 17, 2002), 10, http//www.cpa.ca/epw/epw/Deutsch.pdf (accessed November 20, 2002). See also M. Deutsch, "A Framework for Thinking About Oppression and Its Change," *Social Justice Research* (forthcoming).

11. See W. Ury, *Getting to Peace. Transforming Conflict at Home, at Work, and in the World* (New York, NY: Viking, 1999).

12. B.G. Trigger, *Early Civilizations—Ancient Egypt in Context* (Cairo: AUC, 1993), 52.

13. R.W. Fuller, *Somebodies and Nobodies: Overcoming the Abuse of Rank* (Gabriola Island, Canada: New Societies Publishers, 2003).

14. A. Jones, "Gendercide and Genocide," *Journal of Genocide Research* (2000): 206.

15. F. Fanon, *Black Skin, White Masks* (London: Pluto Press, 1986).

16. A.S. Reber, *The Penguin Dictionary of Psychology,* 2nd ed. (Harmondsworth: Penguin, 1995).

17. Ibid.

18. J. Galtung, *Peace by Peaceful Means* [Oslo and London: PRIO (International Peace Research Institute Oslo) and Sage, 1996], 199.

19. R. Guha and G.C. Spivak, eds. *Selected Subaltern Studies* (New York, NY: Oxford University Press, 1988).

20. A. Miller, *For Your Own Good: Hidden Cruelty in Child-Rearing and the Roots of Violence* (London: Virago Press, 1983). See also the afterword on http://members.xoom.com/childhistory/victim.htm (accessed May 22, 2000).

21. G. Lakoff, and M. Johnson, *Philosophy in the Flesh: The Embodied Mind and Its Challenge to Western Thought* (New York, NY: Basic Books, 1999), 313–314.

22. Ibid., 327.

23. T.W. Adorno, E. Frenkel-Brunswick, D.J. Levinson, and R.N. Sanford, *The Authoritarian Personality,* 1st ed. (New York, NY: Harper, 1950).

24. N. Elias, *The Civilizing Process* (Vol. 1: *The History of Manners;* Vol. 2: *State Formation and Civilization*) (Oxford: Blackwell, 1994).

25. D. Smith, "Organisations and Humiliation: Looking Beyond Elias," *Organization* 8, no. 3 (2001): 537–560.

26. J. Braithwaite, *Crime, Shame and Reintegration* (Cambridge, UK: Cambridge University Press, 1989).

27. Please see Figure 5 with the statistical data at http://www.unfpa.org/swp/2005/english/ch7/index.htm#fig5.

28. United Nations Population Fund (UNFPA), "Gender-Based Violence: A Price Too High," *State of World Population 2005*, 68, http://www.unfpa.org/swp/2005/english/ch7/index.htm.

29. J. Sidanius and F. Pratto, *Social Dominance: An Intergroup Theory of Social Hierarchy and Oppression* (Cambridge, UK: Cambridge University Press, 1999).

30. W.I. Miller, *Humiliation and Other Essays on Honor, Social Discomfort, and Violence* (Ithaca: Cornell University Press, 1993), 175, italics in original.

31. J.O. Lyons, *The Invention of the Self* (Carbondale, IL: Southern Illinois University Press, 1978).

32. I thank Barnett Pearce for making me aware of Lyons's book. I thank Jon Elster for making me aware that the "birth of the self" began much earlier, with Michel de Montaigne (1575), *Essays by Michel De Montaigne Translated by Charles Cotton,* http://eserver.org/philosophy/montaigne-essays.txt (accessed December 15, 2003). See furthermore H. Bloom, *Shakespeare: The Invention of the Human* (London: Fourth Estate, 1999).

33. W. Ury, *Getting to Peace. Transforming Conflict at Home, at Work, and in the World* (New York, NY: Viking, 1999), 108.

34. See Smith, "Organisations and Humiliation," whom I thank for coining the words conquest/relegation/reinforcement/inclusion humiliation.

35. Adapted from Smith, "Organisations and Humiliation," 543.

36. Lindner, "Humiliation—Trauma That Has Been Overlooked."

37. Deutsch, "Oppression and Conflict," 16. See also J. Harvey, *Civilized Oppression* (Lanham, MD: Rowman and Littlefield Publishers, 1999).

38. K.G. Allred, "Anger and Retaliation: Toward an Understanding of Impassioned Conflict in Organizations," *Research on Negotiations in Organizations,* Vol. 7, ed. R.J. Bies, R.J. Lewicki, and B.H. Sheppard (Greenwich, CT: JAI Press, 1999); J.R. Averill, *Anger and Aggression: An Essay on Emotion* (New York: Springer-Verlag, 1982).

39. See Deutsch, "Oppression and Conflict," 31; see also D. Bar-On and A. Nadler, "From Peace Making and Conflict Resolution to Conciliation and Peace Building" (proposal for the International Award of the State of Nordrhine-Westfalia for Research in the Humanities and Social Sciences, where the authors call for more attention to be given to power asymmetry in conflicts, Beer-Sheva, Israel, 1999).

40. M. Sayler, "Humiliation and the Poor: A Study in the Management of Meaning" (PhD dissertation, Fielding Graduate Institute, Santa Barbara, CA, 2004).

41. K.J. Gergen, "Organizational Science in a Postmodern Context," (Swarthmore College: Draft copy for *Journal of Behavioral Science*), 2, http://www.swarthmore.edu/SocSci/kgergen1/text10.html (accessed January 6, 2000).

42. S. Moscovici, "Social Representations Theory and Social Constructionism," Social Representations Mailing List 1 Postings, 28 Apr–27 May 1997, 2, http://www.nsu.ru/psych/internet/bits/mosc1.htm (accessed December 3, 2000).

43. Rostow's linear theory of development is criticized in this line [W.W. Rostow, *The Stages of Economic Growth: A Non-Communist Manifesto* (Cambridge, UK: Cambridge University Press, 1960)]. I thank Roger van Zwanenburg for making me aware of Rostow's work.

44. S.S. Tomkins, *Affect Imagery and Consciousness,* Vols. I–IV (New York, NY: Springer, 1962).

45. D.L. Nathanson, *Shame and Pride: Affect Sex and the Birth of the Self* (New York, NY: Norton, 1992).

46. See, for example, D. Smith, "The Humiliating Organisation: The Functions and Disfunctions of Degradation," in *The Civilized Organisation,* ed. A.v. Iterson, W. Mastenbroek, T. Newton, and D. Smith (Amsterdam: Benjamin, 2002).

47. S.M. Retzinger, *Violent Emotions: Shame and Rage in Marital Quarrels* (Newbury Park, CA: Sage, 1991); T.J. Scheff and S.M. Retzinger, *Emotions and Violence: Shame and Rage in Destructive Conflicts* (Lexington, MA: Lexington Books, 1991).

48. W. Vogel and A. Lazare, "The Unforgivable Humiliation: A Dilemma in Couples' Treatment," *Contemporary Family Therapy* 12, no. 2 (1990): 139–151.

49. R.L. Hale, "The Role of Humiliation and Embarrassment in Serial Murder," *Psychology. A Journal of Human Behaviour* 31, no. 2 (1994): 17–23.

50. D.C. Klein, "The Humiliation Dynamic: Viewing the Task of Prevention from a New Perspective," *The Journal of Primary Prevention* 12, no. 2 (1991): 87–91 and 93–121, and 12, no. 3 (1992): 189–193.

51. L.M. Hartling and T. Luchetta, "Humiliation: Assessing the Impact of Derision, Degradation, and Debasement," *Journal of Primary Prevention* 19, no. 5 (1999): 259–278.

52. See T.J. Scheff, *Emotions, the Social Bond and Human Reality. Part/Whole Analysis* (Cambridge, UK: Cambridge University Press, 1997), 11.

53. H.B. Lewis, *Shame and Guilt in Neurosis* (New York, NY: International Universities Press, 1971).

54. T.J. Scheff, *Bloody Revenge: Emotions, Nationalism and War* (Chicago, IL: University of Chicago Press, 1990).

55. P. Masson, "When Soldiers Prefer Death to Humiliation," *Historia,* no. 596 (1996): 54–56.

56. S. Vachon, "Passer de l'appauvrissement à la pauvreté comme on va de l'humiliation à l'humilité," *Voix et Images* 18, no. 2 (1993): 382–387.

57. V.V. Znakov, "The Comprehension of Violence and Humiliation Situations by Aggressive Adolescents," *Voprosy-Psikhologii* (January–February 1990): 20–27.

58. I.W. Charny, "A Personality Disorder of Excessive Power Strivings," *Israel Journal of Psychiatry* 34, no. 1 (1997): 3–17.

59. J. Gilligan, *Violence: Our Deadly Epidemic and How to Treat It* (New York, NY: Putnam, 1996).

60. See V.D. Volkan, *Blind Trust: Large Groups and Their Leaders in Times of Crisis and Terror* (Charlottesville, VA: Pitchstone Publishing, 2004); V.D. Volkan, D.A. Julius, and J.V. Montville, eds., *The Psychodynamics of International Relationships,* Vol. I: *Concepts and Theories;* Vol. II: *Unofficial Diplomacy at Work* (Lexington, MA: Lexington Books, 1990–1991). See also Blema S. Steinberg, *Shame and Humiliation: Presidential Decision Making on Vietnam* (Montreal/UK: McGill-Queen's, 1996).

61. See E. Staub, *The Psychology of Good and Evil: Why Children, Adults, and Groups Help and Harm Others* (Cambridge, UK: Cambridge University Press, 2003); E. Staub, "The Roots of Evil: Social Conditions, Culture, Personality and Basic Human Needs," *Personality and Social Psychology Review* 3, no. 3 (1999): 179–192.

62. Arien Mack, "The Decent Society—Editor's Introduction," *Social Research* 64, no. 1 (1997): 1-1.

63. A. Margalit, *The Decent Society* (Cambridge, MA: Harvard University Press, 1996).

64. R.E. Nisbett and D. Cohen, *Culture of Honor: The Psychology of Violence in the South* (Boulder, CO: Westview Press, 1996).

65. W.I. Miller, *Humiliation and Other Essays on Honor, Social Discomfort, and Violence* (Ithaca, NY: Cornell University Press, 1993).

66. See A. Honneth, "Recognition and Moral Obligation," *Social Research* 64, no. 1 (1997): 16–35, on related themes.

67. M. Scheler, *Über Ressentiment und moralisches Werturteil* (Leipzig: Engelmann, 1912).

68. M. Scheler, *The Nature of Sympathy* (London: Routledge and Kegan Paul, 1954).

Chapter 3: Globalization and Egalization

1. Thomas L. Friedman, *The World is Flat: A Brief History of the Twenty-First Century* (New York, NY: Farrar, Straus, and Giroux, 2005).

2. See M. Featherstone, ed., *Global Culture: Nationalism, Globalism and Modernity* (London: Sage, 1990).

3. T.H. Eriksen, "Ethnic Identity, National Identity and Intergroup Conflict: The Significance of Personal Experiences," *Social Identity, Intergroup Conflict, and Conflict Reduction,* ed. R.D. Ashmore, L.J. Jussim, and D.A. Wilder (Oxford: Oxford University Press, 2001), 42–70, http://folk.uio.no/geirthe/Identity_politics.html (accessed July 20, 2003).

4. P.T. Coleman, "Power and Conflict," in *The Handbook of Conflict Resolution: Theory and Practice,* ed. M. Deutsch and P.T. Coleman (San Francisco, CA: Jossey-Bass, 2000), 108–130).

5. M. Sherif, O.J. Harvey, B.J. White, W.R. Hood, C.W. Sherif, and D. Campbell, *The Robbers' Cave Experiment: Intergroup Conflict and Cooperation* (Middletown, CT: Wesleyan University Press, 1988).

6. See, for example, http://www.intractableconflict.org/docs/appendix_6.jsp.

7. M.H. Bond, "Unity in Diversity: Orientations and Strategies for Building a Harmonious, Multicultural Society," *Social Psychology and Cultural Context,* ed. J. Adamopoulos and Y. Kashima (Thousand Oaks, CA: Sage, 1998), 17–40.

8. S.L. Gaertner and J.F. Dovidio, *Reducing Intergroup Bias: The Common Ingroup Identity Model* (Hove, UK: Psychology Press, 1999).

9. W. Ury, *Getting to Peace. Transforming Conflict at Home, at Work, and in the World* (New York, NY: Viking, 1999).

10. R.G. Wilkinson, *Unhealthy Societies: The Afflictions of Inequality* (London: Routledge, 1996).

11. S. Mayhew, *A Dictionary of Geography* (Oxford: Oxford University Press, 1997).

12. F. Heider, *The Psychology of Interpersonal Relations* (New York, NY: Wiley, 1958); H.H. Kelley, "The Processes of Causal Attribution," *American Psychologist* 28, no. 107 (1973): 128.

13. See Deutsch, "Oppression and Conflict," 25.

14. See S. Keen, *Faces of the Enemy: Reflections of the Hostile Imagination* (San Francisco, CA: Harper and Row, 1986). I thank Gordon Fellman for this reference.

15. See C.R. Snyder, *Citizen-Soldiers and Manly Warriors: Military Service and Gender in the Civic Republican Tradition* (Lanham, MD: Rowman and Littlefield, 2000).

16. Ury, *Getting to Peace.*

17. Beverly Crawford at the Sommerakademie für Frieden und Konfliktforschung, Loccum, Germany, July 20–25, 1997.
18. J. H. Herz, "Idealist Internationalism and the Security Dilemma," *World Politics* II (1950): 157–180.
19. For example, R. Jervis, R. N. Lebow, and J. G. Stein, *Psychology and Deterrence* (Baltimore, MD: The Johns Hopkins University Press, 1985).
20. F. R. Kluckhohn and F. L. Strodtbeck, *Variations in Value Orientations* (Evanston, IL: Row, Peterson, 1961).
21. P. T. Coleman, "Characteristics of Protracted, Intractable Conflict: Toward the Development of a Metaframework-I," *Peace and Conflict: Journal of Peace Psychology* 9, no. 1 (2003): 1–37.
22. Adapted from Lindner, "The Psychology of Humiliation," 439.
23. Ibid.
24. L. Greenfeld, *Nationalism: Five Roads to Modernity* (Cambridge, MA: Harvard University Press, 1992); L. Greenfeld, "Nationalism and Modernity," *Social Research* 63, no. 1 (1996): 3–40.
25. S. P. Huntington, *The Clash of Civilizations and the Remaking of World Order* (New York, NY: Simon and Schuster, 1996).
26. Janet Shibley Hyde, "The Gender Similarities Hypothesis," *American Psychologist* 60, no. 6 (2005): 581–92.
27. See Mary Douglas, *Purity and Danger: An Analysis of the Concepts of Pollution and Taboo* (London: Ark Paperbacks, 1984).
28. Barrington Moore explains that people persecute those whom they perceive as polluting due to their "impure" religious, political, or economic ideas [B. Moore, Jr., *Moral Purity and Persecution in History* (Princeton, NJ: Princeton University Press, 2000)].
29. With Mike Embley in the BBC World *HARDtalk* program.
30. T. Hobbes (1651), *Leviathan*, The APHIL Library, http://coombs.anu.edu.au/Depts/RSSS/Philosophy/Texts/LeviathanTOC.html (accessed November 9, 2000).
31. J. Locke, *Two Treatises of Government* (London: A. & J. Churchill, 1690).
32. Joseph Preston Baratta, *The Politics of World Federation*, Vol. 1: *The United Nations, U.N. Reform, Atomic Control;* Vol. 2: *From World Federalism to Global Governance* (Westport, CT: Praeger, 2004).
33. "World Conference on Racism, Racial Discrimination, Xenophobia and Related Intolerance," in Durban, South Africa, August 31–September 7, 2001. Read on *intolerance* in L. Noël, *Intolerance: A General Survey* (Montreal: McGill-Queen's University Press, 1994).
34. Coleman, "Power and Conflict," in *The Handbook of Conflict Resolution*, 108–130.
35. Egal also served as Somalia's prime minister from 1967, during the latter period of Somalia's democratic era.
36. See also MoveOn, www.moveon.org/.
37. The International Panel of Eminent Personalities to Investigate the 1994 Genocide in Rwanda and the Surrounding Events. *Rwanda: The Preventable Genocide* (2000), Chap. 16, paragraph 4, www.oau-oua.org/ (accessed September 30, 2000).
38. J. Z. Rubin, D. G. Pruitt, and S. H. Kim, *Social Conflict: Escalation, Stalemate and Settlement*, 2nd ed. (New York, NY: McGraw-Hill, 1994).
39. P. T. Coleman, "Characteristics of Protracted, Intractable Conflict: Toward the Development of a Metaframework-I," *Peace and Conflict: Journal of Peace Psychology* 9, no. 1 (2003): 1–37.

Chapter 4: Humiliation and Misunderstanding

1. E.G. Lindner, *The Relational Anatomy of Humiliation: Perpetrator, Victim, and Third Party* (Human Dignity and Humiliation Studies, 2000), http://www.humiliationstudies.org/documents/evelin/RelationalAnatomyHumiliation.pdf.

2. A. Badiou, *Ethics: An Essay on the Understanding of Evil* (London: Verso, 2001).

3. Immanuel Kant (1724–1804) was a Prussian philosopher, regarded as one of history's most influential thinkers and one of the last major philosophers of the Enlightenment, having a major impact on the Romantic and Idealist philosophies of the 19th century. Emmanuel Lévinas (1906–1995) was a Jewish philosopher from Lithuania, who moved to France and wrote most of his works in French. His work focuses on the ethics of the Other: The Other is not knowable and cannot be made into an object, as is posited by traditional metaphysics.

4. L.D. Ross and J.T. Iost, "Fairness Norms and the Potential for Mutual Agreements Involving Majority and Minority Groups," *Research on Managing Groups and Teams (Vol. 2): Groups in Their Context,* ed. M.A. Neale, E.A. Mannix, and R. Wageman (Greenwich, CT: JAI Press, 1999), 93–114.

5. See, for example, http://www.hri.ca/.

6. T. Pogge, *World Poverty and Human Rights: Cosmopolitan Responsibilities and Reforms* (Cambridge, UK: Polity Press, 2002).

7. J.G. Frazer, *The Golden Bough: a Study in Magic and Religion,* abridged ed. (New York: Macmillan, 1922), Chap. 64, http://www.sacred-texts.com/pag/frazer/ (accessed April 2003).

8. E.G. Lindner, *Lebensqualität im ägyptisch-deutschen Vergleich. Eine interkulturelle Untersuchung an drei Berufsgruppen (Ärzte, Journalisten, Künstler)* (Doctoral dissertation in medicine, Department of Psychological Medicine, University of Hamburg, Hamburg, 1994).

9. F.E. Jandt, *Intercultural Communication: An Introduction* (Thousand Oaks, CA: Sage, 1995), 272.

10. The sources for this statement are provided by the author's network of family relations, but also by close monitoring of the media; for example, in political talk shows this topic "creeps in" and presents itself in its various shades of mutual understanding and misunderstanding that hover between participants from the former East and West.

11. This uttering is condensed from accounts from 12 encounters and media coverage. See also Billig for "everyday thinking," discourse and society, ideology and opinions. M.G. Billig, *Ideology and Opinions. Studies in Rhetorical Psychology* (London: Sage, 1991).

12. I would like to express my thanks for this comment.

13. Quoted from http://www.straightdope.com/mailbag/mpiedpiper.html.

14. I owe this detail to Odd-Bjørn Fure and Jorunn Sem Fure.

15. See also M. Maren, *The Road to Hell: The Ravaging Effects of Foreign Aid and International Charity* (New York, NY: Free Press, 1997); M.B. Anderson, *Do No Harm: How Aid Can Support Peace—or War* (Boulder, CO: Lynne Rienner Publishers, 1999).

16. I thank the reviewer for his remark.

17. See, for example, P.J. O'Halloran, *Humanitarian Intervention and the Genocide in Rwanda* (London: Research Institute for the Study of Conflict and Terrorism, 1995).

18. S.R. Feil, (1998). "Preventing Genocide: How the Early Use of Force Might Have Succeeded in Rwanda," Report to the Carnegie Commission on Preventing Deadly Conflict (Washington, D.C.: April 1998), 3, quoted from The International Panel of Eminent Personalities to Investigate the 1994 Genocide in Rwanda and the Surrounding Events

(2000), *Rwanda: The Preventable Genocide,* chap. 10, paragraph 9, www.oau-oua.org/ (accessed September 30, 2000).

19. See http://www.unicc.org/unrisd/wsp/index.htm.

20. See for a comprehensive discussion D.R.Matsumoto, S. Hee Yoo, and J.A. LeRoux, "Emotion and Intercultural Communication," in *Handbook of Applied Linguistics,* Vol. 7: *Intercultural Communication,* ed. H. Kotthoff and H. Spencer-Oatley (Berlin: Mouton–de Gruyter Publishers, 2005).

Chapter 5: Humiliation and Conflict

1. M.G. Marshall, *Third World War: System, Process, and Conflict Dynamics* (Lanham, MD, and London: Rowman and Littlefield, 1999).

2. W. Brandt, "1945 Different Than 1918" (speech at Harvard University, Cambridge, MA, June 5, 1972, at the commemoration of George Marshall's speech 25 years earlier), http://lcweb.loc.gov/exhibits/marshall/m21.html (accessed December 11, 1999).

3. A. Jan, *Peacebuilding in Somalia* (New York: International Peace Academy, 1996), 1, http://www.ipacademy.inter.net/somalia2.htm (accessed November 1999).

4. See, for example, P.J. O'Halloran, *Humanitarian Intervention and the Genocide in Rwanda* (London: Research Institute for the Study of Conflict and Terrorism, 1995).

5. Eight Red Cross and Red Crescent staff were kidnapped at the airport in Mogadishu North. On January 4, 1999, in Nairobi, I interviewed the head of the group, Ola Skuterud from the Norwegian Red Cross, and later also two other hostages as well as the chief negotiator of the Red Cross who brokered their release.

6. *The Greatest Love of All,* song popularized by Whitney Houston.

7. Marshall, *Third World War,* 62.

8. M. Deutsch, *The Resolution of Conflict: Constructive and Destructive Processes* (New Haven, CT: Yale University Press, 1973), 367.

9. Steven Kull directs the PIPA/Knowledge Networks poll, which conducts ongoing surveys of the U.S. public; see http://www.pipa.org/about.html.

10. E. Hale, "The Return of Anti-Americanism," *USA Today,* August 14, 2002, 2, http://www.canadiandimension.mb.ca/extra/d0816eh.htm (accessed March 15, 2003).

11. P. Legrain, *Open World: The Truth About Globalisation* (London: Abacus, 2002).

12. C.A. Kupchan, *The End of the American Era. US Foreign Policy and the Geopolitics of the Twenty-First Century* (New York, NY: Alfred A Knopf, 2002).

Chapter 6: Humiliation and Terrorism

1. L.A. Parry, *The History of Torture in England* (Montclair, NJ: Patterson Smith Publishing Corp., 1975).

2. W.V. Harris, *Restraining Rage: The Ideology of Anger Control in Classical Antiquity* (Cambridge, MA: Harvard University Press, 2002).

3. D. Kagan, "Honor, Interest, and Nation-State," *Honor Among Nations,* ed. E. Abrams (Washington, D.C.: Ethics and Public Policy Center, 1998).

4. B. Wyatt-Brown, *Southern Honor: Ethics and Behavior in the Old South* (New York, NY: Oxford University Press, 1982).

5. Ibid., 2.

6. D.H. Fischer, *Albion's Seed: Four British Folkways in America* (New York, NY: Oxford University Press, 1989), 843.

7. R.E. Nisbett and D. Cohen, *Culture of Honor: The Psychology of Violence in the South* (Boulder, CO: Westview Press, 1996).

8. S.M. Hersh, "Torture at Abu Ghraib: American Soldiers Brutalized Iraqis. How Far Up Does the Responsibility Go?" *The New Yorker,* May 10, 2004, 5, http://www.newyorker.com/printables/fact/040510fa_fact (posted April 30, 2004).

9. W. Sampson, *Confessions of an Innocent Man: Torture and Survival In a Saudi Prison* (Toronto, Ontario, Canada: McClelland & Stewart, 2005).

10. D. Priest, "CIA Holds Terror Suspects in Secret Prisons," *Washington Post,* November 2, 2005, 4, http://www.washingtonpost.com/wp-dyn/content/article/2005/11/01/AR2005110101644_pf.html.

11. S. Sontag, "Regarding the Torture of Others," *The New York Times,* May 23, 2004, 2, http://www.nytimes.com/2004/05/23/magazine/23PRISONS.html?ei=1&en=c0146bd0d219d6fe&ex=1086188191&pagewanted=print&position=.

12. December 5, 2005, http://news.bbc.co.uk/1/hi/world/americas/4506682.stm.

13. S. Milgram, *Obedience to Authority* (New York: Harper and Row, 1974).

14. M.K. Huggins, M. Haritos-Fatouros, and P.G. Zimbardo, *Violence Workers: Police Torturers and Murderers Reconstruct Brazilian Atrocities* (Berkeley, CA: University of California Press, 2002), 237.

15. Ibid., 239.

16. Ibid.

17. S. Graessner, ed. *At the Side of Torture Survivors: Treating a Terrible Assault on Human Dignity* (Baltimore, MD: The Johns Hopkins University Press, 2001), 13.

18. Ibid., 13.

19. Farida's predicament resonates with what Toni Morrison describes in her novel *Beloved* [T. Morrison, *Beloved: A Novel* (New York, NY: Knopf, 1987)], where she describes the killing of a baby so as to protect it from the fate of slavery. I thank Morton Deutsch for making me aware of this novel.

20. My field of psychological counseling from 1980–1984 was *eating disorders,* and I facilitated therapeutic groups with women with such disorders.

21. Other young women such as Rita, intelligent and promising young pupils and students, may even manage to kill themselves by not eating—the extreme consequence of anorexia nervosa—while others, those who do not induce vomiting, oscillate between asceticism and obesity.

22. A. Hitler, *Mein Kampf* (London: Pimlico, 1999; original work published in 1925–1926).

23. T.J. Scheff, "Shame in Self and Society," *Symbolic Interaction* 26, no. 2 (2003): 239–262.

24. International Committee of the Red Cross Somalia Delegation, *Spared From the Spear: Traditional Somali Behaviour in Warfare* (Nairobi: International Committee of the Red Cross, 1997).

25. In regions that practice blood feud, women are untouched, and they have to assume all the duties that their males cannot carry out anymore are because they have to stay indoors out of fear of being killed. Albania experienced an upsurge of these practices after the downfall of the communist regime that had outlawed them. Thousands of men are currently confined to their own homes, while their women move freely.

26. Human Rights Watch, *Shattered Lives: Sexual Violence During the Rwandan Genocide and Its Aftermath,* September ed. (New York: Human Rights Watch, 1996), 41.

27. Quoted from www.BBCWorld.com, Kimche and Malki talked to Tim Sebastian on BBC World *HARDtalk* on May 22, 2003.

28. F.D. Roosevelt, *Quarantine the Aggressors,* 1937, http://www.nvcc.edu/home/nvsageh/ Hist122/Part4/FDRQuar.htm (accessed July 6, 2003).

29. R. Lemov, *World As Laboratory: Experiments With Mice, Mazes and Men* (New York, NY: Farrar, Straus, and Giroux, 2005).

30. R. Lemov, "The American Science of Interrogation: Debility, Dependency and Dread," *Los Angeles Times,* October 22, 2005, 1, http://www.latimes.com/news/opinion/ commentary/la-oe-lemov22oct22,0,3219677.

31. Ibid., 1.

Chapter 7: The Humiliation Addiction

1. A.S. Reber, *The Penguin Dictionary of Psychology,* 2nd ed. (Harmondsworth: Penguin, 1995).

2. W. Mischel and A.L. De Smet, "Self-Regulation in the Service of Conflict Resolution," *The Handbook of Conflict Resolution: Theory and Practice,* ed. M. Deutsch (San Francisco: Jossey-Bass, 2000), 256–275.

3. Ibid., 259.

4. Ibid., 263.

5. Ibid., 263–264.

6. A. Margalit, *The Ethics of Memory* (Cambridge, MA: Harvard University Press, 2002).

7. J.S. Goldman and P.T. Coleman, *How Humiliation Fuels Intractable Conflict: The Effects of Emotional Roles on Recall and Reactions to Conflictual Encounters* (New York, NY: International Center for Cooperation & Conflict Resolution, Teachers College, Columbia University, 2005), 15.

8. http://www.austin360.com/shared/health/adam/ency/article/000943.html (accessed May 2002).

9. S.C. Eckleberry, *The Dual Diagnosis,* 5, http://www.toad.net/~arcturus/dd/papd.htm (accessed May 20, 2002).

10. Ibid., 5.

11. Ibid., 7.

12. Ibid., 5.

13. Ibid., 7.

14. Read H.C. Kelman, "The Interdependence of Israeli and Palestinian National Identities: The Role of the Other in Existential Conflicts," *Journal of Social Issues* 55 (1999): 581–600, on the role of the other in existential conflicts.

15. Among others, in Lindner, "Humiliation and Reactions to Hitler's Seductiveness in Post-War Germany," and Lindner, "Were Ordinary Germans Hitler's 'Willing Executioners'?"

16. Charny, "A Personality Disorder of Excessive Power Strivings."

17. J. Siegel, "A New Diagnosis for the Power Hungry," *Jerusalem Post,* August 20, 1997, 1-1, 1.

18. T.J. Scheff, (2002). "Emotions and Politics," Eilert Sundt Lecture, University of Oslo, October 24, 2002.

19. Adapted from Lindner, "The Psychology of Humiliation," 183.

20. Ibid., 351.

21. Among others, in Lindner, "Humiliation and Reactions to Hitler's Seductiveness"; Lindner, "Were Ordinary Germans Hitler's 'Willing Executioners'?"

22. B.D. Perry, "Incubated in Terror: Neurodevelopmental Factors in the 'Cycle of Violence,'" *Children, Youth and Violence: the Search for Solutions,* ed. J.D. Osofsky (New York, NY: Guilford Press, 1997), 124–148, http://www.bcm.tmc.edu/civitas/incubated.htm (accessed March 15, 2000).
23. Elliott Leyton, March, 25, 2003, on CBC National radio.
24. A. Miller, *For Your Own Good.*
25. Lindner, "The Psychology of Humiliation," 149.

Chapter 8: The Humiliation Antidote

1. Nelson Mandela in his inaugural address as president, May 10, 1994.
2. Please see, for example, Michael Jesse Battle, *Reconciliation. The Ubuntu Theology of Desmond Tutu* (Cleveland, OH: Pilgrim Press, 1997).
3. M.S. Granovetter, *The Strength of Weak Ties* 78 (May 1973): 1360–1380.
4. Ferdinand Tönnies (1855–1936) was a major contributor to sociological theory and field studies. Tönnies is best known for his distinction between two types of social groups— Gemeinschaft and Gesellschaft.
5. M.H. Bond, "Culture and Aggression—From Context to Coercion," *Personality and Social Psychology Review* 8 (2004): 62–78.
6. M. Volf, *Exclusion and Embrace: a Theological Exploration and Identity, Otherness, and Reconciliation* (Nashville, TN: Abingdon Press, 1996).
7. On May 23, 2002, he was interviewed by Tim Sebastian on BBC World *HARDtalk.*
8. E. Goffman, *Frame Analysis: An Essay on the Organization of Experience* (New York, NY: Harper and Row, 1974).
9. E.R. Borris, "The Healing Power of Forgiveness" (paper, course on Reconciliation Processes, Institute of Conflict Analysis and Resolution, George Mason University, Fairfax, VA, March 13–15, 2000).
10. V.E. Frankl, *Man's Search for Meaning: An Introduction to Logotherapy* (Boston, MA: Beacon Press, 1963).
11. R.J. Lifton, *The Protean Self: Human Resilience in the Age of Fragmentation* (Chicago, IL: University of Chicago Press, 1999).
12. Heffermehl, in N.R. Mandela, "Welcome to Robben Island," *Peace Is Possible,* ed. F.S. Heffermehl [Geneva: International Peace Bureau (IPB) with the support of UNESCO, 2001], 35, 87–89.
13. D.S. Dia, "The Fight Against Female Genital Cutting," *Wal Fadjri Newspaper,* April 3, 2003, 1, received as email text.
14. G. Lakoff and M. Johnson, *Philosophy in the Flesh: The Embodied Mind and Its Challenge to Western Thought* (New York, NY: Basic Books, 1999), 316.
15. R. Axelrod, *The Evolution of Cooperation* (London: Penguin Books, 1990).
16. M. Deutsch, *The Resolution of Conflict: Constructive and Destructive Processes* (New Haven, CT: Yale University Press, 1973), 367.
17. P. Singer, *A Darwinian Left: Politics, Evolution and Cooperation* (London: Weidenfeld & Nicolson, 1999).
18. C. Helfferich, "The Games of Evolutionary Economics," *Alaska Science Forum,* September 1, 1993, Article 1149, 1, http://www.gi.alaska.edu/ScienceForum/ASF11/1149.html (accessed April 15, 2003).
19. C. Nelder, "Envisioning a Sustainable Future," *BWZine (The Online Better World Magazine)* (October/November/December 1996): 10.

20. M. Buber, *I and Thou* (Edinburgh: Clark, 1944).

21. Robert M. Solow, "Technical Change and the Aggregate Production Function," *Review of Economics and Statistics* 39 (1957): 312–320.

22. Deutsch, "Oppression and Conflict," 35–36.

23. Ervin Staub, *The Roots of Evil: The Origins of Genocide and Other Group Violence* (Cambridge, UK: Cambridge University Press, 1989).

24. P.T. Coleman, "Characteristics of Protracted, Intractable Conflict: Toward the Development of a Metaframework-I," *Peace and Conflict: Journal of Peace Psychology* 9, no. 1 (2003): 1–37.

25. D.W. Johnson, R.T. Johnson, and D. Tjosvold, "Constructive Controversy: The Value of Intellectual Opposition," *The Handbook of Conflict Resolution: Theory and Practice,* edited by Morton Deutsch and Peter T. Coleman (San Francisco, CA: Jossey-Bass, 2000), 66.

26. Mischel and De Smet, *The Handbook of Conflict Resolution,* 256–275.

27. Ernest Gellner, *Nations and Nationalism* (Ithaca, NY: Cornell University Press, 1983).

28. From the Web site of the United Nations High Commissioner for Refugees (UNHCR), 2001.

29. See for a recent publication J. Jeffrey Sachs, *The End of Poverty: Economic Possibilities for Our Time* (New York: Penguin Group, 2005). Also, see http://www.un.org/millenniumgoals/.

30. R.H. Jackson, *Quasi-States, Sovereignty, International Relations and the Third World* (Cambridge, UK: Cambridge University Press, 1990).

31. R.D. Kaplan, "The Coming Anarchy," *The Atlantic Monthly* (February 1994), 44–76.

32. On BBC World *HARDtalk* with Jon Sopel.

33. A. Margalit, *The Decent Society* (Cambridge, MA: Harvard University Press, 1996).

Chapter 9: The Future of Humiliation

1. M. Kaku, *Parallel Worlds: A Journey Through Creation, Higher Dimensions, and the Future of the Cosmos* (New York, London, Toronto, Sydney, Auckland: Doubleday, 2005), 361.

2. See the work by Norbert Elias.

3. Friedman, *The World is Flat.*

4. D. Benjamin and S. Simon, *The Next Attack: The Failure of the War on Terror and a Strategy for Getting It Right* (New York, NY: Times Books, 2005).

5. D.A. Hamburg, *No More Killing Fields: Preventing Deadly Conflict* (Lanham, MD: Rowman and Littlefield, 2002).

6. http://www.coexistence.net.

7. N.R. Mandela, *A Long Walk to Freedom: The Autobiography of Nelson Mandela* (London: Little Brown, 1994).

8. Retrieved from http://www.foe.co.uk/pubsinfo/infoteam/pressrel/2001/20011102112007.html, a Web site that informs of a *Trade Justice Parade* in central London on November 3, 2001, as world governments prepared to travel to Doha, Qatar, for *World Trade Organization* talks.

9. To be found, for example, on http://www.tve.org/earthreport/archive/doc.cfm?aid=904.

10. P. Legrain, *Open World: The Truth About Globalisation* (London: Abacus, 2002).

11. J. Sachs, *The End of Poverty: Economic Possibilities for Our Time* (New York: Penguin Group, 2005).

12. U. Beck, *World Risk Society* (Cambridge, UK: Polity Press, 2000); L.M. Hartling, "Strengthening Resilience in a Risky World: It Is All About Relationships," *Work in Progress, No. 101* (Wellesley, MA: Stone Center Working Papers Series, 2003).

13. See for work on the information age M. Castells, *The Information Age: Economy, Society and Culture,* Vol. 1: *The Rise of the Network Society;* Vol. 2: *The Power of Identity;* Vol. 3: *End of Millennium* (Cambridge, MA, Oxford, UK: Blackwell, 1996–1997). See also T.W. Luke and C. Toulouse, eds., *The Politics of Cyberspace: A New Political Science Reader* (New York, NY: Routledge, 1998). The Internet offers many sites with more information on the sociology of cyberspace and issues relating to technoculture and social relations.

14. See, for example, D.A. Hamburg and B.A. Hamburg, *Learning to Live Together: Preventing Hatred and Violence in Child and Adolescent Development* (New York: Oxford University Press, 2004).

15. Mischel and De Smet, *The Handbook of Conflict Resolution.*

16. See, for example, M.L. Minow, "Between Vengeance and Forgiveness: South Africa's Truth and Reconciliation Commission," *Negotiation Journal* 14, no. 4 (1998): 319–355.

17. Howard Zehr pioneered work in transforming our understandings of justice; see, for example, H. Zehr, *The Little Book of Restorative Justice* (Intercourse, PA: Good Books, 2002).

18. Simon Bowen, *The Forgiveness Conference,* October 18, 1999, The Findhorn Foundation, http://www.findhorn.org/events/conferences/archives/forgive/bamber.html (accessed April 2003).

19. I thank Morton Deutsch for this thought, which he communicated to me in a personal conversation in July 2003.

20. Deutsch, "Oppression and Conflict," 21–22.

21. See, for example, W.D. Hartung, *And Weapons for All* (New York, NY: Harper Collins, 1994).

22. There exists a wide spectrum of literature on early warning. For efforts to collect societal indicators that can serve as alarm signals, see, for example, the *Integrated Network for Societal Conflict Research (INSCR)* program at the *Center for International Development and Conflict Management (CIDCM),* University of Maryland.

23. This book is not the place to discuss how exactly such institutions should or could look and how current national sovereignty may be reconciled with democratically anchored global institutions. These are tasks that will take decades to bring about. This book merely wishes to delineate the path.

24. C. Denny and J. Freedland, "New Zealand Warns on 'Law of the Jungle,'" *The Guardian,* May 3, 2003.

25. A. Margalit, *The Decent Society* (Cambridge, MA: Harvard University Press, 1996).

26. Similar to the *Moratorium on Trade in Small Arms* or the *Moratorium on Commercial Whaling.* Read, for example, C. Patten and A. Lindh, "Let's Control the Small Arms Trade," *International Herald Tribune,* June 30, 2001.

REFERENCES

Adorno, T.W., E. Frenkel-Brunswick, D.J. Levinson, and R.N. Sanford. *The Authoritarian Personality.* 1st ed. New York, NY: Harper, 1950.

Allred, K.G. "Anger and Retaliation: Toward an Understanding of Impassioned Conflict in Organizations." *Research on Negotiations in Organizations.* Vol. 7, edited by Robert J. Bies, Roy J. Lewicki, and Blair H. Sheppard. Greenwich, CT: JAI Press, 1999.

Anderson, M.B. *Do No Harm: How Aid Can Support Peace—or War.* Boulder, CO: Lynne Rienner Publishers, 1999.

Averill, J.R. *Anger and Aggression: An Essay on Emotion.* New York: Springer-Verlag, 1982.

Axelrod, R. *The Evolution of Cooperation.* London: Penguin Books, 1990.

Badiou, A. *Ethics: An Essay on the Understanding of Evil.* London: Verso, 2001.

Baratta, Joseph Preston. *The Politics of World Federation.* Vol. 1: *The United Nations, U.N. Reform, Atomic Control;* Vol. 2: *From World Federalism to Global Governance.* Westport, CT: Praeger, 2004.

Bar-On, D., and A. Nadler. *From Peace Making and Conflict Resolution to Conciliation and Peace Building.* Proposal for the International Award of the State of Nordrhine-Westfalia for Research in the Humanities and Social Sciences. Beer-Sheva, Israel: 1999.

Battle, Michael Jesse. *Reconciliation. The Ubuntu Theology of Desmond Tutu.* Cleveland, OH: Pilgrim Press, 1997.

Bauman, Z. *Intimations of Postmodernity.* London: Routledge, 1992.

Beck, U. *World Risk Society.* Cambridge, UK: Polity Press, 2000.

Benjamin, D., and S. Simon. *The Next Attack: The Failure of the War on Terror and a Strategy for Getting It Right.* New York, NY: Times Books, 2005.

Billig, M.G. *Ideology and Opinions. Studies in Rhetorical Psychology.* London: Sage, 1991.

Bloom, H. *Shakespeare: The Invention of the Human.* London: Fourth Estate, 1999.

Bond, M.H. "Unity in Diversity: Orientations and Strategies for Building a Harmonious, Multicultural Society." *Social Psychology and Cultural Context.* Edited by John Adamopoulos and Yoshihisa Kashima, 17–40. Thousand Oaks, CA: Sage, 1998.

Bond, M.H. "Culture and Aggression—From Context to Coercion." *Personality and Social Psychology Review* 8 (2004): 62–78.

Borris, E.R. "The Healing Power of Forgiveness." Paper prepared for course on Reconciliation Processes, Institute of Conflict Analysis and Resolution, George Mason University, Fairfax, VA, March 13–15, 2000.

Braithwaite, J. *Crime, Shame and Reintegration.* Cambridge, UK: Cambridge University Press, 1989.

Brandt, W. "1945 Different Than 1918." Speech at Harvard University, Cambridge, MA, June 5, 1972, at the commemoration of George Marshall's speech 25 years earlier. German Information Center, ed. *The Marshall Plan and the Future of U.S.-European Relations,* 13–24. New York, NY: German Information Center. http://lcweb.loc.gov/exhibits/marshall/m21.html (accessed December 11, 1999).

Briggs, Robin. *Witches and Neighbors: The Social and Cultural Context of European Witchcraft,* 262. New York: Penguin, 1998.

Buber, M. *I and Thou.* Edinburgh: Clark, 1944.

Castells, M. *The Information Age: Economy, Society and Culture.* Vol. 1: *The Rise of the Network Society;* Vol. 2: *The Power of Identity;* Vol. 3: *End of Millennium.* Cambridge, MA, Oxford, UK: Blackwell, 1996–1997.

Charny, I.W. "A Personality Disorder of Excessive Power Strivings." *Israel Journal of Psychiatry* 34, no. 1 (1997): 3–17.

Coleman, P.T. "Power and Conflict." *The Handbook of Conflict Resolution: Theory and Practice.* Edited by Morton Deutsch and Peter T. Coleman, 108–130. San Francisco, CA: Jossey-Bass, 2000.

Coleman, P.T. "Characteristics of Protracted, Intractable Conflict: Toward the Development of a Metaframework-I." *Peace and Conflict: Journal of Peace Psychology* 9, no. 1 (2003): 1–37.

Coser, L.A. *Masters of Sociological Thought: Ideas in Historical and Social Context.* 2nd ed. Fort Worth, TX: Harcourt Brace Jovanovich, 1977.

Denny, C., and J. Freedland. "New Zealand Warns on 'Law of the Jungle.'" *The Guardian,* May 3, 2003.

Des Forges, A.L., and Human Rights Watch. *Leave None to Tell the Story. Genocide in Rwanda.* New York, NY: Human Rights Watch, 1999.

Deutsch, M. *The Resolution of Conflict: Constructive and Destructive Processes.* New Haven, CT: Yale University Press, 1973.

Deutsch, M. "Oppression and Conflict." Plenary address given at the annual meetings of the International Society of Justice Research, Skovde, Sweden, June 17, 2002. http//www.cpa.ca/epw/epw/Deutsch.pdf (accessed November 20, 2002).

Deutsch, M. "A Framework for Thinking About Oppression and Its Change." *Social Justice Research* (2006).

Dia, D.S. "The Fight Against Female Genital Cutting." *Wal Fadjri Newspaper,* April 3, 2003 (received as email text).

Douglas, Mary. *Purity and Danger: An Analysis of the Concepts of Pollution and Taboo.* London: Ark Paperbacks, 1984.

Dutton, D.G., E.O. Boyanowsky, and M.H. Bond. "Extreme Mass Homicide: From Military Massacre to Genocide." *Aggression and Violent Behavior* 10 (2005): 437–473.

Eckleberry, S.C. *The Dual Diagnosis,* 2000. http://www.toad.net/~arcturus/dd/papd.htm (accessed May 20, 2002).

Elias, N. *The Civilizing Process.* Vol. 1: *The History of Manners;* Vol. 2: *State Formation and Civilization.* Oxford: Blackwell, 1994.

Eriksen, T.H. "Ethnic Identity, National Identity and Intergroup Conflict: The Significance of Personal Experiences." *Social Identity, Intergroup Conflict, and Conflict Reduction.* Edited by Richard D. Ashmore, Lee J. Jussim, and David A. Wilder, 42–70. Oxford: Oxford University Press, 2001. http://folk.uio.no/geirthe/Identity_politics.html (accessed July 20, 2003).

Fanon, F. *Black Skin, White Masks.* London: Pluto Press, 1986.

Featherstone, M., ed. *Global Culture: Nationalism, Globalism and Modernity.* London: Sage, 1990.

Feil, S.R. "Preventing Genocide: How the Early Use of Force Might Have Succeeded in Rwanda." Report to the Carnegie Commission on Preventing Deadly Conflict, Washington, D.C., April 1998.

Fischer, D.H. *Albion's Seed: Four British Folkways in America.* New York, NY: Oxford University Press, 1989.

Frankl, V.E. *Man's Search for Meaning: An Introduction to Logotherapy.* Boston, MA: Beacon Press, 1963.

Frazer, J.G. *The Golden Bough: A Study in Magic and Religion.* Abridged edition. New York: Macmillan, 1922. http://www.sacred-texts.com/pag/frazer/ (accessed April 2003).

Friedman, Thomas L. *The World is Flat: A Brief History of the Twenty-First Century.* New York, NY: Farrar, Straus, and Giroux, 2005.

Fuller, R.W. *Somebodies and Nobodies: Overcoming the Abuse of Rank.* Gabriola Island, Canada: New Societies Publishers, 2003.

Gaertner, S.L., and J.F. Dovidio. *Reducing Intergroup Bias: The Common Ingroup Identity Model.* Hove, UK: Psychology Press, 1999.

Galtung, J. *Peace by Peaceful Means.* Oslo and London: PRIO (International Peace Research Institute Oslo) and Sage, 1996.

Gellner, Ernest. *Nations and Nationalism.* Ithaca, NY: Cornell University Press, 1983.

Gergen, K.J. "Organizational Science in a Postmodern Context." Swarthmore College: Draft copy for *Journal of Behavioral Science,* 2000. http://www.swarthmore.edu/SocSci/kgergen1/text10.html (accessed January 6, 2000).

Gergen, K.J., and M.M. Gergen. "Toward a Cultural Constructionist Psychology." Swarthmore College, Pennsylvania State University: 2000. http://www.swarthmore.edu/SocSci/kgergen1/tccp.html (accessed January 6, 2000).

Gilligan, J. *Violence: Our Deadly Epidemic and How to Treat It.* New York, NY: Putnam, 1996.

Goffman, E. *Frame Analysis: An Essay on the Organization of Experience.* New York, NY: Harper and Row, 1974.

Goldman, J.S., and P.T. Coleman. *How Humiliation Fuels Intractable Conflict: The Effects of Emotional Roles on Recall and Reactions to Conflictual Encounters.* New York, NY: International Center for Cooperation & Conflict Resolution, Teachers College, Columbia University, 2005.

Graessner, S., ed. *At the Side of Torture Survivors: Treating a Terrible Assault on Human Dignity.* Baltimore, MD: The Johns Hopkins University Press, 2001.

Granovetter, M.S. "The Strength of Weak Ties." *American Journal of Sociology* 78 (May 1973): 1360–1380.

Greenfeld, L. *Nationalism: Five Roads to Modernity.* Cambridge, MA: Harvard University Press, 1992.

Greenfeld, L. "Nationalism and Modernity." *Social Research* 63, no. 1 (1996): 3–40.

Guha, R., and G.C. Spivak, eds. *Selected Subaltern Studies.* New York, NY: Oxford University Press, 1988.

Haas, J. "Warfare and the Evolution of Culture." Working Papers 98-11-088. Santa Fe, NM: Santa Fe Institute, 1998. http://www.santafe.edu/sfi/publications/Working-Papers/98-10-088.pdf (accessed November 15, 2002).

Hale, E. "The Return of Anti-Americanism." *USA Today,* August 14, 2002. http://www.canadiandimension.mb.ca/extra/d0816eh.htm (accessed March 15, 2003).

Hale, R.L. "The Role of Humiliation and Embarrassment in Serial Murder." *Psychology. A Journal of Human Behaviour* 31, no. 2 (1994): 17–23.

Hamburg, D.A. *No More Killing Fields: Preventing Deadly Conflict.* Lanham, MD: Rowman and Littlefield, 2002.

Hamburg, D.A., and B.A. Hamburg. *Learning to Live Together: Preventing Hatred and Violence in Child and Adolescent Development.* New York: Oxford University Press, 2004.

Harris, M. *Culture, People, Nature: An Introduction to General Anthropology.* London and New York, NY: Longman, 1997.

Harris, W.V. *Restraining Rage: The Ideology of Anger Control in Classical Antiquity.* Cambridge, MA: Harvard University Press, 2002.

Hartling, L.M. "Strengthening Resilience in a Risky World: It Is All About Relationships." Work in Progress, No. 101, Wellesley, MA: Stone Center Working Papers Series, 2003.

Hartling, L.M. "Humiliation: Real Pain, a Pathway to Violence." Preliminary draft of a paper prepared for Round Table 2 of the 2005 Workshop on Humiliation and Violent Conflict, Columbia University, New York, December 15–16, 2005. www.humiliationstudies.org/documents/HartlingNY05meetingRT2.pdf.

Hartling, L.M. and T.Luchetta. "Humiliation: Assessing the Impact of Derision, Degradation, and Debasement." *Journal of Primary Prevention* 19, no. 5 (1999): 259–278.

Hartung, W.D. *And Weapons for All.* New York, NY: HarperCollins, 1994.

Harvey, J. *Civilized Oppression.* Lanham, MD: Rowman and Littlefield Publishers, 1999.

Heider, F. *The Psychology of Interpersonal Relations.* New York, NY: Wiley, 1958.

Helfferich, C. "The Games of Evolutionary Economics." *Alaska Science Forum,* Article 1149 (September 1, 1993). http://www.gi.alaska.edu/ScienceForum/ASF11/1149.html (accessed April 15, 2003).

Hersh, S.M. "Torture at Abu Ghraib: American Soldiers Brutalized Iraqis. How Far Up Does the Responsibility Go?" *The New Yorker,* May 10, 2004. http://www.newyorker.com/printables/fact/040510fa_fact (posted April 30, 2004).

Herz, J.H. "Idealist Internationalism and the Security Dilemma." *World Politics* II (1950): 157–180.

Hitler, A. *Mein Kampf.* London: Pimlico, 1999; original work published in 1925–1926.

Hobbes, T. *Leviathan.* The APHIL Library, 1651. http://coombs.anu.edu.au/Depts/RSSS/Philosophy/Texts/LeviathanTOC.html (accessed November 9, 2000).

Hofstede, G.H. *Culture's Consequences: International Differences in Work-Related Values.* Beverly Hills, CA: Sage, 1980.

Honneth, A. "Recognition and Moral Obligation." *Social Research* 64, no. 1 (1997): 16–35.

Hudnall, A.C., and Evelin G. Lindner. "Crisis and Gender: Addressing the Psychosocial Needs of Women in International Disasters." In *Handbook of International Disaster Psychology,* Vol. 4: *Interventions With Special Needs Populations,* edited by Gilbert Reyes and Gerard A. Jacobs, 1–18. Westport, CT: Praeger, 2005.

Huggins, M.K., M. Haritos-Fatouros, and P.G. Zimbardo. *Violence Workers: Police Torturers and Murderers Reconstruct Brazilian Atrocities.* Berkeley, CA: University of California Press, 2002.

Human Rights Watch. *Shattered Lives: Sexual Violence During the Rwandan Genocide and Its Aftermath.* September edition. New York: Human Rights Watch, 1996.

Huntington, S.P. *The Clash of Civilizations and the Remaking of World Order.* New York, NY: Simon and Schuster, 1996.

Hyde, Janet Shibley. "The Gender Similarities Hypothesis." *American Psychologist,* 60, no. 6 (2005): 581–92. http://www.apa.org/journals/releases/amp606581.pdf.

International Committee of the Red Cross Somalia Delegation. *Spared From the Spear: Traditional Somali Behaviour in Warfare.* Nairobi: International Committee of the Red Cross, 1997.

International Panel of Eminent Personalities to Investigate the 1994 Genocide in Rwanda and the Surrounding Events. *Rwanda: The Preventable Genocide.* 2000. www.oau-oua.org/ (accessed September 30, 2000).

Jackson, R.H. *Quasi-States, Sovereignty, International Relations and the Third World.* Cambridge, UK: Cambridge University Press, 1990.

Jan, A. *Peacebuilding in Somalia.* New York: International Peace Academy, 1996. http:// www.ipacademy.inter.net/somalia2.htm (accessed November 1999).

Jandt, F.E. *Intercultural Communication: An Introduction.* Thousand Oaks, CA: Sage, 1995.

Jervis, R., R.N. Lebow, and J.G. Stein. *Psychology and Deterrence.* Baltimore, MD: The Johns Hopkins University Press, 1985.

Johnson, D.W., R.T. Johnson, and D. Tjosvold. "Constructive Controversy: The Value of Intellectual Opposition." *The Handbook of Conflict Resolution: Theory and Practice,* edited by Morton Deutsch and Peter T. Coleman, 65–85. San Francisco, CA: Jossey-Bass, 2000.

Jones, A. "Gendercide and Genocide." *Journal of Genocide Research,* 2, no. 2 (June 1, 2000): 185–211.

Kagan, D. "Honor, Interest, and Nation-State." *Honor Among Nations,* edited by Elliot Abrams. Washington, D.C.: Ethics and Public Policy Center, 1998.

Kaku, M. *Parallel Worlds: A Journey Through Creation, Higher Dimensions, and the Future of the Cosmos.* New York, London, Toronto, Sydney, Auckland: Doubleday, 2005.

Kaplan, R.D. "The Coming Anarchy." *The Atlantic Monthly* (February 1994): 44–76.

Keen, S. *Faces of the Enemy: Reflections of the Hostile Imagination.* San Francisco, CA: Harper and Row, 1986.

Kelley, H.H. "The Processes of Causal Attribution." *American Psychologist* 28, no. 107 (1973): 128.

Kelman, H.C. "The Interdependence of Israeli and Palestinian National Identities: The Role of the Other in Existential Conflicts." *Journal of Social Issues* 55 (1999): 581–600.

Klein, D.C. "Introduction to the Issue." *The Journal of Primary Prevention* 12 (December 2, 1991): 87–91.

Klein, D.C. "The Humiliation Dynamic: An Overview." ("The Humiliation Dynamic: Viewing the Task of Prevention From a New Perspective." Part I Section One: The Humiliation Dynamic.) *The Journal of Primary Prevention* 12 (December 2, 1991): 93–121.

Klein, D.C. "Introduction to the Issue." *The Journal of Primary Prevention* 12 (March 3, 1992): 189–193.

Kluckhohn, F.R., and F.L. Strodtbeck. *Variations in Value Orientations.* Evanston, IL: Row, Peterson, 1961.

Kupchan, C.A. *The End of the American Era. US Foreign Policy and the Geopolitics of the Twenty-First Century.* New York, NY: Alfred A. Knopf, 2002.

Lakoff, G., and M. Johnson. *Philosophy in the Flesh: The Embodied Mind and Its Challenge to Western Thought.* New York, NY: Basic Books, 1999.

Legrain, P. *Open World: The Truth About Globalisation.* London: Abacus, 2002.

Lemov, R. (2005a). The American Science of Interrogation: Debility, Dependency and Dread. *Los Angeles Times,* October 22, 2005. http://www.latimes.com/news/opinion/commentary/la-oe-lemov22oct22,0,3219677.

Lemov, R. (2005b). *World As Laboratory: Experiments With Mice, Mazes and Men.* New York, NY: Farrar, Straus, and Giroux, 2005.

Lewis, H.B. *Shame and Guilt in Neurosis.* New York, NY: International Universities Press, 1971.

Leyton, E. *Touched by Fire. Doctors Without Borders in a Third World Crisis.* Toronto: McClelland and Stewart, 2000.

Lifton, R.J. *The Protean Self: Human Resilience in the Age of Fragmentation.* Chicago, IL: University of Chicago Press, 1999.

Lindner, Evelin G. "Lebensqualität im ägyptisch-deutschen Vergleich. Eine interkulturelle Untersuchung an drei Berufsgruppen (Ärzte, Journalisten, Künstler)." Doctoral dissertation in Medicine, Department of Psychological Medicine, University of Hamburg, 1994.

Lindner, Evelin G. "Women in the Global Village: Increasing Demand for Traditional Communication Patterns." *Towards a Women's Agenda for a Culture of Peace,* edited by Ingeborg Breines, Dorota Gierycz, and Betty Reardon, 89–98. Paris: UNESCO, 1999.

Lindner, Evelin G. (2000a). "The Psychology of Humiliation: Somalia, Rwanda/Burundi, and Hitler's Germany." Doctoral dissertation in Psychology, Department of Psychology, University of Oslo, 2000.

Lindner, Evelin G. (2000b). "The Relational Anatomy of Humiliation: Perpetrator, Victim, and Third Party." Human Dignity and Humiliation Studies, 2000. http://www.humiliationstudies.org/documents/evelin/RelationalAnatomyHumiliation.pdf.

Lindner, Evelin G. (2000c). "Were Ordinary Germans Hitler's 'Willing Executioners'? Or Were They Victims of Humiliating Seduction and Abandonment? The Case of Germany and Somalia." *IDEA: A Journal of Social Issues* 5, no. 1 (2000). http://www.ideajournal.com/lindner-willing-executioners.html.

Lindner, Evelin G. (2000d). *What Every Negotiator Ought to Know: Understanding Humiliation.* Coalition for Global Solidarity and Social Development, Peace and Conflicts, 2000. http://globalsolidarity.transcend.org/articles/what.pdf.

Lindner, Evelin G. (2001a). "How Research Can Humiliate: Critical Reflections on Method." *Journal for the Study of Peace and Conflict,* Annual edition (2001–2002): 16–36. http://jspc.library.wisc.edu/.

Lindner, Evelin G. (2001b). "Humiliation—Trauma That Has Been Overlooked: An Analysis Based on Fieldwork in Germany, Rwanda/Burundi, and Somalia." *TRAUMATOLOGYe* 7, no. 1 (2001): Article 3 (32 pages). http://www.fsu.edu/%7Etrauma/v7/Humiliation.pdf.

Lindner, Evelin G. (2001c). "Humiliation and the Human Condition: Mapping a Minefield." *Human Rights Review* 2, no. 2 (2001): 46–63.

Lindner, Evelin G. (2001d). "Humiliation as the Source of Terrorism: A New Paradigm." *Peace Research* 33, no. 2 (2001): 59–68.

Lindner, Evelin G. (2001e). "Women and Terrorism: The Lessons of Humiliation." *New Routes: A Journal for Peace Research and Action. Special Issue: Targeting Women* 6, no. 3

(2001): 10–12. See full text in www.life-peace.org under http://www.life-peace.org/newroutes/newroutes2001/nr200103/lessonsofhum0301.htm.

Lindner, Evelin G. "Healing the Cycles of Humiliation: How to Attend to the Emotional Aspects of 'Unsolvable' Conflicts and the Use of 'Humiliation Entrepreneurship.'" *Peace and Conflict: Journal of Peace Psychology* 8, no. 2 (2002): 125–138.

Lindner, Evelin G. "Humiliation or Dignity: Regional Conflicts in the *Global Village*." *The International Journal of Mental Health, Psychosocial Work and Counselling in Areas of Armed Conflict* 1, no. 1 (January 2003): 48–63. See also http://www.transnational.org/forum/meet/2002/Lindner_RegionalConflicts.html.

Lindner, Evelin G. (2004a). "Humiliation in a Globalizing World: Does Humiliation Become the Most Disruptive Force?" Paper prepared for the "Workshop on Humiliation and Violent Conflict," Columbia University, New York, NY, November 18–19, 2004. http://www.humiliationstudies.org/whoweare/evelin13.php.

Lindner, Evelin G. (2004b). "Gendercide and Humiliation in Honor and Human-Rights Societies." *Gendercide and Genocide,* edited by Adam Jones. Nashville, TN: Vanderbilt University Press, 2004.

Lindner, Evelin G. (2005a). "Die Psychologie der Demütigung." *Punktum, Fach- und Verbandszeitschrift des Schweizerischen Berufsverbandes für angewandte Psychologie SBAP* (März 2005): 3–8.

Lindner, Evelin G. (2005b). "Human Rights, Humiliation, and Globalization." *Symbolik, Gesellschaftliche Irrationalität und Psychohistorie, Jahrbuch für Psychohistorische Forschung,* Vol. 5, edited by Ludwig Janus, Florian Galler, and Winfried Kurth, 143–172. Heidelberg: Mattes Verlag, 2004.

Lindner, Evelin G. (2005c). "Mature Differentiation as Response to Terrorism and Humiliation: Refrain from the Language of 'War' and 'Evil.'" *Transnational Foundation for Peace and Future Research.* http://www.transnational.org/tff/people/e_lindner.html.

Lindner, Evelin G. (2006a). "Emotion and Conflict." *The Handbook of Conflict Resolution: Theory and Practice,* edited by Morton Deutsch, Peter T. Coleman, and Eric C. Marcus. 2nd ed. San Francisco, CA: Jossey-Bass, 2006.

Lindner, Evelin G. (2006b). "Humiliation and Reactions to Hitler's Seductiveness in Post-War Germany: Personal Reflections." Special issue "Humiliation and History in Global Perspectives," *Social Alternatives* 25, no. 1, first quarter (2006).

Lindner, Evelin G. (2006c). "Humiliation, Killing, War, and Gender." *The Psychology of Resolving Global Conflicts: From War to Peace.* Vol. 1: *Nature Vs. Nurture,* edited by Mari Fitzduff and Chris E. Stout, 137–174. Westport, CT, London: Praeger Security International, 2006.

Lindner, Evelin G., Judy Kuriansky, and N.R. Walsh. "Humiliation or Dignity in the Israeli-Palestinian Conflict." *Psychosocial Approaches to the Israeli/Palestinian Conflict,* edited by Judy Kuriansky. Westport, CT: Praeger, 2006.

Locke, J. *Two Treatises of Government.* London: A. & J. Churchill, 1690.

Luke, T.W., and C. Toulouse, eds. *The Politics of Cyberspace: A New Political Science Reader.* New York, NY: Routledge, 1998.

Lyons, J.O. *The Invention of the Self.* Carbondale, IL: Southern Illinois University Press, 1978.

Mandela, N.R. *A Long Walk to Freedom: The Autobiography of Nelson Mandela.* London: Little Brown, 1994.

Mandela, N.R. "Welcome to Robben Island." *Peace Is Possible,* edited by Fredrik S. Heffermehl, 87–89. Geneva: International Peace Bureau (IPB) with the support of UNESCO, 2001.

Maren, M. *The Road to Hell: The Ravaging Effects of Foreign Aid and International Charity.* New York, NY: Free Press, 1997.

Margalit, A. *The Decent Society.* Cambridge, MA: Harvard University Press, 1996.

Margalit, A. *The Ethics of Memory.* Cambridge, MA: Harvard University Press, 2002.

Marshall, M.G. *Third World War: System, Process, and Conflict Dynamics.* Lanham, MD, and London: Rowman and Littlefield, 1999.

Masson, P. "When Soldiers Prefer Death to Humiliation." *Historia* no. 596 (1996): 54–56.

Matsumoto, D.R., S. Hee Yoo, and J.A. LeRoux. "Emotion and Intercultural Communication." *Handbook of Applied Linguistics.* Vol. 7: *Intercultural Communication,* edited by Helga Kotthoff and Helen Spencer-Oatley. Berlin: Mouton–de Gruyter Publishers, 2005.

Mayhew, S. *A Dictionary of Geography.* Oxford: Oxford University Press, 1997.

McLuhan, H.M. *The Gutenberg Galaxy: The Making of Typographic Man.* Toronto: University of Toronto Press, 1962.

Milgram, S. *Obedience to Authority.* New York: Harper and Row, 1974.

Miller, A. *For Your Own Good: Hidden Cruelty in Child-Rearing and the Roots of Violence.* London: Virago Press, 1983. See also the afterword at http://members.xoom.com/childhistory/victim.htm (accessed May 22, 2000).

Miller, W.I. *Humiliation and Other Essays on Honor, Social Discomfort, and Violence.* Ithaca, NY: Cornell University Press, 1993.

Minow, M.L. "Between Vengeance and Forgiveness: South Africa's Truth and Reconciliation Commission." *Negotiation Journal* 14, no. 4 (1998): 319–355.

Mischel, W., and A.L. De Smet. "Self-Regulation in the Service of Conflict Resolution." *The Handbook of Conflict Resolution: Theory and Practice,* edited by Morton Deutsch, 256–275. San Francisco: Jossey-Bass, 2000.

Montaigne, M.d. *Essays by Michel De Montaigne Translated by Charles Cotton.* 1575. http://eserver.org/philosophy/montaigne-essays.txt (accessed December 15, 2003).

Moore, B., Jr. *Moral Purity and Persecution in History.* Princeton, NJ: Princeton University Press, 2000.

Morrison, T. *Beloved: A Novel.* New York, NY: Knopf, 1987.

Moscovici, S. (1997). "Social Representations Theory and Social Constructionism." Social Representations Mailing List 1 Postings, 28 Apr–27 May 1997. http://www.nsu.ru/psych/internet/bits/mosc1.htm (accessed December 3, 2000).

Nathanson, D.L. *Shame and Pride: Affect Sex and the Birth of the Self.* New York, NY: Norton, 1992.

Nelder, C. "Envisioning a Sustainable Future." *BWZine (The Online Better World Magazine)* (October/November/December 1996).

Nisbett, R.E., and D. Cohen. *Culture of Honor: The Psychology of Violence in the South.* Boulder, CO: Westview Press, 1996.

Noël, L. *Intolerance: A General Survey.* Montreal: McGill-Queen's University Press, 1994.

O'Halloran, P.J. *Humanitarian Intervention and the Genocide in Rwanda.* London: Research Institute for the Study of Conflict and Terrorism, 1995.

Parry, L.A. *The History of Torture in England.* Montclair, NJ: Patterson Smith Publishing Corp., 1975.

Patten, C., and A. Lindh. "Let's Control the Small Arms Trade." *International Herald Tribune,* June 30, 2001.

Perry, B.D. "Incubated in Terror: Neurodevelopmental Factors in the 'Cycle of Violence.'" *Children, Youth and Violence: the Search for Solutions,* edited by Joy D. Osofsky, 124–148. New York, NY: Guilford Press, 1997. http://www.bcm.tmc.edu/civitas/incubated.htm (accessed March 15, 2000).

Pogge, T. *World Poverty and Human Rights: Cosmopolitan Responsibilities and Reforms.* Cambridge, UK: Polity Press, 2002.

Priest, D. "CIA Holds Terror Suspects in Secret Prisons." *Washington Post,* November 2, 2005. http://www.washingtonpost.com/wp-dyn/content/article/2005/11/01/AR2005110101644_pf.html.

Reason, P., ed. *Participation in Human Inquiry.* London: Sage, 1994.

Reber, A.S. *The Penguin Dictionary of Psychology.* 2nd ed. Harmondsworth: Penguin, 1995.

Retzinger, S.M. *Violent Emotions: Shame and Rage in Marital Quarrels.* Newbury Park, CA: Sage, 1991.

Richerson, P.J., R. Boyd, and R.L. Bettinger. *The Origins of Agriculture As a Natural Experiment in Cultural Evolution.* Davis, CA: University of California, Center for Agricultural History, 1999. http://www.des.ucdavis.edu/faculty/Richerson/Origins_Ag_IV3.htm (accessed November 2002).

Roosevelt, F.D. *Quarantine the Aggressors.* 1937. http://www.nvcc.edu/home/nvsageh/Hist122/Part4/FDRQuar.htm (accessed July 6, 2003).

Ross, L.D., and J.T. Iost. "Fairness Norms and the Potential for Mutual Agreements Involving Majority and Minority Groups." *Research on Managing Groups and Teams (Vol. 2): Groups in Their Context,* edited by Margaret A. Neale, Elizabeth A. Mannix, and Ruth Wageman, 93–114. Greenwich, CT: JAI Press, 1999.

Rostow, W.W. *The Stages of Economic Growth: A Non-Communist Manifesto.* Cambridge, UK: Cambridge University Press, 1960.

Rubin, J.Z., D.G. Pruitt, and S.H. Kim. *Social Conflict: Escalation, Stalemate and Settlement.* 2nd ed. New York, NY: McGraw-Hill, 1994.

Sachs, J. *The End of Poverty: Economic Possibilities for Our Time.* New York: Penguin Group, 2005.

Sampson, W. *Confessions of an Innocent Man: Torture and Survival in a Saudi Prison.* Toronto, Ontario, Canada: McClelland & Stewart, 2005.

Sayler, M. "Humiliation and the Poor: A Study in the Management of Meaning." PhD dissertation, Fielding Graduate Institute, Santa Barbara, CA, 2004.

Scheff, T.J. *Bloody Revenge: Emotions, Nationalism and War.* Chicago, IL: University of Chicago Press, 1990.

Scheff, T.J. *Emotions, the Social Bond and Human Reality. Part/Whole Analysis.* Cambridge, UK: Cambridge University Press, 1997.

Scheff, T.J. "Emotions and Politics." Eilert Sundt Lecture 2002, University of Oslo, Oslo, October 24, 2002.

Scheff, T.J. "Shame in Self and Society." *Symbolic Interaction* 26, no. 2 (2003): 239–262.

Scheff, T.J., and S.M. Retzinger. *Emotions and Violence: Shame and Rage in Destructive Conflicts.* Lexington, MA: Lexington Books, 1991.

Scheler, M. *Über Ressentiment und moralisches Werturteil.* Leipzig: Engelmann, 1912.

Scheler, M. *The Nature of Sympathy.* London: Routledge and Kegan Paul, 1954.

Sherif, M., and H. Cantril. *The Psychology of Ego-Involvements, Social Attitudes and Identifica-tions.* New York, NY: Wiley, 1947.

Sherif, M., O.J. Harvey, B.J. White, W.R. Hood, C.W. Sherif, and D. Campbell. *The Robbers' Cave Experiment: Intergroup Conflict and Cooperation.* Middletown, CT: Wesleyan University Press, 1988.

Sidanius, J., and F. Pratto. *Social Dominance: An Intergroup Theory of Social Hierarchy and Oppression.* Cambridge, UK: Cambridge University Press, 1999.

Siegel, J. "A New Diagnosis for the Power Hungry." *Jerusalem Post,* August 20, 1997, 1-1.

Singer, P. *A Darwinian Left: Politics, Evolution and Cooperation.* London: Weidenfeld & Nicolson, 1999.

Smith, D. "Organisations and Humiliation: Looking Beyond Elias." *Organization* 8, no. 3 (2001): 537–560.

Smith, D. "The Humiliating Organisation: The Functions and Disfunctions of Degradation." *The Civilized Organisation,* edited by Ad v. Iterson, Willem Mastenbroek, Tim Newton, and Dennis Smith. Amsterdam: Benjamin, 2002.

Snyder, C.R. *Citizen-Soldiers and Manly Warriors: Military Service and Gender in the Civic Republican Tradition.* Lanham, MD: Rowman and Littlefield, 2000.

Solow, Robert M. "Technical Change and the Aggregate Production Function." *Review of Economics and Statistics* 39 (1957): 312–320.

Sontag, S. "Regarding the Torture of Others." *The New York Times,* May 23, 2004. http://www.nytimes.com/2004/05/23/magazine/23PRISONS.html?ei=1&en=c0146bd0d219d6fe&ex=1086188191&pagewanted=print&position=.

Staub, E. *The Psychology of Good and Evil: Why Children, Adults, and Groups Help and Harm Others.* Cambridge, UK: Cambridge University Press, 2003.

Staub, E. "The Roots of Evil: Social Conditions, Culture, Personality and Basic Human Needs." *Personality and Social Psychology Review* 3, no. 3 (1999): 179–192.

Staub, Ervin. *The Roots of Evil: The Origins of Genocide and Other Group Violence.* Cambridge, UK: Cambridge University Press, 1989.

Steinberg, B.S. *Shame and Humiliation: Presidential Decision Making on Vietnam.* Montreal/UK: McGill-Queen's, 1996.

Tomkins, S.S. *Affect Imagery and Consciousness (Volumes I - IV).* New York, NY: Springer, 1962.

Trigger, B.G. *Early Civilizations—Ancient Egypt in Context.* Cairo: AUC, 1993.

United Nations Population Fund (UNFPA). "Gender-Based Violence: A Price Too High." *State of World Population 2005.* http://www.unfpa.org/swp/2005/english/ch7/index.htm.

Ury, W. *Getting to Peace. Transforming Conflict at Home, at Work, and in the World.* New York, NY: Viking, 1999.

Vachon, S. "Passer de L'Appauvrissement à la Pauvreté comme on va de l'Humiliation à l'Humilité." *Voix Et Images* 18, no. 2 (1993): 382–387.

Vogel, W., and A. Lazare. "The Unforgivable Humiliation: A Dilemma in Couples' Treatment." *Contemporary Family Therapy* 12, no. 2 (1990): 139–151.

Volf, M. *Exclusion and Embrace: A Theological Exploration and Identity, Otherness, and Reconciliation.* Nashville, TN: Abingdon Press, 1996.

Volkan, V.D. *Blind Trust: Large Groups and Their Leaders in Times of Crisis and Terror.* Charlottesville, VA: Pitchstone Publishing, 2004.

Volkan, V.D., D.A. Julius, and J.V. Montville, eds. *The Psychodynamics of International Relationships.* Vol. I: *Concepts and Theories;* Vol. II: *Unofficial Diplomacy at Work.* Lexington, MA: Lexington Books, 1990–1991.

Wilkinson, R. G. *Unhealthy Societies: The Afflictions of Inequality.* London: Routledge, 1996.

Wisconsin Institute for Peace and Conflict Studies, UWM Peace Studies Program, and UWM Center for International Education. Invitation to the Conference "New Paths to Peace: Innovative Approaches to Building Sustainable Peace and Development, November 6–8, 2003." Milwaukee, WI: Wisconsin Institute for Peace and Conflict Studies, 2003.

Wyatt-Brown, B. *Southern Honor: Ethics and Behavior in the Old South.* New York, NY: Oxford University Press, 1982.

Zehr, H. *The Little Book of Restorative Justice.* Intercourse, PA: Good Books, 2002.

Znakov, V. V. "The Comprehension of Violence and Humiliation Situations by Aggressive Adolescents." *Voprosy-Psikhologii* (January–February 1990): 20–27.

INDEX

ABOUT THE SERIES

As this new millennium dawns, humankind has evolved—some would argue has devolved—exhibiting new and old behaviors that fascinate, infuriate, delight, or fully perplex those of us seeking answers to the question, "Why"? In this series, experts from various disciplines peer through the lens of psychology telling us answers they see for questions of human behavior. Their topics may range from humanity's psychological ills—addictions, abuse, suicide, murder, and terrorism among them—to works focused on positive subjects including intelligence, creativity, athleticism, and resilience. Regardless of the topic, the goal of this series remains constant—to offer innovative ideas, provocative considerations, and useful beginnings to better understand human behavior.

Chris E. Stout
Series Editor

About the Series Editor and Series Advisory Board

CHRIS E. STOUT, Psy.D., MBA, holds a joint governmental and academic appointment in Northwestern University Medical School and serves as Illinois's first Chief of Psychological Services. He served as an NGO Special Representative to the United Nations, was appointed by the U.S. Department of Commerce as a Baldridge Examiner, and served as an advisor to the White House for both political parties. He was appointed to the World Economic Forum's Global Leaders of Tomorrow. He has published and presented more than 300 papers and 29 books. His works have been translated into six languages.

BRUCE E. BONECUTTER, Ph.D., is Director of Behavioral Services at the Elgin Community Mental Health Center, the Illinois Department of Human Services state hospital serving adults in greater Chicago. He is also a Clinical Assistant Professor of Psychology at the University of Illinois at Chicago. A clinical psychologist specializing in health, consulting, and forensic psychology, Bonecutter is also a longtime member of the American Psychological Association Task Force on Children and the Family.

JOSEPH FLAHERTY, M.D., is Chief of Psychiatry at the University of Illinois Hospital, a Professor of Psychiatry at the University of Illinois College of Medicine, and a Professor of Community Health Science at the UIC College of Public Health. He is a Founding Member of the Society for the Study of Culture and Psychiatry. Dr. Flaherty has been a consultant to the World Health Organization, to the National Institutes of Mental Health, and also the Falk Institute in Jerusalem.

MICHAEL HOROWITZ, Ph.D., is President and Professor of Clinical Psychology at the Chicago School of Professional Psychology, one of the nation's leading not-for-profit graduate schools of psychology. Earlier, he served as Dean and Professor of the Arizona School of Professional Psychology. A clinical psychologist practicing independently since 1987, his work has focused on psychoanalysis, intensive individual therapy, and couples therapy. He has provided Disaster Mental Health Services to the American Red Cross. Dr. Horowitz's special interests include the study of fatherhood.

SHELDON I. MILLER, M.D., is a Professor of Psychiatry at Northwestern University and Director of the Stone Institute of Psychiatry at Northwestern Memorial Hospital. He is also Director of the American Board of Psychiatry and Neurology, Director of the American Board of Emergency Medicine, and Director of the Accreditation Council for Graduate Medical Education. Dr. Miller is also an Examiner for the American Board of Psychiatry and Neurology. He is Founding Editor of the *American Journal of Addictions* and Founding Chairman of the American Psychiatric Association's Committee on Alcoholism.

DENNIS P. MORRISON, Ph.D., is Chief Executive Officer at the Center for Behavioral Health in Indiana, the first behavioral health company ever to win the JCAHO Codman Award for excellence in the use of outcomes management to achieve health care quality improvement. He is President of the Board of Directors for the Community Healthcare Foundation in Bloomington and has been a member of the Board of Directors for the American College of Sports Psychology. He has served as a consultant to agencies including the Ohio Department of Mental Health, Tennessee Association of Mental Health Organizations, Oklahoma Psychological Association, the North Carolina Council of Community Mental Health Centers, and the National Center for Health Promotion in Michigan.

WILLIAM H. REID, M.D., MPH, is a clinical and forensic psychiatrist and consultant to attorneys and courts throughout the United States. He is a Clinical Professor of Psychiatry at the University of Texas Health Science Center. Dr. Miller is also an Adjunct Professor of Psychiatry at Texas A&M College of Medicine and Texas Tech University School of Medicine, as well as a clinical faculty member at the Austin Psychiatry Residency Program. He is chairman of the Scientific Advisory Board and medical advisor to the Texas Depressive & Manic-Depressive Association, as well as an examiner for the American Board of Psychiatry and the Law, as chairman of the Research Section for an International Conference on the Psychiatric Aspects of Terrorism, and as medical director for the Texas Department of Mental Health and Mental Retardation.

About the Author

EVELIN LINDNER is a Social Scientist and Founding Manager of Human Dignity and Humiliation Studies based at the Columbia University Conflict Resolution Network. She is also Guest Professor in the Department of Psychology at the University of Oslo and a Senior Lecturer of Psychology at the Norwegian University of Science and Technology. She holds dual doctorates, in social medicine and social psychology. Her research on humiliation and its role in genocide, war, and violent conflict began in 1996 and has taken her to locations including Rwanda and Somalia.

Recent Titles in Contemporary Psychology

MAHLER

AND HIS WORLD

EDITED BY KAREN PAINTER

PRINCETON UNIVERSITY PRESS
PRINCETON AND OXFORD

Published by Princeton University Press, 41 William Street,
Princeton, New Jersey 08540
In the United Kingdom: Princeton University Press,
3 Market Place, Woodstock, Oxfordshire OX20 1SY

Library of Congress Control Number 2002104405

ISBN 0-691-09243-5 (cloth)
ISBN 0-691-09244-3 (paperback)

British Library Cataloging-in-Publication Data is available

This publication has been produced by the Bard College Publications Office:
Ginger Shore, Director
Mary Smith, Art Director
Composed in Baskerville by Natalie Kelly
Text edited by Paul De Angelis
Music typeset by Don Giller
Printed on acid-free paper. ∞
www.pupress.princeton.edu
Printed in the United States of America
1 3 5 7 9 10 8 6 4 2

Dedicated to
Gilbert Kaplan
Henry-Louis de La Grange
Donald Mitchell

Contents

PART III
MAHLER'S AMERICAN DEBUT:
The Reception of the Fourth and Fifth Symphonies, 1904–1906
EDITED BY ZOË LANG

PART IV
MAHLER'S GERMAN-LANGUAGE CRITICS
EDITED AND TRANSLATED BY KAREN PAINTER AND BETTINA VARWIG

Contents

Preface and Acknowledgments

Like the other volumes associated with the Bard Music Festival, this book seeks to place its protagonist in the context of general cultural, political and social developments as well as offer new approaches to musical analysis. It is appropriate at the very beginning to acknowledge the debt that everyone who ventures into the field of Mahler research owes to the three individuals to whom this volume is dedicated. Without Henry-Louis de La Grange's vast and authoritative biography of the composer, the contributors to this volume, or any scholars of Mahler, could not have developed their own research in such far-ranging areas. Donald Mitchell has provided a similar inspiration through an awesome range of publications, including brilliant work on the chronology of Mahler's compositions. And Gilbert Kaplan's passion for the Second Symphony as well as his philanthropy have helped sustain the wider public audience for Mahler's music that encourages scholars to continue their own investigations.

Gustav Mahler held a special fascination among contemporaries not only during his lifetime but also following World War I, when the celebrated Mahler festival in Amsterdam in 1920 marked an important step toward the cultural reconciliation of recent enemies. Mahler was the public persona par excellence—the innovative and dictatorial artistic director of a preeminent opera theater—and yet an impassioned Romantic who composed in the isolation of his lakeside and mountain huts. While contemporaries generally applauded his innovative activity as director and conductor, Mahler's compositions drew sharply polarized reactions. His facility in polyphonic writing, inventiveness of orchestration, and strong rhythmic capacity all became the object of heated debate. The frequent reliance on folk music themes, taken up in both his song cycles and his symphonies where they were woven into opulently scored marches and counterpoint, left him open to charges of excess and banality. Both detractors and champions—at the time and ever since—debated musical quality in terms of the political issues that roiled early twentieth-century Europe. His Jewish origins made the stakes even higher in Central Europe. His music seemed to have immense consequences for the contest between progress and reaction. Even when listeners recognized an immensely poignant and subjective content to the later symphonies and song cycles, the duration and emotional scope of the works, their clear claim to continue the line from Beethoven, Wagner, and Brahms, endowed his work with ideological as well as strictly musical consequence.

As serious music in the interwar years evolved toward greater experimentation and toward a more defiant modernism, it became easier to focus on what seemed anachronistic in Mahler's enterprise. After his death in 1911, indeed after moving his podium to New York three years earlier, the talents of the conductor were no longer present to second the achievements of the composer. The National Socialist regime in Germany and annexed Austria dictated the disappearance of the repertory in its homeland. Slowly accepted into the canon beginning in the 1960s, both in concert halls and in the academy, Mahler has reemerged as a giant figure. His work and its meaning still remain at the center of ideological and musical debates. Indeed, Mahler's inherently controversial deployment of mass, duration, timbre and populist sources has made this corpus of work a privileged object of aesthetic and historical as well as strictly musical analysis. Commentators and scholars remain drawn by the conviction that somehow Mahler's legacy encapsulates the achievement and ripeness of a bourgeois culture poised in the early twentieth century between decay or the need for renewal—a cumulative legacy too defiant (and sometimes humorous) to be purely elegiac, and too anchored in tradition to become revolutionary.

This volume brings together scholars on both sides of the Atlantic with the widest possible range in methodology. Several of the essays incorporate some of the interdisciplinary approaches that have left such a strong mark on American musicology over the last decade or so. Contributors examine Mahler's music and career against the backdrop of the pressing transformations of his wider world: Peter Franklin takes up questions of gender, Talia Pecker Berio interrogates Mahler's Jewish identity, Leon Botstein examines the ironic consequences of the late twentieth-century embrace of Mahler, Charles S. Maier explores the theatricality of his art and the political world, and Karen Painter examines the impinging confrontation with mass society, in particular with the Eighth Symphony.

Another set of essays places Mahler's work at their center. Thomas Peattie shows how philosophical and literary concepts of memory can illuminate some of the processes in Mahler's music, especially the celebrated moments of pastoral evocation. Turning toward the private realm that the composer distilled into the controlled sonic dialogue of voice and orchestra, Camilla Bork examines the structures of meaning in Mahler's celebrated "Ich bin der Welt abhanden gekommen," and Peter Revers analyzes the *Kindertotenlieder,* which took on a mythic significance after the death of Mahler's daughter. The intimate connection between autobiography and music in late Mahler is explored by Stephen Hefling.

Mahler's symphonies provide one of the richest sites on which to construct a history of musical listening. In both Europe and America, critics debated not only specific pieces and performances but the nature of musical meaning, as the composer's brilliant orchestration drew reviewers into polemics over how to listen to symphonic structures. Thus it seems appropriate to offer a sample of the rich and lively debates that played so important a role in the cultural sections of the Central European press but have found only a pale counterpart in the more austere tradition of Anglo-American criticism. Zoë Lang presents documents from the first performances of his music in America. Karen Painter and Bettina Varwig translate reviews of the leading German-language critics of Mahler's world.

* * *

Several colleagues and friends were helpful in the shaping of this volume, in particular Reinhold Brinkmann. Conversations with Leon Botstein, as well as his exemplary interdisciplinary work combining history, criticism, and aesthetics, left their mark on the conception of the volume. My thanks to Zoë Lang for her editorial assistance, and David Black, with his gift for research and reconstruction. I am especially grateful to Ginger Shore for her assured leadership in the production of the volume. The book benefited from Paul De Angelis's patience and wisdom in editorial matters, Natalie Kelly's excellent composition and Don Giller's setting of the musical examples. Members of the planning committee of the Bard Music Festival were helpful throughout, especially Christopher Gibbs, Mark Loftin, and Irene Zedlacher. A special thanks to Fred Appel and Walter Lippincott at the Princeton University Press for their encouragement and advice. Finally, I would like to thank the staff of the Harvard Music Department for their assistance, above all Karen Rynne.